# A
# Series of Lectures

*on*

# Social Justice

as broadcast by

Rev. Charles E. Coughlin

over a National Network

March, 1935

# A
# SERIES OF LECTURES

*on*

# SOCIAL JUSTICE

*by*

## The Rev. Chas. E. Coughlin

*of the*

Shrine Of The Little Flower,
Royal Oak, Michigan
and Broadcast
Over a National Network

Published by
THE RADIO LEAGUE OF THE LITTLE FLOWER
ROYAL OAK, MICHIGAN
March, 1935 A.D.

Imprimatur

MICHAEL JAMES GALLAGHER, D. D.

✠ BISHOP OF DETROIT

Detroit, Michigan, March, 1935

Published by

THE RADIO LEAGUE OF THE LITTLE FLOWER

Printed in the United States of America by
THE CONDON PRINTING CO., DETROIT

# Dedication

This book is dedicated
to the members
of the

## National Union for
## Social Justice

whose moral and financial
support have made possible the
broadcasting of these addresses.

CHARLES E. COUGHLIN

# Contents

# THE NATIONAL UNION FOR SOCIAL JUSTICE

### (Sunday, November 11, 1934)

SIXTEEN years ago this afternoon, my friends, I mingled with thousands of my fellow citizens who were celebrating the termination of a war that was fought to end wars. As I look back upon these years—years identified with the Peace Treaty of Versailles, with the League of Nations, with assassinations of men in high office, with the birth of Bolshevism, with repudiations of debts and with universal poverty—I honestly believe that in all history such destruction of ideals and such miscarriage of justice were never chronicled save during the years which witnessed the assassination of Christ.

Instead of making the world safe for democracy, the bells which tolled their message sixteen years ago this afternoon were sounding its requiem. Instead of announcing that here was the end of all war, we were being ushered into a new conflict too terrible to contemplate.

No nation and but few individuals have escaped the atrocities identified with the last sixteen years. Waste and destruction of property, the desolation of homes and farms, the decay of factories and industries, which are associated with this period through which we have passed, are beyond our reckoning. They were years when innocent civilians of all countries were bowed down by the regimented forces of greed, of selfishness, of crass ignorance and of obstinacy.

Thus, it is almost with a cynical smile that we hope for peace when we recognize the feverish efforts of every great nation as they are busy manufacturing cannons and shells, war ships and lethal gases. The stage is being set for the last act of that tragedy which will mark the passing of a prostituted civilization unless our course is suddenly changed. Peace conferences and naval conferences failed miserably as did the hypocritical efforts of the League of Nations. In their laboratories of destruction the chemists of greed and of poverty, of hate and of lying propaganda are mingling their poisons of warfare. The old diplomacies, the ancient rivalries which were left wounded unto death upon the battle fields of Flanders today are rising in their ghostly forms to sound a new call to arms. To these menaces we are not blind. Their ghastly presence must not be ignored.

## I

On this Sunday following the signal political victory of the new deal, perhaps, my friends, you are expectant to hear soft words of praise and glorification. I shall not be one, either today or at any future date, to break down your confidence in the outcome of this new deal. My constant prayer is for its success. Soft words and insincere praise, however, must have no more place at this present hour than had our empty rejoicing sixteen years ago. Thus, I wish to re-assert my belief that, although the old Republican party with its rugged individualism is as dead as Benedict Arnold, nevertheless, it is true that the Democratic party, now composed of progressive men and women of all political affiliations, is merely on trial. Two years hence it will leave the courtroom of public opinion vindicated and with a new lease on life, or will be condemned to political death if it fails to answer the simple question of why there is want in the midst of plenty.

Truly, democracy itself is on trial. It has been given the final mandate to face the real causes of this depression and to end them instead of temporizing with useless efforts for the preservation of a system, both economic and political, which once before watered the fields of Europe with blood and the highways of America with tears.

Today the American people are the judge and jury who will support this administration and accord it a sportman's chance to make good. It has already subscribed to the principle that human rights must take precedence over financial rights. It recognizes that these rights far outweigh in the scales of justice either political rights or so-called constitutional rights. It appears to be an Administration determined to read into the Constitution the definition of social justice which is already expressed within its very preamble. There we are taught that the object of this Government is to establish justice, to insure domestic tranquillity, to promote the general welfare and to provide the blessings of liberty for ourselves and for our posterity.

The task confronting this government consists first, in recognizing and utilizing this constitutional truth; and, second, in eliminating and destroying, once and for all, the well known and well established unconstitutional causes of this depression. This afternoon I plan to address you on its first cause viewed from a material standpoint.

## II

This has to do with a just and living annual wage for all citizens who care to earn their own livelihood. I will deal with the substantial error associated with modern industrialism—an error which, if not eradicated, will logically lead us into the perpetuation of the dole system and thence into communism. After all, the economic analysis of communism teaches us that the State is absolutely supreme; is absolute master and proprietor of all material goods; is the sole industrialist and capitalist, and its citizens are the recipients of chocolate coated doles. Communism is nothing more than a candied pill of glorified *"doleism."*

Thus, at the outset of this discussion, let me rehearse for you a few facts relative to the history of labor and of industry, of production and of unemployment. As we turn back the pages which tell us the story of the World War, we are convinced that it was one organized and operated for commercial purposes and commercial gains. Every cannon forged, every shell exploded was trade-marked with the sign of decadent capitalism. It was a war fought to make the world safe for Wall Street and for the international bankers.

Are you not aware of the fact that in 1914 England's financial and commercial supremacy were in jeopardy due to the rapid advance of German commerce? Are you ignorant of the fact that during the first two years of the World War the United States industrialists and bankers had poured billions of credit dollars into the war chests of Great Britain? Need I remind you of the pleading on the part of English statesmen for us to enter the war or of the letters sent by Ambassador Page to President Wilson demanding that we should join the allies for the sole reason of preserving our bankers' foreign investments—bankers, who in league with England, had wagered on the losing horse; powerful bankers who, in a few months after the outbreak of hostilities, perverted the mind of President Wilson to such an extent that, although elected to his high office on the promise of keeping us out of the war, he now submitted to the fallacy that it was more sacred to protect the capitalistic dollar than to preserve the life of a mother's son!

The years in which all this was happening were identified with the date when the monstrous dragon of want had been slain by the new St. George of modern scientific machinery. Before the advent of the World War we were not troubled with the problem of unemployment. Eighteen or twenty years ago industry was well operated under a system of economics devised for the upkeep of a civilization which, until then, was engaged in solving the problem of production. With our clumsy machinery and unskilled mechanics we could not produce enough shoes, bath tubs, locomotives, motor cars or, for that matter, any other mass production commodity to supply the practical demands of a world which was still struggling to free itself from the deprivations of the past. By 1914 Watt and his steam engine, Edison and his electric motor and the thousand inventors who followed them had not completely conquered the problem of want in the midst of need—the problem of production.

Now what has all this to do with the World War of 1914 and with the present depression which was born in 1918? Be patient

9

for a moment and I shall try to weave a few thoughts relative to this subject into a simple fabric of understanding.

For the first two years of the war we found practically the full manpower of France, of England, of Italy, of Belgium and of the European allies clothed in the uniforms of soldiers. This meant that the flower of European youth ceased to be producers. This meant that suddenly the production power of Europe was perverted into a force of destruction.

Meanwhile America was called upon to supply wheat and corn, pork and cotton, food and wearing apparel not only for these 10-million allied soldiers but also for their wives and children and fellow citizens who remained at home—citizens who were not so much engaged in farming and in producing the demands of a peaceful life—but regimented citizens who were occupied in manufacturing shrapnel and bullets, rifles and munitions. These, too, must be cared for, at least in part, by American labor and agriculture.

Perhaps mathematical, official figures are more eloquent than words to amplify this statement.

In 1912, even while preparations for the World War were going on in Europe, we exported less than $1-billion worth of goods. In 1915 our exports amounted to more than $2½-billion. Nineteen hundred and sixteen saw this rise to practically $4-billion. This figure of $4-billion held good for the years 1917 and 1918. When the war ceased our exports to Europe dropped below the $1-billion mark—$849,762,607 for 1933 to be exact; For 1934, ending with September, our exports were only $696,620,471.

During this period of bloated exportation which was identified with the World War, several substantial effects are to be noted. We in America passed from the normalcy of 1914 production into the abnormalcy of 1916 and 1918 production and accomplished twice as much work with millions of fewer laborers! As a matter of fact we had 4½-million soldiers and sailors actually subtracted from our farms and factories, from our trade and commerce. These men were not only non-producers. They were occupied with destruction and not with production. They, as well as their non-producing wives and children, had to be cared for. Thus, approximately 30-million men, at the most, were engaged here in America to produce the ordinary necessities and conveniences for the United States as well as clothing and foodstuffs, munitions, and battleships for a great portion of the allied forces and allied citizens. Handicapped though we were with a shortage of help in our factories and in our fields, I repeat, that in 1918 we were forced to produce more than twice as much as we did in 1913.

Now if fewer men, both farmers and mechanics, kept both America and a great part of Europe supplied with foodstuffs and with war materials during this period of artificial prosperity while the flower of America and of the allied youth was busied with destruction, how was this accomplished?

Well, naturally, these were days when unemployment was unheard of. But more than that these were days when the disciples of Watt and Edison so perfected steam and electricity, when the scientists and engineers so perfected the lathe and mass production machinery that, between the years of 1914 and 1918, we find science and engineering making it possible for one man to do the work of approximately two and one-half men.

Keep that fact in mind as you turn your calendar to the date of November 11, 1918! Armistice Day—the day when there was born from the womb of war the new problem of distribution.

That was the day when the soldiers and sailors began to return to their respective homes. That was the day when Europe's task, at least from an economic viewpoint, was to resume producing for herself without the help of America. We, in this country, were expected to return to normal housekeeping. But when more than 4-million soldiers and sailors came back to our shores seeking employment they found young girls and married women occupying positions in office and in factory. More than that, they discovered mass production machinery so perfected that no longer was it possible to continue with the same program of production in 1919 as had been in vogue in 1914.

These were the facts which confronted the so-called statesmen in 1920. They were the known facts which maliciously and purposely were avoided as Wall Street, which had long since moved into the Treasury Department, launched a program of credit inflation at home and of bond inflation abroad hoping to stimulate European purchasing by post war loans. Wall Street, which owned almost all the industries, was determined to keep itself going. They were loans made in the shape of credit notes—not in actual dollars. They were loans made with bankers' checks which were expected to be repaid in ounces of gold. More than that, they were loans made upon the presumption that European factories would remain idle and that European people would buy American goods.

Of this insane practice, which necessarily dug itself into the trenches of repudiation, I shall speak to you on a following Sunday. But for the time being I shall not digress from the labor, the unemployment, the industrial problem.

When we weave together the threads which the loom of fact has so clearly fabricated, to what conclusions are we forced as we view the labor situation between 1919 and 1929?

First: Unemployment on a huge scale was an absolute certainty, if we still held to the proposition that a laborer should be paid 50 cents an hour while he worked and then be left to seek refuge in a dole line until the motor cars, the locomotives, the shoes and other products of a factory were being consumed.

Second: The theory that production for a profit existed for industrialists and stockholders only, and not for laborers and mechanics, was no longer tenable. If laborers were required to work only six or eight months in the year under a wage scale that paid them while they worked and starved them while they were idle, then a new annual wage scale must be adopted.

This, then, was no depression. It simply marked the end of an era where man's problem was formerly one of production. It announced the birth of a new era where henceforth our problem shall be one of distribution of the profits not only to the owners and stockholders but also to the laborers and mechanics, enabling all to live prosperously even when the wheels of industry have ceased operating.

### III

Now let me speak about this problem of distribution which we must solve within the next two years or else witness a new form of government that will face it and attempt to solve it by some communistic means.

As far as production is concerned, we have more acreage under cultivation, more factories equipped with the finest machinery, more educated scientists and skilled mechanics than any other nation in all history. Our struggle against the blind forces of destructive nature, as well as against the ignorance of the past, has been successful. The Great War has driven in and riveted down this nail of progress so firmly that no longer shall there be want in the midst of need. Today there is want in the midst of plenty.

Before speaking further about the distribution of wealth may I be emphatic in my opposition to the philosophy of destructionism or of sabotage. To all purposes destructionism says: *"Let us go back to the year 1900 or to the year 1850. Let us take land out of cultivation. Let us destroy pigs and cotton and wheat and corn."*

If that philosophy were logical, it would also say: *"Let us destroy one out of every three automobile plants; permanently lock the doors of one out of every three steel mills; burn down half our textile factories; flood one-third of all our coal mines and pay a bounty to every Dillinger and desperado for removing scientists from our universities."*

It is the philosophy which refuses to face the problem of distribution. It is the philosophy which is attempting to hold us manacled to an obsolete system of finance and of production for a profit only. It is the final attempt on the part of a decadent capitalism to destroy us into prosperity. It is similar to the program of the bankers who, for ten years following the war, attempted to bond us with paper into gold prosperity.

Now, my friends, let no one deceive you with the economic lie that there is over-production when millions are hungry, when millions more are in the bread line and when 16-million homes in America are deprived of the ordinary conveniences of life—running water, modern plumbing, electricity and modern heat.

There is simply a lack of distribution.

Distribution of wealth is substantially associated with the problem of money—with the problem of 50 cents an hour while you work and the soup line while you are idle; with the problem of a destroyed purchasing power; with the problem of organized doles and disorganized taxation; with the problem of impending communism.

If there is plenty for all in this country—plenty of fields of wheat and of cotton, plenty of factories, mechanics and scientists —the only reason why this plenitude of God's blessing is not shared by all is because our Government has not, as yet, faced the problem of distribution. In other words, it may boast that it has driven the money changers from the temple but it permits industry to cling tenaciously to the cast-off philosophy of the money changers. Our Government still upholds one of the worst evils of decadent capitalism, namely, that production must be only at a profit for the owners, for the capitalist, and not for the laborer. This philosophy of finance, or of distribution of profits, based on the theory of *"pay-while-you-work"* for the laborer can only be identified with destruction of the entire system of capitalism.

## IV

Were I addressing a group of industrialists I would inquire of them whether or not they were of the opinion that this technical unemployment—an unemployment brought about by the scientific development of machinery and of men—could continue. Surely, they must recognize that industrial competition must produce newer inventions, newer machinery and longer bread lines.

I would ask the industrialists whether or not they and their children could logically anticipate a time in the not distant future when they will become targets for the wrath of a despoiled people. Do they not remember the French Revolution, the Russian Revolution? Do they know that human nature does not change?

I would plead with them, for their own self-preservation, if for no other reason, to co-operate with the Government as it will move, we hope, towards the shortening of hours for all engaged in mass-production activity and towards an annual wage system

13

that is just and equitable and thus permit American workmen to preserve the American standard of living.

The annual wage shall not be one that will permit us merely to subsist. It must be one that will keep us on the level of the American standard of living. That is why our foreparents forsook Europe to come to America. That is what we and our children shall fight for.

By no means shall we despairingly admit that all is lost. All is not lost if we only have the courage to adopt the policy of producing for use at a profit for all—the owner and the laborer.

Indeed, we must find room in the ranks of agriculture, of science, of art and of labor for every American citizen who wishes to earn his livelihood and retain his self-respect. We can ill afford to have 12-million men, 2-million women and well over 2-million never-employed youths in this nation idle and angry. From a practical standpoint, I repeat, their number will increase in proportion as our science is perfected. From a practical standpoint, they and the millions, who will gradually be added to their ranks, will become unable to share the tax burden of this nation—a burden which ultimately will mean the break-down of government and the confiscation of all industry and the communizing of property.

You industrialists, surrounded as you are by your economists, are anxious to form organizations for the protection of your property rights and for the perpetuation of your profit system. But, may I ask you, of what value are property rights unless they are firmly established upon the sanctity of human rights?

Are those of you who own and control wealth ignorant of the fact that labor owes no rights to capital unless capital performs its duty towards labor?

Are you forgetful, ye princes of this world's goods, that you are no better than stewards designated to manage justly and fairly the property of this world which belongs not to you but to the God who created you?

In the event of strikes produced under an unjust economic system where men are forced to starve because there is no work at a profit for the owner, are you men foolish enough to think that the moral law of God shall force the working men to disobey the first command of all—the command of self-preservation—and follow, in its stead, your man-made precept of property preservation?

Are you so misguided by your advisers as to believe that, because you own a factory, or a bank, or a fortune, you can use it as you will to the detriment of the common good?

And on this Armistice Day, when the murmurings of discontent are rumbling throughout the capitals of this world, when

14

armies are being marshaled and new cannons forged, are you so bereft of reason as to think for a moment that the men and women, whom your system has starved for five long years, will shoulder arms to protect your rights and your property and your rotten policies?

Modern capitalism is destroying itself at both ends. It speaks to the youth of the nation with this bright sentence: *"You are inexperienced. We do not want you."* To the matured laborers in industry who are forty-five years of age, it says: *"You must retire simply because the compensation insurance rate is too high for us and the insurance companies of this nation do not care to risk you."*

There are 21-million boys and girls in our public school system. Approximately 1-million in our colleges and universities soon will be knocking at your doors for employment. For the older ones you will try to re-write the natural law of God as you preach to them the reasonableness of birth control when you really mean the godlessness of wealth control.

*"Increase and multiply"* was the command of God—a command that has been sterilized in the heart of every thinking young man who dares not marry because he dares not inflict poverty upon his children.

And this in a nation where the birth rate and the death rate are sparring for supremacy; this in a nation that dares not invite the immigrant to enter because already there is too much unemployment!

Yes, *"increase and multiply"* was the command which echoed over the flowering fields and the towering forests. It was heard in the sheep-folds and on the pasture-lands. It broke forth in holy emotions as lovers clasped in fond embrace.

*"Increase and multiply and I shall kiss your fields with the lips of the sun and water them with the fountains of rain. I will unfold to you the secrets of nature. And I shall teach your nimble fingers to work and labor as I do the wings of a bird to fly."*

Oh! how this Sacred Scripture has become perverted as, in the midst of plenty, we struggle to create want—we struggle to create profits—all for the purpose of perpetuating a slavery which has been so often described as the concentration of wealth in the hands of a few!

My friends, the outworn creed of capitalism is done for. The clarion call of communism has been sounded. I can support one as easily as the other. They are both rotten! But it is not necessary to suffer any longer the slings and arrows of modern capitalism any more than it is to surrender our rights to life, to liberty and to the cherished bonds of family to communism.

15

The high priests of capitalism bid us beware of the radical and call upon us to expel him from our midst. There will be no expulsion of radicals until the causes which breed radicals will first be destroyed!

The apostles of Lenin and Trotzky bid us forsake all rights to private ownership and ask us to surrender our liberty for that mess of pottage labeled "prosperity," while it summons us to worship at the altar where a dictator of flesh and blood is enthroned as our god and the citizens are branded as his slaves.

Away with both of them! But never into the discard with the liberties which we have already won and the economic liberty which we are about to win—or die in the attempt!

My friends, I have spent many hours during these past two weeks—hours, far into the night, reading thousands of letters which have come to my office from the young folks and the old folks of this nation. I believe that in them I possess the greatest human document written within our times.

I am not boasting when I say to you that I know the pulse of the people. I know it better than all your newspaper men. I know it better than do all your industrialists with your paid-for advice. I am not exaggerating when I tell you of their demand for social justice which, like a tidal wave, is sweeping over this nation.

Nor am I happy to think that, through my broadcasts, I have placed myself today in a position to accept the challenge which these letters carry to me—a challenge for me to organize these men and women of all classes, not for the protection of property rights as does the American Liberty League; not for the protection of political spoils as do the henchmen of the Republican or Democratic parties. Away with them too!

But, happy or unhappy as I am in my position, I accept the challenge to organize for obtaining, for securing and for protecting the principles of social justice.

To organize for action, if you will! To organize for social united action which will be founded on God-given social truths which belong to Catholic and Protestant, to Jew and Gentile, to black and white, to rich and poor, to industrialist and to laborer.

I realize that I am more or less a voice crying in the wilderness. I realize that the doctrine which I preach is disliked and condemned by the princes of wealth. What care I for that! And, more than all else, I deeply appreciate how limited are my qualifications to launch this organization which shall be known as the NATIONAL UNION FOR SOCIAL JUSTICE.

But the die is cast! The word has been spoken! And by it I am prepared either to stand or to fall; to fall, if needs be, and

16

thus, to be remembered as an arrant upstart who succeeded in doing nothing more than stirring up the people.

How shall we organize? To what principles of social justice shall we pledge ourselves? What action shall we take? These are practical questions which I ask myself as I recognize the fact that this NATIONAL UNION FOR SOCIAL JUSTICE must be established in every county and city and town in these United States of America.

It is for the youth of the nation. It is for the brains of the nation. It is for the farmers of the nation. It is for everyone in the nation.

Establishing my principles upon this preamble, namely, that we are creatures of a beneficent God, made to love and to serve Him in this world and to enjoy Him forever in the next; that all this world's wealth of field, of forest, of mine and of river has been bestowed upon us by a kind Father, therefore I believe that wealth, as we know it, originates from natural resources and from the labor which the children of God expend upon these resources. It is all ours except for the harsh, cruel and grasping ways of wicked men who first concentrated wealth into the hands of a few, then dominated states, and finally commenced to pit state against state in the frightful catastrophes of commercial warfare.

Following this preamble, these shall be the principles of social justice towards whose realization we must strive:

1. I believe in liberty of conscience and liberty of education, not permitting the state to dictate either my worship to my God or my chosen avocation in life.

2. I believe that every citizen willing to work and capable of working shall receive a just, living, annual wage which will enable him both to maintain and educate his family according to the standards of American decency.

3. I believe in nationalizing those public resources which by their very nature are too important to be held in the control of private individuals.

4. I believe in private ownership of all other property.

5. I believe in upholding the right to private property but in controlling it for the public good.

6. I believe in the abolition of the privately owned Federal Reserve Banking system and in the establishment of a Government owned Central Bank.

7. I believe in rescuing from the hands of private owners the right to coin and regulate the value of money, which right must be restored to Congress where it belongs.

8. I believe that one of the chief duties of this Government owned Central Bank is to maintain the cost of living on an even keel and arrange for the repayment of dollar debts with equal value dollars.

9. I believe in the cost of production plus a fair profit for the farmer.

10. I believe not only in the right of the laboring man to organize in unions but also in the duty of the Government, which that laboring man supports, to protect these organizations against the vested interests of wealth and of intellect.

11. I believe in the recall of all non-productive bonds and therefore in the alleviation of taxation.

12. I believe in the abolition of tax-exempt bonds.

13. I believe in broadening the base of taxation according to the principles of ownership and the capacity to pay.

14. I believe in the simplification of government and the further lifting of crushing taxation from the slender revenues of the laboring class.

15. I believe that, in the event of a war for the defense of our nation and its liberties, there shall be a conscription of wealth as well as a conscription of men.

16. I believe in preferring the sanctity of human rights to the sanctity of property rights; for the chief concern of government shall be for the poor because, as it is witnessed, the rich have ample means of their own to care for themselves.

These are my beliefs. These are the fundamentals of the organization which I present to you under the name of the NATIONAL UNION FOR SOCIAL JUSTICE. It is your privilege to reject or to accept my beliefs; to follow me or to repudiate me.

Hitherto you have been merely an audience. Today, in accepting the challenge of your letters, I call upon everyone of you who is weary of drinking the bitter vinegar of sordid capitalism and upon everyone who is fearsome of being nailed to the cross of communism to join this Union which, if it is to succeed, must rise above the concept of an audience and become a living, vibrant, united, active organization, superior to politics and politicians in principle, and independent of them in power.

This work cannot be accomplished in one week or two weeks or in three months, perchance. But it must begin today, at this moment. It shall be a Union for the employed and the unemployed, for the old and the young, for the rich and the poor, independent of race, color or creed. It is my answer to the challenge received from the youth of the nation; my answer to those who have dared me to act!

All I ask of you today is that you voluntarily subscribe your name to this Union. In addressing your letter to me, please be careful to note well the county in which you live as well as the State. Information will be sent to you for your organization within your own county and your own district.

Tremendous opposition will be aroused against us. Obstacles will be thrown in our path to prevent our success. Every public utility shall besiege us. But all of those who still wish to leave behind them a better country than they found are invited today and this week to unite their hearts and minds for the establishment of social justice.

I have spoken to some of you for nine years over this microphone and to most of you for more than three years.

Today I call upon you to assemble your ranks for action. Thus, in the name of the God of our fathers, we can look forward to better days to come. But without His principles of justice and of charity reduced into practice there is little hope either for ourselves or for the children who will follow us.

There are no fees being exacted from you to belong to this NATIONAL UNION FOR SOCIAL JUSTICE. I am not in it for the commercial profit, because I am talking to the poor, talking to the dispossessed, talking to the jobless and talking against those who possess the means to sustain this broadcast. It will be supported by the voluntary offerings of those who can afford to support it.

In this Union fear no man, employer or employe. For in this crusade we cannot rise to a realization of the principles of social justice without the unremitting and sacrificing toil on the part of all our members.

Do not entertain the thought that, because you are a housewife engaged in your daily duties, a student at his books, an unemployed person, a nun in a convent, a hobo in the jungle or an industrialist in the seat of the mighty, your moral support in this Union is not welcome. All I ask is that those who apply for membership will be men and women of courageous heart and intrepid spirit willing and ready to suffer.

God wills it!

This is the new call to arms—not to become cannon fodder for the greedy system of an outworn capitalism nor factory fodder for the slave whip of communism.

This is the new call to arms for the establishment of social justice!

God wills it! Do you?

# MORE ON THE NATIONAL UNION

*(Sunday, November 18, 1934)*

Y WAY of introduction, I feel obligated to develop a few thoughts for the thousands of persons who wrote to me last week, as well as for the many other thousands in this audience, relative to the NATIONAL UNION FOR SOCIAL JUSTICE.

As you already know, I was impelled to launch this organization chiefly because I was deluged by a multitude of letters coming from Catholics and Protestants and Jews, from shopkeepers, industrialists, farmers and laborers. These letters insisted that the people are surfeited with mere promises; that they are demanding action. More than that, these letters taught me that there is scarcely a man or a woman in this nation who does not recognize the fact that this is no depression from which we are suffering. It is an absolute break-down of the old economic system, both industrial and financial, through which we and our foreparents struggled for the past one hundred and fifty years for prosperity and succeeded in getting it despite capitalism.

No matter how logically and sanely it was conceived, capitalism became so infested with abuses that its nature became identified with the abuses themselves.

Knowing these things, the patience of the majority of the people is becoming exhausted with all these efforts made on the part of those who are hopelessly striving to restore prosperity by preserving the financial and industrial forces which existed in this country before 1929.

By no means are the people unanimous in demanding a change or the establishment of a new economic system. The most powerful group in the nation is solidly opposed to any change. These are the American Bourbons of banking and of industry who, like their predecessors in Royalist France, never learned anything and never forgot anything until the Revolution occurred. This group desires to patch up both the industrial and financial system of yesterday and retain it with only a few accidental modifications. *"If they have no bread, let them eat cake"*—is still their idea of social justice.

Another group, which is rapidly growing, is seeking the extreme measure of communism which advocates the total abolition of all private property together with the nationalization, not only of natural resources but also of trade, of commerce and of industry under a form of government which is technically known as an oligarchy or the rule of a handful of powerful commissars.

Besides the doctrines of these two groups—modern capitalism and modern communism—I believe there can be established a new school of thought where the vast majority of the American people are willing to learn and then rebuild their nation on the age old principles of positive morality. I believe that neither capitalism, as we know it, nor communism, as it operates in Russia, is desired by the ordinary American man or woman. One is just as obnoxious as the other. They are both bad trees which can do nothing better than bear bad fruit. They are both breeders of poverty, both founded upon unjust principles as they both lead inevitably to revolution.

While we refuse to adopt the plans or the philosophy of the communist, we also refuse to support any policy or any group of men who endeavor to restore to power the system of American capitalism which is associated with want in the midst of plenty. The regimented poverty of communism and the created poverty of capitalism are both equally unnecessary.

With this idea in mind, I accepted the challenge of millions of letters received during the past two years to give you people something else besides talk—to give you an outlet for action. The people want a new deal that is a new deal, where the old kings and queens of finance and the legal jokers of politics are thrown into the discard. They want no marked cards. They simply want to play the game of commercial, industrial and financial life, if you care to call it such, honestly and fairly according to the rules of social justice—rules based upon the inalienable rights of human nature and not upon its sordid basis of warped individualism.

This organization known as the NATIONAL UNION FOR SOCIAL JUSTICE is in its cradle.

The word *"national"* implies that it is not for Michigan or for New York only. It is for every State in the nation.

The word *"union"* implies that it is not for Catholic or for Protestant or for Jew alone. Nor is it for laborer or farmer or for industrialist only. It is for all of our citizens irrespective of race, of color, of creed or of profession. It is to be dominated not by Catholic priest or Protestant minister or Jewish rabbi but by American citizens as such.

The words *"social justice"* point out that it is, first of all, opposed to the absolute injustices which are rampant in our midst, and signify that it stands for a fair and equitable distribution of wealth, of profits and the establishment of those principles which will guarantee us a right to life, to liberty and to the pursuits of happiness. Lastly, it is an active organization which will not be contented to talk about these things, but which plans to reduce these things into practice, so that we citizens, who form this nation, shall be enabled, without fear of exploitation, to enjoy the plenitude of God's blessings which have been poured upon us and which are being withheld because of a famine, not of food, not of scientific ability, but of social justice.

I have laid down sixteen principles, the realization of which is our ultimate objective. These principles are so substantially related to this NATIONAL UNION FOR SOCIAL JUSTICE that anyone who is not willing to accept them in their entirety is not welcome in this Union. They represent the solid ground upon which the majority of us will march to victory. They define clearly our hostility to both communism and American capitalism as we know them. But they can never be realized under our form of government unless we can number at least 5-million adherents to these principles and thereby establish a balance of power independent of parties and of politics.

This is no new political party any more than the United States Steel Trust or the United States Chamber of Commerce or the American Bankers' Association or the coal or oil or textile interests constitute a political party, despite the fact that they retain powerful lobbies at Washington.

But it will be a Union to be reckoned with by every Senator, by every Congressman and by every President whom we elect to legislate and to execute the laws of this country for the welfare of the majority of the people in this country.

I openly admit that this Union pretends to be nothing less than an articulate, organized lobby of the people, to bring united pressure upon the representatives at Washington for the purpose of securing the passage of those laws which we want passed, solely with the end in view of breaking down the concentration of wealth, of eliminating the abuses which have been identified with capitalism, and of building up legislation for social justice instead of legislation that breeds communism.

You have elected Representatives. But once they occupy their seats at Washington they are buttonholed by every selfish interest working against your interest. The purpose of this organization is to tell them what laws you want passed and to give you, the laborer, the agriculturist, and the forgotten man, just as much influence as is possessed by the vested powers of wealth.

It is a sorry day that such a move on our part is necessary. But an openly avowed rubber-stampism has made this necessary. Listen to the feet that sound on the steps of the Capitol! Visualize those who enter the Senators' offices or the voices that plead for privileged legislation! No one walks or speaks for labor or agriculture, as a handful of Senators and Representatives fight your losing battles. We are finished surrendering to the mighty lobbies of wealth!

We are anxious to give expression to our definition of the new deal in such a manner that our Representatives will not be mere rubber stamps but will truly represent us in what we want and not accept our tax money for salaries to represent the lobbies of wealth, of power and of greed in what they want.

This is not planned to be an organization which is satisfied with empty, vacuous meetings which are liable to fall under the control of self-seekers. Meetings mean nothing. We have had them for the past one hundred and fifty years and have experienced the growth of two parties whose representatives, despite all their meetings, have failed to accomplish the purpose for which they were assembled.

The old political gatherings were entirely out-moded at the birth of radio. When I present to you the NATIONAL UNION FOR SOCIAL JUSTICE I present a new forum as modern as the radio, uncontrolled and uncontrollable by the machinations of politicians who will not be able to return from Washington and alibi, as they kiss your babies, that they did not know your wishes. More than that, with the carefully selected board of legal advisers, consisting of Catholic, Protestant, Jew and non-conformist, with whom I am surrounding myself, I will from time to time actually draw up suitable, definite concrete bills for legislation which will be presented to your Representatives with the backing of every member of the NATIONAL UNION FOR SOCIAL JUSTICE. They dare not alibi!

The days for alibi and for misrepresentation have passed if you care to utilize this common denominator of the radio.

In unity there is strength. There is no dissipation of our strength through intermediaries who need pass your wishes on to me. You can deal directly.

Therefore I invite you in the name of social justice to unite on the sixteen basic principles which were enumerated last Sunday afternoon.

My friends, I prefer professional politicians to remain outside this Union. There is not one professional politician in this nation who can conscientiously sign up with these sixteen points. Politicians are not going to use us. We plan to use them. They have had their chance and they have failed. Too often their motto, *"to the victor belong the spoils,"* is not in harmony with our motto, *"to the American public belongs social justice."*

Thus if you are in harmony with this proposal; if you believe in the adoption of these principles which I have just recited to you; if you are willing to utilize the well established, the long established and the efficacious method employed by the power trusts, the steel trusts and every other lobby at Washington, I ask that you do not delay in making it your personal business to write a letter to me at Royal Oak, Michigan, stating that you are willing to join this Union. There are no fees attached to it. Its expenses will be borne by voluntary contributions. Moreover, organizers for members of this Union will be going about at a later date to secure more members. Please do not contribute one penny to them. If you care to contribute towards the maintenance of this open radio forum, do it directly. This is your chance. I accept the challenge to do my best to secure the principles of social justice.

# SOCIAL JUSTICE AND A
# LIVING WAGE

*(Sunday, November 18, 1934)*

## I

AY I address this audience on the subject of the justice associated with a living wage and, inferentially, with the injustice of our modern capitalistic structure which prevents the laborer from receiving this wage.

I shall begin with a quotation from the pen of Mr. Lammot duPont, the President of E. I. duPont de Nemours & Company. This quotation, which I shall read for you, expresses clearly and concisely the philosophy of the modern capitalist and industrialist in relation to the rest of their fellowmen. It reads as follows:

*"I mean that all government regulation of business, as such, and as distinguished from any other forms of activity, should be abolished. I mean that business should not be prohibited by government, or compelled by government to do things which private individuals are not prohibited or compelled to do. . . . Business should be treated as an individual is treated—no better, no worse."*

More than one hundred and thirty years ago Mr. duPont's ancestor came to the shores of Rhode Island and brought with him the germ of this cold-blooded, selfish, unsocial philosophy. He was a member of an organization in France known as the Physiocrats. Their chief motto was *"laissez faire"* which, roughly translated, means *"let us alone. Let us do as we please. Let us manufacture what we will."* If not expressed, there was at least implied the belief that government should be regulated by industry; that the citizens of a nation must be subjected to the whims and fancies of the manufacturer; and that the laboring class should be considered as nothing more than pawns to be played with, to be used and cast into the discard in the mad struggle for individualistic wealth.

It was the principle of anarchy reduced to business and for the welfare of business. Laws for everything but none for business! No law over business! It is a law unto itself!

I am not quoting this publicized statement to single out Mr. duPont, America's foremost industrialist. He is only representative of his class which, as long as it retains its belief in this anarchical and unsocial creed, is inviting upon its own head the wrath of an aroused people. I am referring to it merely to quote alongside of it a statement from the pen of Donald Richberg, the Executive Director of the National Emergency Council under Mr. Roosevelt. He says:

*"Nothing has been more clearly proved in the last twenty years than that in the intricacies of modern trade and industry, with personal responsibility largely concealed behind a 'screen of corporate complexities,' it has become possible for businessmen to prey upon each other and the public by methods that are just as vicious in their ethical quality and in their social results as such time-dishonored practices as forgery and embezzlement."*

These, my friends, are two statements which are contradictory. The one is representative of a class which refuses to admit the existence of social justice, which opposes the idea that industry has social duties. The other is more in keeping with the thoughts which I have tried to express, namely, that the old order of industry must be abolished, that its independence, its superiority to government, its lack of obligation to its laborers, its profit for stockholders and "bread-lines-for-workers" theory must be upheld.

*"I mean that all government regulation of business should be abolished!"* So says this mighty prince of industry in one breath while in another he commissions his agents to sell munitions to all governments and his lobbyists to influence protective legislation!

## II

Before discussing further these two contradictory theories may I submit to you a few principles in which I believe and which are either directly or indirectly associated with a just and living wage.

1. This or any other government which is duly instituted exists only at the sufferance of the people and for the common welfare of all the people—not for the particular welfare of any individual class be it industrialist or financial.

2. Therefore, it is the business of government not only to regulate reasonably the conduct of individuals in their dealings with each other, but also to regulate the conduct of the manufacturer to the laborer whether the manufacturer is an individual or a corporation of individuals.

3. Although there are two kinds of property rights, namely, private property owned by private individuals and public property owned by the nation, nevertheless, the ownership of private property does not argue that the owner of it may do with his property what he pleases. If I own a shotgun that is no argument why I may kill my neighbors' child. If I own a factory that is no argument why I may starve the laborers to make profits and profits only for the stockholders. All property is subject to control. All property is owned primarily by Almighty God Who gave us this earth and the fulness thereof—its fields and its forests, its mines and its factories—to be used, if not owned, for the common welfare of every person. This, the Physiocrat, the

26

duPont, the laissez faire philosopher denies as he places himself not only on a par with Almighty God but above Him in that he claims the unlimited use of those properties which he privately owns. This is the doctrine which is twin brother to atheism, This is the doctrine which is anti-social in that it disbelieves by its practice that we are our brothers' keepers. Finally, this is the doctrine which protests against liberty as wealthy manufacturers reduce the laboring class into the bondage of economic slavery and forced, unprofitable idleness.

4. If it is the duty of government to regulate business with the thought in mind that this nation and its wealth primarily belong to God and was bestowed upon us for the common welfare of the common people, I believe that, in the present state of human society, it is advisable that the hourly wage contract should be abolished. In its stead legislation should be passed by which the laborer would receive an annual wage which would enable him to live in decency and according to the American standard. I further believe that this annual wage should not be siphoned from the earnings of the worker only while he works. It should be paid to him primarily from the profits which he has helped to create for the manufacturer. Moreover, instead of the hourly wage contract, there should be a contract of partnership— partnership not in the ownership of the business, but partnership in the profits of the business by which both laborer and industrialist shall reap their just reward.

5. I believe that modern industry is by its very nature related to the social order. It is composed of capital, of labor and of brains. Unless, therefore, these three combine together for the common good; unless this social and individual character of labor be recognized, business itself shall fail and labor shall never be adequately recompensed. Capital cannot do without labor and, least of all, it cannot subsist with an indigent element of labor existing in our country.

6. I further believe that although private industry is privately owned, nevertheless, because of its social character, it depends upon the laborer for its operation. Thus, the representatives of labor should have a voice in the management of the business. Hitherto the management has been left in the hands of those who were interested solely in profits for the stockholders and not in conveniences for human beings.

7. I further maintain that it is not only the right of every laborer to plan for the day when he can support his wife and his children from the revenue of his pay envelope, but he has a further right to look towards that future day when, from the savings derived from his pay envelope, he can become an owner of property himself.

This nation or no other nation can subsist unless there is a wide distribution of private ownership. Today the majority of our homes and farms are held under a form a servile contract and not under deeds of ownership. This is the result of the concentration of profits in the hands of a few, namely, the concentration of property in the hands of a few.

8. I uphold the principle that it is unjust on the part of the laborer to demand wages so high that an employer cannot pay them without ruin and without consequent distress to the working people themselves. Wages must not be so high that they shall drain industry of its working capital and shall force the capitalist to the conclusion that it is safer and more economical to lock up his factory than to operate it. But, in conjunction with this, I equally uphold the principle that if business finds itself making only meager profits on account of bad management, exorbitant salaries to the executives, want of enterprise, or out of date methods, these are not just reasons for reducing the workingmen's wages. The American workingman must not be sentenced to live in poverty because of the philosophy that all profits are to be retained by the stockholders.

9. Lastly, I uphold the principle that if both manufacturers and laborers complain that either there is no *business* or that present business does not provide sufficient profits to enable all of us to live according to the American standard, then those financiers who are responsible for the famine of money are they who are perpetrating a grievous wrong on both industry and labor and, consequently, are responsible for an unjust wage. If, therefore, both industry and labor recognize that finance, or rather, the lack of finance, is the impediment to progress, they are justified in demanding the removal of that obstacle; for why should the vast masses of labor and of industry be forced to suffer and to live in want and indigence because of the mismanagement of financial affairs or because the financial system itself is so obsolete that no valid hope is presented for a restoration of prosperity? The sooner we damn and destroy a bad financial philosophy, the happier this nation will be.

In the litany of my beliefs relative to a just and living wage I shall not fail to mention that it is the business of the government, which has been elected by the people, to so regulate industry that work will be provided for all those who are willing to work, and to so regulate the wage scale, that, independent of the hours spent by the laborer at his employment, it is commensurate with those annual expenses necessitated for a decent American standard of livelihood.

These are the nine principles related to the second point in my program for a just and living annual wage for all American citizens who are willing and able to work.

# III

My friends, man is a social creature. Everywhere about us this fact is self-evident. There are tailors and butchers, shoemakers and tool-makers, shipwrights and physicians, bakers and attorneys—ten thousand different vocations necessary for the sustenance of the life of this nation or of any other nation. No man is sufficient unto himself. Every human activity is dependent upon our common labors. They who are working in the bowels of the earth fetching out coals to warm our homes, or plowing in distant fields the furrows which will cradle the wheat to bring us nourishment—they are all bound together.

Who denies that man is a social creature?

Who dares uphold the theory that he who controls one industry or one form of agriculture, or one factory, is so independent of his fellow citizens that he dares use his produce, though he owns it, to suit his own caprices, careless of the needs and of the rights to life and to happiness of his fellow citizens?

"Laissez faire" may have been the motto of a Robinson Crusoe as, with his man Friday and his unintelligent parrot, he lived a hermit's life far from the paths of trade and commerce and distant from his fellow beings. But in America with its dense population, its manifold complexities of life, its necessary dependencies of one citizen upon the other, its intense specializations of activity, only one blinded by greed and stimulated by avarice dares to profess the doctrine that ownership and use are identical things—the same doctrine which proclaims that I may do as I please with my own property and to the devil with the rest of my fellow citizens.

I may not do as I please with my own property. Because I am a social creature, I may use my property only in so far as it will be of positive use and of no detriment to my fellow creatures. I may not lock up my property against human needs. I may not lock my factory and prevent people from working when people need work and while there is purchasing power to consume the product. I may not be unsocial. I may not be a Dillinger either by taking a life by means of a gun or by the slow process of starvation. One is as bad as the other. Man is a social creature. That is the way that God has created us. We will suffer no philosophy emanating from the brain of a creature to overturn the Creator's plans.

I ask you, ladies and gentlemen, to choose between the statement issued by the prince of industry, Mr. duPont, and the one spoken by Donald Richberg, the Executive Director of the National Emergency Council. Are you for the old deal with its industrial dictatorship and its doctrine of laissez faire-ism or are you for a new deal whereby the government shall legislate against unjust competition, against concentration of profits in the hands of stockholders? Are you for the unlimited and unqualified protection of property rights plus use rights or do you believe in the doctrine of private property but in the equally important doctrine of governmental limitation of its use and of its profits?

As long as the heresy upheld by the modern industrialist is adhered to, namely, that use and ownership are identical, there shall follow in its wake indigence and poverty, loss of homes and of farms and, eventually, strife and bloodshed.

Today, perhaps, the industrialist is empowered to call upon the local and the State police forces to protect his factories and his privately owned industries. But, unless the doctrine of *"laissez faire-ism,"* of *"do as you please-ism,"* takes its place with the theories of slavery, the day will come when neither State nor local police will be able to protect the right to property let alone to the use of it as one pleases.

## IV

It is the primary duty of the government and of all good citizens to abolish conflict between classes and divergent interests. It is our duty to foster and promote harmony among the various ranks of society. No sane man believes in the possibility of creating harmony by bandaging the festered sores of modern industry. No intelligent person preaches effectively against radicalism if he does not first destroy the causes which create it.

Social justice cries aloud to heaven for the workingmen to unite together with the industrialist, not against him. Social justice cries just as loudly to heaven for the industrialist to unite with the workingmen, not against them. The industrialist must recognize that the laborers in his factory are not mere chattels, nor are they to be treated less and insured less against the destructive forces of poverty than are his machines, his lathes and his furnaces which are housed against the inclemencies of all weather and are insured, in season and out of season, against fire and destruction. Labor is not something that can be bought and sold like any piece of merchandise. Labor is something human, something sacred. When you employ a man you are not hiring his muscles or his skill. You are engaging the services of his very soul which gives life and activity to hs skill; of a soul that was inspired by Almighty God to love and to bring little babies into the world; of a soul made to the image and likeness of God before Whose common court you will commonly stand. You are employing the soul of one who is little less than an angel. In one sense you are attempting to purchase the services of something that is unpurchasable, of something that is immortal. The protection of that human life which, leaving all things else, surrenders itself to your just commands, imposes a duty upon you to care for its just rights even more sacredly than you care for your property rights. By all the precepts of social justice, you are forbidden to exclude the laborer from a share in the profits just as much as is this same social justice violated by a propertyless earning class who, in the excesses of communism, perhaps, would demand for themselves not only a share in the use of your produce but a total ownership of your private property.

While we uphold the doctrine of private ownership we will not permit you industrialists to forget the equally sacred doctrine of stewardship. One cannot exist without the other. Destroy the stewardship doctrine and your doctrine of private propertyism is as empty as a sucked egg. The doctrine of stewardship means this: That the earth and the fulness thereof belongs to God; that you who acquire private property have done so only under God; that you cannot exclude from its just usage your fellowmen. Never forget that from the natural resources about us and from the unremitting toil of our citizens springs all wealth. It is a toil that is expended upon either one's own private property or the private property belonging to some other person where capital and labor unite. When labor is willing to supply its brawn and its brain to work at your property, Mr. Industrialist, that same labor cannot be denied a just and living wage which enables it to share reasonably in the produce of American inventions, of American conveniences as well as in decent necessities of life. That is God's doctrine, not mine. You who fight against it are fighting against the Omnipotence of the hand that created you.

I ask you industrialists, if and when you arrive at that point in production where it is necessary to shut down your factories, do you cancel the insurance on your machinery, do you let it become a prey to rust and to destruction? Foolish question for anyone to entertain when, at this very moment—when tomorrow morning, because of these words which I have spoken—you will go running to insurance agencies to purchase riot insurance. Your United States Chamber of Commerce and your other organizations which you have so ably built up for yourselves never had the sagacity and the intelligence to estimate the superior value of the hands, the horned hands, that worked your machines in your factory without which your private property would be worth no more than a scrap heap. You can get along without machinery but you cannot get along without men. More than that, you can get along without advice from your bankers and their outworn philosophy but you dare not attempt to get along without advice from your laborers upon whose purchasing power and good-will you depend.

I am not excoriating you industrialists, nor casting upon you the burden of blame altogether for this condition in which we find ourselves. You, too, have been victimized. But I do castigate you because, like parrots, you have repeated the sophistry of your bankers, your competing manufacturers, if you will, because they manufacture money. You have been foolish enough to let them get away with it. I do blame you for refusing to face facts and for attempting to dwell in realms of fancy. Today your only salvation is identified with the establishment of social justice. Today your only redemption is for capital to join labor instead of perpetuating its harlotry with finance.

See what this union with finance has accomplished.

The J. P. Morgan and Company and Drexel and Company of Philadelphia, who are really no more distinct that a double yolked egg, have twenty partners as members of the board of directors or trustees of fifteen great banks in this nation, having total assets of $3,811,411,000.

On seven holding companies they control fourteen directorships. The assets of these companies total $83,786,475.39.

This same colossus of Wall Street has twelve directorships in ten railroad companies which represent assets of $3,436,666,000.

Five public utility companies representing assets of $3,404,-555,000 have nine Morgan partners as directors.

Eight operating utility companies with ten Morgan controlled directors are valued at $2,818,147,000.

Thirty-eight of our largest industrial corporations in America have fifty-five of Morgan's partners acting as directors or trustees. These corporations are valued at $6,037,644,000.

Six partners of the J. P. Morgan Company are directors or trustees of six insurance companies whose total assets are listed at $337,187,000.

Moreover, there are over one thousand corporations related to the Morgan Company where the colossus acts in the capacity of non-partner directors and trustees.

Leaving these latter aside and listing only the former corporations in which the partners of Morgan and Company and Drexel and Company—the twin yolk egg—are listed as being members of the board of directors or trustees, we have assets representing approximately $20-billion. Include the others, the one thousand corporations, and the assets add to a total of approximately $40-billion—one-sixth of the wealth of the nation—controlled by one man who is a banker and by his directors who direct industry for him. The wedding of the industrialist and the financier has been the destruction of American capitalism.

These are governmental figures—not my compilation. This is the financial giant, the Cyclops, with its one eye intent upon gazing at profits. This is the monster of money control against whose fantastic powers we are fighting for a nation's financial independence!

This is the brains and the brawn of the financial harlotry which controls the industry of the nation, the transportation of the nation, the telephonic and telegraphic communication of the nation, the insurance companies of the nation, while it holds us in the hollow of its hand and, through its puppets, endeavors to hold on to the old financial system which has made slaves of civilized people.

This is only a sample of the concentration of wealth in the hands of the financial element, because capital, intended by nature to remain faithful to labor, has gone forth to dwell with the prostitute of finance who manufactures money.

See what has occurred in our midst when capital and industry permitted the bankers to dictate the policy of labor. Twelve million unemployed; seven million part time employed; seventeen million Americans living on doles; debts multiplying, taxation mounting—all because you industrialists have conspired with the so-called sound money manufacturers against the farmer and the laborer—and against your own best interests. At this moment these same financiers who wrecked our country are emerging from their hiding places to plead recognition for their plans of restoration.

Do we plan to be placid and apathetic and not unite against them? Are the just and living wage and the rights of labor subjects only to be discussed and not reduced to practice? If you believe in these principles which I have unfolded, I ask you to join the NATIONAL UNION FOR SOCIAL JUSTICE.

# WHAT PREVENTS A JUST
# AND LIVING WAGE?

*(Sunday, November 25, 1934)*

## I

IN HIS book entitled *"On Our Way"* Mr. Roosevelt, our President said:

*"We are not going through another winter like the last. I doubt if ever any people so bravely and cheerfully endured a season half so bitter. We cannot ask America to continue to face such needless hardships. It is time for courageous action, and the Recovery Bill gives us the means to conquer unemployment with exactly the same weapon that we have used to strike down child labor.*

*"The proposition is simply this:*

*"If all employers will act together to shorten hours and raise wages we can put people back to work. No employer will suffer, because the relative level of competitive cost will advance by the same amount for all. But if any considerable group should lag or shirk, this great opportunity will pass us by and we will go into another desperate winter. This must not happen."*

This quotation seems to be closely related to a recent development in our national affairs. Just last week it was decided by the United States Chamber of Commerce, which body is acting as spokesman for the industrialists and financiers of this nation, to co-operate in a more noble manner with the activities of our Administration. This is a pleasant and wholesome change which is worthy of recording. Until last week the banker and the banker-controlled industrialist spent millions of dollars obstructing the new deal. I hope their conversion of heart is not patterned after the Greek heroes who entered the city of Troy by posing as its benefactors. Somehow or other, sagacious citizens always fear Greeks even when bearing gifts.

It is not fair to interpret this gesture on the part of American business as one that is linked to subterfuge and hypocrisy. Nor is it fair for our citizens to suspect even momentarily the motives of our President. He is endeavoring to bring about a union of forces, a union of efforts. He is not entrusting, I hope, to the hands of the old dealers the outcome of the new deal. He is not surrendering our destinies to those who believe in the sacred right of privately manufacturing money, of expanding credit and of contracting currency at their own wills. Above all, it would only be a vile misinterpretation to charge him with the betrayal of the interests of the American people by letting loose once more the four horsemen of the Apocalypse as they mount their steeds of slavery, of famine, of pestilence and of war.

If industry and finance are determined that now is the time to co-operate for progress and prosperity, it is honestly expected that they alter their entire philosophy which characterized their activities in the past. No longer dare they be riders of ruin and of rabid individualism. If yesterday they identified all wealth with money and all progress with gold and profits, today they must become converts to the forgotten doctrines of social justice.

This nation has arrived at that point in its history where on this eve of Thanksgiving Day we can honestly return thanks to our God for having bestowed upon us the science and the mechanics of the ages, the blessings of forests, of fields, of mines, of orchards—blessings never paralleled in the past. Besides all that, in His bounty God has filled our hearts with liberty and with a love of happiness which were never equalled in the annals of the world. For those things we are grateful as on this day we sound the clarion call to farmer, to laborer and to industrialist to unite and sever, once and for all, the fetters which bind us to the slavery of finance. All these benedictions bestowed upon us by Almighty God will be useless if we permit a money policy of scarcity to dominate us in the midst of plenty.

Thus, at this moment, if there is honesty of purpose in the hearts of those who formerly were so strong in their opposition, they will not be content to gage success except insofar as they are able to place 12-million idle men at profitable work instead of exploiting the laborer.

Candidly, our citizens are not in total sympathy with the American Liberty Leaguers and the fossilized Chamber of Commerce members, who, in the past, openly professed their beliefs in the supremacy of property rights to the neglect of human rights.

If those beliefs still predominate in the months and years to come then I can say:

*"Go back to your plow, Mr. Farmer, and dig deep your furrows not at a profit but at a loss. Take your place on the mass production line, Mr. Laborer, at fifty or eighty cents an hour for six months in the year as you look forward to lay-offs and bread lines. Wipe from your brow those deepening lines of worry, Mr. Merchant, and become reconciled to your disease of debt and famine of currency as you wonder how you can save your homes, pay your taxes and retain your self-respect."*

If these gentlemen of industry and of finance refuse to reconcile their old policies with the new program of distribution; if they are determined to continue mumbling their meaningless incantations relative to sound money, to printing press money, to gold standardism and to a thousand other superstitious fears with the hope of practicing their black art and magic with any degree of success before our people, they are doomed to failure.

† It is to be hoped that we are really on our way to solving this problem of want in the midst of plenty. We must not be on our way backwards. I ask the industrialist, therefore, if he can hire one more man in his factory; if he can produce one more shoe, one more motor car, one more suit of clothes, unless the purchasing power of this country is restored; unless we revamp our financial philosophy.

I further ask the industrialist, who admittedly is in business to make profits for the stockholders, if he hopes to continue with the worn-out policies of 1929 which, over a period of years, have been proven to be obstacles in the path of the laborer and of the farmer. Finally, I ask the sincere bankers and manufacturers if the time has not arrived for them to put aside an economic system which was devised for production only and to adopt one which aims not only at production but also at distribution.

From this day forward industry, as represented by the United States Chamber of Commerce, must break the shackles of its obsolete theories and must recognize that a new day has dawned. If it fails to do this, I dare prophesy that before another November comes to pass the manufacturer and the industrialist will recognize that they have been betrayed by finance. They must line up with labor and with agriculture instead of holding fast to the program of the international bankers and the money manufacturers.

## II

If we are to look to the United States Chamber of Commerce to help restore prosperity to our nation let us investigate the record of this organization and hear what its spokesmen had to say in the past. I believe that I shall be able to point out to you that its former thoughts on progress and prosperity; its former theories relative to the problem of distribution and its former credo upon which prosperity should be built—all must be scuttled. After I point out these things to this audience with words definite and concrete from the pens and lips of the gentlemen who have pledged to lend their support to the new deal, I challenge them either to give pronouncement to a new philosophy or else to stand by their old. If they stand by the old honest men are forced to regard them as nothing more than mere obstructionists.

In January, 1932, at Decatur, Illinois, Silas H. Strawn, then president of the Chamber of Commerce, said:

*"Let those who are complaining of their lot here go to some other country, any other country, and see how much better off we are than the people of any other nation on earth.*

*"Let us cease to whine about depression and devote ourselves to the diligent performance of our daily duties."*

On that date Mr. Strawn advocated travel and Dr. Coueism for our 12-million unemployed who were going about their duties of producing smiles on empty stomachs.

In June, 1932, Mr. Strawn again gave voice to the following formula for prosperity:

*"We must balance the budget ... The first step towards achieving this balanced budget should be not increased taxation but decreased federal expenditures."*

The only feasible way to decrease federal expenditures is to throw to the mercies of the unkind elements the 17-million persons on our national dole. That is the way to get prosperity.

Again, in July, 1932, the United States Chamber of Commerce simply slays us with this platitude:

*"We call upon the officials of our federal, state and local governments to balance their budgets both by the elimination of all unnecessary expenditures and the increasing of such equitably levied taxes as may be necessary as an emergency measure."*

Just two years ago the depression could have been ended, according to these gentlemen, by increasing taxation upon the home owners, the small business man, the laborer and the farmer. That was their philosophy.

Finally, in July, 1932, Mr. Henry I. Harriman, President of the United States Chamber of Commerce, issued his magnanimous fourteen point program for recovery. Here it is synopsized:

1. The budget must be balanced by raising more taxes.

2. The President of the United States should be given power to veto or reduce appropriation bills of Congress.

3. The Federal Reserve Banks must have control over credit.

4. Amend the anti-trust laws.

5. Enlarge the power of trade associations.

6. Let business establish its own economic councils free from government interference.

7. Repeal that portion of the Farm Board Act which authorizes the attempt to equalize prices by government purchases.

8. Reduce the hours of labor.
(Nothing is said about increasing the pay of labor.)

9. Keep the Reconstruction Finance Corporation loaning to public and private works.

10. Amend the Volstead Act—do not repeal it.

11. Refers to our ex-soldiers. Let the government give care to the dependents of those who lost their lives. But the name *"veteran"* must not be sullied by its use as a cloak to cover the demands for pension, bonus or hospitalization.

12. Give the President the power of a dictator, of a Mussolini, so that when Congress is not in session he can suspend the operation of existing laws and provide for emergency measures required by the public welfare.

13. Keep out of the League of Nations but enter into the World Court.

14. The depression of 1929 was caused by a loss of moral perspective and a collapse of common honesty. The Sermon on the Mount and the Ten Commandments will always be the true guide to real and lasting prosperity.

These, my friends, are the fourteen points in a program for the restoration of prosperity. They were published by Mr. Harriman, the present president of the United States Chamber of Commerce. Pleasant news to the ears of the farmer, the laborer, the veteran and the democracy-loving American.

No suggestion for a living wage! No conception for agricultural profits! No intimation of restoring to Congress the right to coin and regulate the value of money! No plan to produce except for a profit! No relief to the taxpayer! No program for removing the causes of the depression! In fact, no depression but simply a collapse of honesty!

Does the United States Chamber of Commerce seriously regard the collapse of honesty on the part of bankers and brokers, of bogus bond salesmen and hide-out holding companies? Does it wish to protect the depositors' money?

In May, 1933, the United States Chamber of Commerce went on record in favor of the bankers and against the depositors when it said:

*"The Chamber is specifically against government guaranty of deposits. The Chamber of Commerce recommends that the federal and state governments enact laws permitting, under careful regulation, the extension of branch banking."*

This, my friends, is the Bourbonism, the laissez faire-ism, the do-as-you-please-ism of which I spoke last Sunday. This is the philosophy of the United States Chamber of Commerce which is demanding that death sentence be passed upon the National Recovery Act and contends that, while unions among workingmen are permissable, the industrialist needs pay no attention to the demands of the union.

In January, 1934, Mr. Harriman, President of the United States Chamber of Commerce, wrote an article in a magazine known as *"The Nation's Business"* which he titled *"Faith in Money is Essential."* Although every child in this nation knows that we are suffering from a lack of money and from an unbearable burden of debt money, Mr. Harriman propounded this financial program:

+ 1.   Promptly establish a fixed gold standard, revaluing the gold dollar if necessary.

2.   Stabilize our currency with the currency of Great Britain through the medium of our privately owned Federal Bank and the privately owned Central Banks of England.

3.   Change the legislation for the so-called permanent plan for insurance of bank deposits.

4.   Remove all the burdens which the National Recovery Act is now placing upon small business.

This, then, is the skeleton of a program totally opposed to the program for which we stand. It is the avowed proposal on the part of the United States Chamber of Commerce to keep us tied to the privately owned central banks and to permit these privately owned central banks to continue with our famine of money and the regulation of our currency.

Again I challenge the United States Chamber of Commerce to scuttle this philosophy or their silence will force us to conclude that they still cling to it and are, therefore, nothing more than Greeks bearing gifts into the city which they would destroy.

All these charges and statements which I made relative to the United States Chamber of Commerce, have been written or subscribed to by spokesmen for this organization in the volumes of its publication known as *"The Nation's Business."*

My friends, now you know the new deal that this body proposes to give you if it retains the philosophy so clearly expressed by its spokesmen during the past two years. You know its avowed opposition to financial reform and its hostility to industrial and agricultural reform. Between the lines it is easy for you to read that it is still wedded to its belief in production for profit and profit only. Here is one lobby which, apparently, has succeeded in expressing its views.

However, I ask you if there is enough red blood left in the American people, including the industrialists, to protest against these policies which are detrimental to our interests, to our happiness and to our rights, as American citizens, to a decent livelihood, not one of which rights can be obtained if the philosophy of the United States Chamber of Commerce is reduced to practice. The challenge still holds good!

I have no personal quarrel with any of these members of the United States Chamber of Commerce. But steadfastly I shall quarrel with their philosophy as long as they retain it. Unfortunately, they have been educated in a school that knew little and cared less for the practical interpretation of the Sermon on the Mount. It was the same school which protected slavery; the same school which often identified virtue with the cunning of squeezing through loopholes of conscience which led to the practices of mass exploitation.

Keenly apprehensive, flawlessly organized, they worked in silence, always careful to avoid a display of their power or an exhibition of their plans. But now you know their plans!

Today, with their backs against the tottering wall of the old deal, they must accept the challenge either to help produce prosperity or cease opposing any and all policies which aim to make of the Sermon on the Mount a practical norm of life instead of a platitude to be played with.

The new philosophy of social justice I shall defend against their exaggerated interpretation of property rights. I shall oppose their old theories of financial bondage as long as it is my privilege to utilize the facilities of this radio.

## III

While discussing the man-made poverty which has been inflicted upon the people of the United States by reason of such philosophy as was formerly advocated by the United States Chamber of Commerce, let me forewarn these gentlemen that their old sophistry of supply and demand is no safe rule in economics today or tomorrow. There is the most plenteous supply that ever existed in this nation and, at the same time, the greatest demand which ever existed in this world. There is simply a lack of money for the supply to reach the demand.

According to circular 296 of the United States Department of Agriculture—the same Department which supports the policy of destruction, I am sorry to say—we have the following facts to substantiate the statement I just made. There is disclosed an annual deficiency of approximately 27-billion pounds of milk, or 13-billion quarts; a deficiency of 1-1/3-billion pounds of tomatoes and citrus fruits; a deficiency of more than 12-billion pounds of fruits and green vegetables; a deficiency of 2-billion pounds of meat; a shortage of more than 13-billion eggs and 2½-billion pounds of sugar. These deficiencies and shortages do not exist because there is not a supply or because there is not a demand but simply because the people who want to use this supply have not the money to buy it. We have millions of untilled acres which could be devoted to the raising of cattle and to the supplying of milk, of fruits and of vegetables, and yet our farmers are forced to forego their agricultural pursuits because the philosophy of scarce money has ordained that they operate at a loss.

If 527-millions of acres and 6-million American farmers are partially idle and fail to meet the adequate food requirements of our people to the astonishing extent of nearly 100-billions of pounds of foodstuffs, it is not logical to say that there is an under-supply or an over-demand. Were these acres and these farmers permitted to work under a decent financial system there would be no need of importing foodstuffs and no under-supply in actual products. We have a superabundance of potential supply and an equal demand for foodstuffs. The people of this nation know this. All the sophistry that you can preach will be nothing more than buncombe in the future.

While we are slaughtering cattle, burning wheat and plowing under cotton, we have imported 22-billion pounds of foodstuffs at prices cheaper than our farmers could afford to produce. How can the United States Chamber of Commerce and the so-called sound money advocates face these facts of want in the midst of plenty, of want created by their modern financial system?

As for a demand or a supply of wearing apparel: In the prosperous year of 1929, not to mention the depression year of 1934, the men of this nation were supplied on a per capita basis of a bare one-third of a garment of new out-wear. In other words, in this land of plenty where two new suits of clothes per year might be reasonably expected by each man, there was a deficiency of some 66-million suits of clothes. And this in a country where our American ability to produce could supply two suits for each man!

For the female population, which fared much better, there was barely one-half garment, including skirts, ensembles and suits. On a minimum living standard basis of two new outer garments for each woman in this country the deficiency was in excess of 52-million garments. This had nothing to do either with supply or demand. The deficiency is totally related to a lack of purchasing power, to a famine of money!

If you care to express the same thought in another manner, all this lack of clothing and this undernourishment were due to the damnable philosophy of production for profit instead of for profitable use.

I repeat that we had both the acreage and the mechanical capacity to supply two full garments each to every individual which would increase our cotton and wool production by 5-billion pounds. This means an increase of six times our present number

41

of sheep and an additional 17-million acres of cotton in cultivation, if our farmers were allowed to operate for profitable use and if our factories were allowed to keep open and supply the necessary clothing required by our people.

What does the United States Chamber of Commerce think when confronted by these facts placed alongside their philosophy?

Are they under the impression that our laborers in the factory and our farmers on the soil will continue to produce only for the benefit and the profit of the stockholders and the bankers who control our industries, and, through their mortgages, control our farms?

Shall we go on forever with rules and regulations invented for an economy of scarcity when today we are confronted with an economy of abundance?

Of our 527-million acres of workable land only 280-millions are devoted to the production of food. If our 125-million people in this nation were eating a decent American diet we would have need of 335-million acres in production. Yet we purposely attempt to commit the sacrilege of *"less-and-less-ism"* by clinging to the falsities of scarce money when God has blessed us with the abundance of *"more-and-more-ism."* No wonder that the Scriptures remind us that *"money is the root of all evil!"*

A plenitude is within our very grasp, but the acquisition of it is obstructed because the United States Chamber of Commerce's philosophy of production for profit and not for human needs is again in the saddle.

Meantime you will starve. You will clothe yourselves just on this side of nakedness because those who control money pervert the law of supply and demand. God's law of justice and of charity, I am afraid, has become out-moded and, in its stead, man's law of greed reigns supreme.

The international bankers, the privately owned Federal Reserve bankers, the industrialists who continue to subscribe to the philosophy of *"profit for stockholders at any price and production for profit only,"* certainly are not only refusing to face the facts of modern existence. They are refusing to face and recognize the very principles which relate to their own self-preservation.

## IV

Last Sunday I partly developed for you the second point in the program of the National Union for Social Justice relative to a decent living, annual wage. In connection with this I pointed out that one of the chief functions of our government is to supply opportunities for work for those who are willing and able to work. I intimated that a scale of wages, based only on payment while you work and bread lines while you don't work is one of the first causes for unemployment and is contrary to social justice.

Today may I emphasize three more principles which must be adopted before a living and a fair wage can be secured.

1. There is demanded of the workingmen, of the industrialists and of the farmers of this nation a union of effort and wood will, to the end that a scale of wages will be set up which will enable the greatest number of our citizens to secure the greatest opportunities to purchase the necessities and conveniences of modern American life. That is the first principle.

2. Besides advocating a union between the laborer, the farmer and the industrialist, I might add this further principle that a reasonable relation between the prices obtained for the products of the farm and the wages paid for the products of labor must be established, if there will be such a thing as a just wage. Call this the commodity dollar, if you will. But we must work towards this end, namely, that we shall not be deprived of our goods which the wealth and the resources of nature, of our scientists and of our factories supply us because of a scarcity of dollars or because of dear dollars. Money must no longer be our master and we, its slaves. The supply of money and the regulated value of money must be in proportion to the supply of nature's products and to human demands.

It is not Christianity to teach that men and women are supposed to live in poverty. Poverty is the breeder of holdups, brigandry, immorality and vice. Prosperity and culture, provided they be used with prudence, are singular helps to virtue. That is our teaching.

3. I contend that it is impossible to have a just and living wage or an equitable price level established for the commodities of the farm or of the factory under the system of modern capitalism.

I am practical enough to forget the dictionary definition of capitalism and to accept its definition as translated by the actual facts which today are identified with capitalism. I take this stand against capitalism for the following reasons:

(a) Modern capitalism violates right order because it so employs the working of wage earning classes as to divert business and economic activity to its own advantage without any regard to the human dignity of the workers, the social character of economic life, social justice, and the common good.

(b) It is evident in our days that capitalism not only accumulates wealth but also immense power and despotic economic domination into the hands of a few, and that those few are frequently not the owners but only the trustees and directors of invested funds and administer these funds at their own good pleasure. It is absolutely erroneous to say that the public utility corporations, for example, are owned by hundreds of thousands of stockholders; that a steel corporation possesses 500,000 owners and General Motors 300,000 owners. As a matter of fact most of the stock in public utilities, in the steel industry and in the motor industry is controlled by a very small group of men and these, in turn, by three other men—Mellon, Morgan and duPont—whose representatives out-vote the hundreds of thousands of so-called stockholders.

(c)   This capitalistic power has become particularly irresistible because it has been exercised by those who held and controlled money and who governed and determined the allotment of credit. For that reason, upon bended knee, industry and labor and agriculture were forced, in the past, to beg from them for the supply of the life blood, so to speak, to the entire economic body. These financiers grasp, as it were, in their hands the very soul of production so that no one dares breathe, let alone live, against their will.

(d)   Free competition is a further characteristic note of modern capitalism. This permits the survival only of those who are the strongest and means that those who fight most relentlessly, careless of the Commandments and of social justice, are the victors to whom belong the spoils.

(e)   Modern capitalism, as suggested by Mr. Harriman, whom I quoted for you, has always been identified with the dictatorship of economic domination. It was chiefly due to this phase of modern capitalism that fierce battles arose to acquire control of the nation so that its resources of power, of light, of water and of money, as well as the House of Representatives, could be abused in the struggle for existence.

It was this same economic dictatorship which could not brook a rival; for by its very nature it created wars amongst the nations.

(f)   This well known characteristic of modern capitalism is one of unbridled ambition—ambition for domination which has succeeded the desire for profits. As a result of this, the whole economic life has become hard, cruel and relentless in a ghastly measure.

Furthermore, the multiplication of federal and state officers, the intermingling and scandalous confusion of duties and offices of civil authority, have been created under capitalism to protect the privileged classes. No wonder our government sometimes is regarded as a slave who, if he attempts to rebel against this economic system of capitalism, is confronted with capital on strike and is forced to kiss the hand of the banker who holds the lash.

44

(g)  From modern capitalism, as from a poisoned fountain-head, there flows that stream of detestable internationalism, by which the Warburgs, the Rothschilds and the Morgans dominate affairs not only in America but also in the Central Banks of Europe and fly from their mastheads the flag which bears this emblem *"My Country! 'tis where my fortune is."* It is an internationalism which cares not for the righteousness of social justice or of sound philosophy, but is willing for the protection of its private property, to become a bed-fellow with the harlot of the ages. This was done by capitalistic France who, the day before yesterday, wedded her destinies to those of communistic Russia.

These seven statements are associated with the second principle in our platform for social justice. These are the seven obstacles that prevent a just and living wage and these are the obstacles that must be removed. It is impossible for the laborer, for the farmer or for the honest industrialist to presume that there is such a thing as a just wage or purchasing power in this nation when all profits are siphoned into the hands of a few. It is presumptuous to discuss questions relative to a just and honest wage as long as the working people of America support the system of modern capitalism that is not one whit better than Russian communism.

If I advocate its dissolution, I come to you people to teach you the philosophy of social justice.

The testing hour has arrived. The challenge has gone out to the bankers and to the industrialists who supported modern capitalism less than two weeks ago to forget their philosophy and to line up with God's philosophy. Every plank in the platform for social justice is founded upon the Commandments, on the Scriptures and upon the dignity of God's fatherhood and man's brotherhood.

My friends, there was a time when I was peacefully reconciled to privation and want, to the existence of undernourished children, barefoot men and broken-hearted women.

Caught as I was in the whirlpool of a hideous philosophy of money which I had accepted as something inevitable like sunrise and sunset, I dared preach patience to my people, when the only patience that should have been in their hearts was tolerance for me, who was a blind leader leading the blind.

But those days of defending modern capitalism have gone. I have dared to reject that philosophy of finance which breeds unnecessary poverty, which generates tubercular children and universal misery.

# SHARE THE PROFITS WITH LABOR

*(Sunday, December 2, 1934)*

AFTER five years of so-called depression, the capitalist and the laborer are both convinced that industrial affairs have arrived at a deadlock. Under the present capitalistic, financial, industrial and scientific arrangements there is nothing left for this nation to do except proceed backwards like a snail. Our experiment of borrowing ourselves out of debt with bankers' bonds has proven to be a miserable failure. The 500,000 more men who are out of work this year than last year constitute an appalling fact as does the kindred fact that our national dole for emergency relief has doubled from August, 1933, to August, 1934.

There is only one way of reading scientifically the thermometer of prosperity. This method is definitely related to how many men we have put back to profitable work. A correct reading forces us to conclude that the mercury has been on the downward trend. This is true despite the fact that business is better and that dividends for stockholders have increased. But 85 per cent of the American people will always be more concerned with the profits accruing to the laborer and to the farmer than with the capitalistic profits which are pouring into the pocketbooks of the fortunate few.

America cannot prosper unless labor prospers!

This truism is as well known to the United States Chamber of Commerce as it is to every citizen. Thus, the Chamber is about to marshal its forces for the purpose of ending the depression by putting the millions of unemployed back to work.

*"Back to work,"* say I? But upon what basis?

*"Back to profitable work"* or merely *"back to work?"* *"Back to work"* so that the family can live according to the American standard and enjoy both the necessities and the conveniences of those things which are within our grasp; or *"back to work"* on the basis of a lower standard from whose depths we will bid farewell to the things we dreamed about and to the life we planned?

I seriously doubt the ability of industry under the present policies to put one million men back to work let alone the eleven or twelve million idle men who are in our nation. But granting the ability of the Chamber of Commerce to accomplish this Herculean task, what method will it employ?

All we have to judge by is its official pronouncement which, was published in September, 1932. In that issue of *Nation's Business* it said:

*"Adjustment in working hours in industry is having the attention of the Special Committee of the Department of Manufacture. This Committee is endeavoring to suggest general policies which should govern business men in making the necessary adjustments in industrial operations brought about by present conditions. As one of its activities the Committee is participating in and giving assistance to the national 'share the work' movement."*

Now let us see what is wrong with this seemingly sane proposal.

My friends, the bald fact is this: We are not so much interested in any *"share-the-work"* movement as we are vitally interested in a *"share-the-profit"* movement. This is the point that the gentlemen from the Chamber of Commerce totally overlook. *"Share-the-work-ism"* is the Siamese twin to *"share-poverty-ism."* To share the work without sharing the profits, as contemplated by the Chamber of Commerce, means that a laborer who now obtains $25.00 a week must be satisfied with approximately $15.00 a week.

This assertion I shall substantiate in a moment by undeniable facts.

Not once did it enter into the concept of these Aristotelian geniuses, who preside over the destinies of the Chamber of Commerce, that mass production machinery is constantly displacing labor and, therefore, the constant displacement of labor inevitably leads to more sharing of work and to more sharing of depleted pay envelopes. This holds true unless "share-the-work" is accompanied by a substantial sharing of profits. This, their capitalistic money system cannot afford to face. This, their capitalistic economic system, that was designed for production at a profit to the owner of a factory, cannot do.

I forewarn you, my friends: be not misled by any half-truth and half-baked policy which will advocate a thirty hour week or even a twenty hour week unless it envisions a yearly salary sufficient to meet the requirements of your standard of living.

Be not misled by any such trick legislation which will be proposed. It offers you a rainbow bubble which will vanish into thin air the moment you attempt to grasp it.

*"Share-the-work"* means *"share-the-poverty,"* It is a fallacy which, like a hidden dagger, lies beneath the cloak of beneficence —a dagger which will strike you down in the cold blood of abject poverty if you succumb to its arguments.

## II

And now for the facts to substantiate these statements. The following figures were taken from the *Official Federal Reports* and from the *Report on the National Income and Its Purchasing*

*Power* as prepared by our National Bureau of Economic Research.

1. In 1919 we had in the United States of America 274,402 manufacturing establishments. By 1927—eight years later—despite our increase in population and our increase in exports these manufacturing establishments decreased by 30 per cent leaving only 191,866 manufacturing plants in operation.

These figures prove to you that there was a tendency towards monopolization; that business, as conducted in this nation, was programmed and geared only for the few.

It was fast becoming a grim reality that, in the United States, there was no place for the small business man. Only that plant which was associated with a large banking house could secure loans to purchase labor-saving machinery. The little industrialist, who refused to sell his birthright and share his profits, not with the laborer but with the banker, gradually was being eased out of industry.

All this might fall under the heading of unjust competition.

2. In 1919 these manufacturing plants employed 9,039,171 wage earners. Eight years later this wage earning group was reduced to 8,349,755. Here again we find, despite our increased population and exports, fewer laborers were required — a decrease of 689,416.

3. According to official figures, the factories in the past ten years ending with 1933, produced 42 per cent more merchandise with 500,000 fewer factory workers than they did in the ten previous years.

And in the prosperous year of 1929, industries upon which 40 per cent of our wage earners depended for a living, employed 900,000 fewer wage earners than they did in 1919 although the 1929 production was 50 per cent greater.

Our railroads, for example, increased their business 7 per cent with 250,000 fewer employes. Our coal mines surrendered 23 per cent more coal with approximately 100,000 fewer miners. A tremendous increase in the production of textiles, or motor cars, of practically every mass production article was noticeable while there was a marked decrease in the number of laborers employed.

Perhaps you are beginning to see why I condemn that program of share-the-work. Year by year, despite a decrease in the number of manufacturing institutions, there was a gradual increase in the number of articles produced, accompanied by a falling off in the number of men employed.

In this year of 1934 do the proponents of *"share-the-work"* propose to turn back the hands of the clock of progress? Dare they suggest that we go back to the hand saw and scrap the power saw? Why, such a suggestion is hostile to reason!

The scientist is not going to vanish. The engineer of tomorrow does not plan to put his brains in cold storage. The fact is, there will be fewer factories and fewer laborers required five years hence than there are today. And there will be greater production five years hence than there is today.

Are you in favor of share the work and share the poverty when it is a proven truth that there is less need for mass production manual labor? My friends, we have arrived at that period in the cycle of development when idleness must be translated into leisure.

Man has won his victory over the menacing mysteries of the unkind elements. The old tools have given place to the new. The wheel, the nail, the spade and the broad axe belong to the past! Steam, electricity, the power lathe, a myriad number of automatic devices have out-moded them all. The battle for production has been won! Henceforward less and less factory labor is required.

If that be so, are we prepared to adopt the program of share-the-work, share-the-pay-envelope and share-the-poverty with all profits gravitating towards those who own the factories?

This is the cycle of development which cries aloud for a share in the profits.

4. Now let us change our point of vantage and view these facts from a different angle.

In 1914 the value of the products manufactured in our industrial establishments was approximately $24-billion. In 1921 this value increased to $44-billion. In 1923 it skyrocketed to $60-billion. While in 1929 it reached the stupendous figure of $69-billion.

Not only was power concentrated in the hands of fewer industrialists; not only did our population increase by more than 25-million persons; not only did the wealth produced by these industrialists increase by almost 300 per cent! The astounding and frightful figure associated with all this is that there was a steady, devastating decrease in employment and in wages also. The more business carried on, the fewer people were employed!

5. As far as the wage decrease, which accompanied the wealth increase, is concerned, let us put these official figures on the books of our memories.

In 1923 when modern capitalism was in bloom the total volume of wages paid to working men in the manufacturing industries was $11,007,000,000. In 1929 when the annual value of our manufactured products had increased $9-billion over the 1923 total the volume of wages in the manufacturing industries was still approximately $11-billion.

Need I ask you who shared in this profit of $9-billion more wealth? It was not the working man. It was the financially controlled industrialist who appears before you today with his program of share-the-work as he shirks the inevitable program of the sharing the profits.

To emphasize this point let me explain to you that while the total wages paid to the working men during these years of increased production scarcely varied, in 1922 the total dividends paid to the owners of industry by all corporations in the United States was $930,648,000. In 1929 these dividends increased to $3,478,000,000—an increase of 356 per cent for the owners of industry—but hardly a dollar's increase for the laborers employed in industry.

Do not these figures impress you with the fact that what the laboring man requires in this nation is not so much a share-the-work program as a share-the-profit program?

6. To express this same thought with figures as recent as 1929 we learned from the Federal Deposit Insurance Corporation (just last week) that out of 50-million bank depositors 800,000 of them control two-thirds of the total bank deposits in the nation. We learned that 71 percent of American families had incomes in 1929, a prosperous year, mind you, of less than $2,500 when the sum of $2,500 is necessary to maintain a decent American standard of living. Today in the year 1934 the average laborer is receiving less than $1,000 a year and the cost of living is well proportioned to $1,500 a year. To state it conservatively, 71 per cent of our people are living in abject poverty. There is no other name for it. We learn that 1-1/5 per cent of our American families received one-fourth of the total income produced by the United States and the remaining three-fourth of that income was left to the 98-4/5 per cent balance of the American public. This was in 1929. Today it is far more acute than it was in that year.

This is what I so often referred to as the concentration of wealth in the hands of a few. This is the system of modern capitalism, which from governmental analysis, proves beyond dispute or question that there is no just sharing of profits in this nation. This is the capitalistic system which the United States Chamber of Commerce endeavors to foist upon you men and women with their damnable slogan of *"share-the-work."* Finally these are the figures known by everybody in Washington from President to page boy as they enter the halls of Congress to rectify the ills of a so-called depression.

I ask you, ladies and gentlemen, if you will be patient with your Representatives or your Senators as they argue and debate over negligible matters and refuse to outlaw this legally protected banditry of capitalism?

+ The ever-increasing number of propertyless wage earners and the superabundant riches of the fortunate few are unanswerable arguments that the earthly goods, so lavishly produced in this age of mass productionism, are far from rightly distributed and shared amongst the various classes of men.

Over a period of more than fifty years capitalism forgot that it could not survive unless purchasing power and profitable private ownership were shared with the laboring class.

Industry, with its savage individualism, was in business for the profits to be gained therefrom. Its god was the gold of profits, its high priest, the banker; and its Bible was the gospel of greed.

The time has arrived when both citizen and Congressman are well informed, I repeat, as to the inherent rottenness of capitalism. The time has come when, if these Congressmen refuse to legislate against the concentration of wealth and for the distribution of profits, then we are perfectly justified in accusing them of playing politics with misery and of having sold the temple back to the bankers.

### III

We are through, at least for this afternoon, with the citation of figures. Saving our sanity, we dare not reject them. Under the compulsion of reason we must face the two realities which they unfold to us. First: there is the blessing of technical unemployment as we clumsily call it.. Tools have been perfected. Science has progressed. We have arrived at that point in civilization when it is no longer necessary to figure out how to get 12-million men back to steady, constant factory labor. That is a problem similar to the one of trying to make a square peg fit into a round hole. Our task is identified with how to distribute the profits which have been piled up through the use of mechanical devices. Watt and Stephenson, Fulton and Edison—these and a thousand other scientists, by harnessing the forces of nature, have taught us how to share-the-work with machinery long before the United States Chamber of Commerce revived the heresy of sharing the work with our already impoverished fellow citizens.

*"The blessing of technical unemployment,"* I call it. But the system of modern capitalism, which pays the laborer only while he works and lets him work only while he produces at a profit for the owner of the machine, is endeavoring to change a blessing into a curse.

Second: There is the inescapable conclusion that capitalism tends to concentrate all profits in the purses of machine owners and to scatter poverty over the face of the earth. It is a peculiar poverty, if you will. It is a poverty which forces humanity to stand helplessly starving, before the baker's shop window with its plenitude of good things.

## IV

Now you are interested in learning for what principles the National Union for Social Justice stands when confronted with the problems and abuses which have grown out of capitalistic mass productionism.

1. We maintain that it is not only the prerogative but it is also the duty of the government to limit the amount of profits acquired by any industry.

2. We maintain that it is the function of the government to see that industry is so operated that every laborer engaged therein will secure those goods which will be sufficient to supply all needs for an honest livelihood.

3. We further maintain that it is the duty of government to secure the production of all those industrial goods—food, wearing apparel, homes, drugs, books and all modern conveniences— which the wealth of the nation, the natural resources of the land and the technical ability of our scientists are able to produce until all honest human needs within the nation are amply supplied. This principle is contrary to the theory of capitalism. Capitalism produces for a profit to the individual owner. Social justice advocates the production for use at a profit for the national welfare as well as for the owner.

4. We maintain the principle that there can be no lasting prosperity if free competition exists in any industry. Therefore, it is the business of government not only to legislate for a minimum annual wage and a maximum working schedule to be observed by industry, but also so to curtail individualism that, if necessary, factories shall be licensed and their output shall be limited. For it is not in accordance with social justice that the owner of an industry will so operate his factory as to destroy free competition and thereby use his private property to the detriment of society.

5. It is the aim of the National Union for Social Justice to assist in the re-establishment of vocational groups. By this I mean that the laboring class who practice the same trade or profession should combine in units independent, if they so choose, of the factory where they work or of the industry in which they are employed.

May I expand upon this point: At present we have approximately 45-million citizens who are eligible to join forces in unionized labor.

At the most there are no more than 6-million persons identified with labor unions. In other words just barely more than 12 per cent of the artisans, the mechanics and the laborers of America are united for common action. Despite the lesson that you have learned over the ages, you do not seem to profit by your years of perpetual betrayal. I mean that you have constantly listened to high-binding politicians speak their pre-election promises to labor. I mean that you have been constantly deceived. Are you not aware that this so-called democratic country of ours has been controlled by the capitalist and the plutocrat? Have you not learned through bitter experience that no political party seriously cares for your welfare. The mockery of your vote was all that counted. I mean that you have been victims of class legislation —of legislation designed to protect the rich and the property rights of the rich; legislation which sneered at the poor and at human rights.

Diabolical loopholes were written into a thousand laws to protect the capitalist. See the Insull case in Chicago last week. Because the little word "intent" was slipped into a law Mr. Insull will very likely go free. Ingenious devices were set up in as many more laws to entrap the laborer, the farmer and the uninitiated.

Need I ask you to unite? In the past you had not the sagacity to organize among yourselves.

But that is not true of the banker, of the industrialist, of the plutocrat! They are organized almost 100 per cent against you for the protection of those very principles of exploitation which have succeeded in reducing more than 70 per cent of our population to a standard of living that is best described as economic slavery.

You men and women of the laboring class! You not only have the right to organize. It is your duty to establish vocational groups. In no sense does the National Union for Social Justice wish to overthrow unionism. It is our aim to perfect and to sustain it. It is our aim to uphold vocational unionism.

But as long as you good people remain disunited; as long as you fail to agree upon a common, basic program, you need never hope to enjoy the inalienable rights of a just and living wage or an equitable share in the bountiful wealth of our nation. The money and the interest arrayed against you are too powerful for your undivided, pigmy efforts to succeed.

In the past, whether you knew it or not, you were forced to take up arms against each other in an industrial warfare of slave against slave—a warfare more heinous in its results of human suffering than was the Civil War which disgraced our nation.

6. It is the aim of the National Union for Social Justice to

so work towards a reform in government that the Department of Labor shall not only protect labor but shall counsel and guide it in its negotiations with capital.

What part has this Department of Labor played in your lives? For years it joined hands with the banking fraternity and knelt before the shrine of the Department of Commerce to learn its lessons from the directors of capitalism as to how it could perpetuate a department of slavery. For years this branch of our government has been the most inefficient, hypocritical and foreflushing department in operation at Washington. Even during the automobile strike in Detroit last year the head of the Department was speaking at $400 an hour here or elsewhere when she should have been in Washington. Ordinarily it was presided over by a sphinx who dared not open his mouth in defense of labor. Silently the Secretary of Labor sat in his office while unemployment increased, while the coal miners slaved in the pits, while the textile industry sweat blood out of children and women; while long hours and short wages were the portion of millions of our citizens and while wealth was concentrated in the hands of a few. The Department of Labor was the department of slavery.

It was the department which exacted from the laboring man twelve months of taxation while it permitted him to work for six months of starvation.

Now do not misunderstand me! I am not advocating that you form a labor party any more than I am upholding the existence of the capitalist party which has been in power under the Wilsons and the Hardings throughout the years. We had enough class legislation under capitalism. I am not advocating class legislation to favor the laborer and to disparage the capitalist. All I am asking is that you unite to obtain social justice.

7. The seventh principle: The National Union for Social Justice contends that strikes and lock-outs are absolutely unnecessary. For in the case of disagreement between employer and employe it is the business of the public authority to intervene and settle such disputes which can be settled amicably by the parties involved. For it is our observation that both strikes and lock-outs have occasioned more harm to the common good of the nation than any benefit which has been derived. But in the case of the government's neglecting its duty to settle such industrial disputes, always keeping in mind that there is no settlement without a just and living wage for the laborer and an equitable distribution of profits to all, then there is nothing left except for united labor to refuse to sell its services at a loss just the same as it is unreasonable to expect the farmer to plow his ground and sow his seed at a loss.

Strikes have been most unprofitable for the common welfare of this nation. Strikes were not necessary had labor been organized and had the industrialists learned that their welfare was associated not with the financiers but with the men employed in their factories.

If a government fails to legislate a program of sharing the profits and of supplying the willing working men of this nation with that portion of its abundance with which God has blessed us then there is no recourse left to the laboring man except to strike and strike until he wins. It is nothing more than the self-same spirit of 1776 which impelled Washington to strike against taxation without representation. Today it is worse than in 1776 because we have both taxation and starvation without representation.

For the past two Sundays I have devoted this hour to the various principles associated with a just and living wage.

After all, they are only principles irrelevant and useless in themselves unless they are reduced to practice. And this putting of them into practice is definitely dependent upon your organizing. Bear in mind that there is arrayed against you an army of wealth more powerful than the combined forces of Caesar, Napoleon and Foche. To ask or expect reform from this force is like asking a hungry lion with a lamb beneath its paws to subscribe to the beauties of vegetarianism. No reform, no social justice shall come except you wrest it from the hands of the exploiters by your united moral force.

There is no need for revolution in this country but there is need to break down the obstacles which prevent our normal evolution.

Capitalism, as we know it, must depart! No better than communism, it seeks to identify all wealth in the hands of a few. The communist claims all for the State and none for the individual. The capitalist claims all for his class and none for the laborer or the farmer as he gains control over the State.

Social Justice seeks and demands a just distribution of the nation's wealth and a just distribution of the profits for the laborer as well as for the industrialist.

Capitalism and communism both destroy private ownership. Social justice seeks to multiply it.

It is yours to choose! It is yours to struggle for!

# THE AMERICAN LIBERTY LEAGUE

*(Sunday, December 9th, 1934)*

**D**URING the past week there came to my desk copies of the promotional literature being used by the American Liberty League in securing new memberships.

From a pamphlet entitled *"American Liberty League, A Statement of Its Principles and Purchases,"* I glean this statement of their aims and ideals:

*"The particular business and objects of the Society shall be to defend and uphold the Constitution of the United States and to gather and disseminate information that (1) will teach the necessity of respect for the rights of persons and property as fundamental to every successful form of government, and (2) will teach the duty of government to encourage and protect individual and group initiative and enterprise, to foster the right to work, earn, save and acquire property, and to preserve the ownership and lawful use of property when acquired."*

This is typical of the whole bundle of propaganda. The founders of the Liberty League make a patriotic salute to the Constitution, pledge themselves to defend and uphold it, and then immediately forget every other provision of the Constitution to concentrate on the right of ownership and use of property.

This fixation on property rights should be sufficient warning to the seventy-one per cent of our people who are existing below the American standard of a decent living.

Literally, my friends, that is all I can glean from a study of the Liberty League's promotional material.

In a folder entitled, *"Why—The American Liberty League?"*, from the gifted pen of Jouett Shouse, formerly the chairman of the Democratic National Committee, you will find a bit of philosophy of almost Aristotelian profundity. Mr. Shouse gives us the interpretation of what the Liberty League means by property rights. Listen to it attentively because the gifted front-man of the Liberty League has coined a new philosophy that was never preached in the circles of civilized men since the days of the Neros, the Vespasians and the other emperors of slavery.

Jouett Shouse says: *"It will be noted that the statement of principles links the 'rights of persons and property.' There is a very good reason for the conjunction. In the view of those who comprise the membership of the League, the superficially drawn distinction between 'human rights' and 'property rights' is a catchphrase and nothing more. The two so-called categories of rights are inseparable in any society short of Utopia or absolute communism. To protect a man's so-called human rights and strip him of his property rights would be to issue him a fishing license and then prohibit him from baiting his hook."*

That is the doctrine of Mr. Shouse and the so-called Liberty League. That is the doctrine which I said was neither preached nor practiced on the face of the earth since the days of the Neros and Vespasians.

My friends, if that doctrine is sound then all you citizens of the United States who do not own property have no rights as human beings, for Mr. Shouse says that human rights and property rights are identical and inseparable.

You who own no property, therefore, possess no human rights. You are an economic slave, a financial peon compared to whom the contemporaries of Uncle Tom, who immortalized the cabin, were freed men and brave.

Well, that may be the belief of the millionaire leaders of the American Liberty League. But it was not the belief of the founders of this Republic when, in the first session of the First Congress, they wrote the Ninth Amendment to the Constitution of the United States.

The Ninth Amendment says: *"The enumeration in the Constitution of certain rights shall not be construed to deny or disparage others retained by the people."*

The doctrine of the Liberty Leaguers was, therefore, not the doctrine of those who founded this nation insofar as they attempt to identify property rights and human rights to such an extent that, if you lack the former, the latter must necessarily vanish into nothingness.

✝ The doctrine of the Liberty Leaguers is not the doctrine of the Catholic Church. I say this for the benefit of Mr. Alfred E. Smith and Mr. John Raskob and also for the benefit of any other Catholics who care to join the American Liberty League. Moreover, I say this without fear of contradiction from any person high or low, cardinal or priest, who has spent at least a dozen hours of honest study on the doctrine of the Church as interpretated by Pius XI on this subject. Pope Pius XI wrote the Encyclical, *"Quadragesimo Anno"*:

*"When the civil authority adjusts ownership to meet the needs of the public good it acts not as an enemy, but as the friend of private owners; for thus it effectively prevents the possession of private property, intended by Nature's Author in His Wisdom for the sustaining of human life, from creating intolerable burdens and so rushing to its own destruction."*

57

In other words the state can take away private property and should take away private property if for no other reason than to protect those who have too much property, from the just wrath of those who have no private property.

Someone has said that there are two sides to every question. Be he high or be he low, be he prince or be he pauper, there is only one side to this question. It is God's question and it is God's side!

You cannot be a scarlet-cloaked pussy-footer when the cries of downtrodden humanity in their inarticulate form are mounting above the platitudinous pronouncements of rhetorical spellbinders.

Finally and emphatically the belief of the Liberty Leaguers is not my belief. Witness the sixteenth principle of the National Union for Social Justice.

*"I believe in preferring the sanctity of human rights to the sanctity of property rights. I believe that the chief concern of government shall be for the poor because, as it is witnessed, the rich have ample means of their own to care for themselves."*

Be not deceived, my friends, by the lip service which the devisers of the Liberty League pay at the shrine of the Constitution.

Such principles as the one I have quoted from Mr. Shouse reveal with terrifying clarity what is in their hearts.

The Declaration of Independence blazoned forever on the record of civilization that *"All men are endowed by their Creator with certain inalienable rights—life, liberty and the pursuit of happiness."* It is the primary duty of government to preserve these rights.

The founders of this government wrote the Constitution expressly *"to promote the general welfare."*

But it is a strange, narrow, dangerous form of liberty that is outlined by the League which has assumed her glorious name.

To those who wish to identify themselves with the American Liberty League, Mr. Shouse sends a little bronze button about the size of a dime. On its face there is stamped the replica of the Liberty Bell that once sounded the vibrant notes of independence when our American forefathers protested against the so-called property rights of a George III. Across the front of this Liberty Bell are the letters A.L.L. which inadvertently spell the word *"all."* All for the rich and none for the poor! All for the concentrators of wealth and the dregs of life's bitter chalice for the dispossessed and unemployed! All for the international bankers and only the crumbs that they drop from their table for the rest of us!

On the day when the lineal ancestors of the American Liberty Leaguers vitiated our Constitution and handed over the right to coin and regulate money to private individuals despite the doctrine which proclaims that *"Congress and Congress alone has the right to coin and regulate money"*—on that day the Liberty Bell, now solemnly hanging in Philadelphia, was cracked and its joyous notes of liberty were silenced.

Alas poor Liberty Bell! The clarion purity of your original melody is no more! Cracked and discordant, today you are a fit symbol for the duPonts, the Raskobs and the rest of them as they have the effrontery to use you in perpetuating a financial and industrial system which is pauperizing the people of this land.

If the founders of the American Liberty League have the common honesty not only to protect our Constitution but to restore the coinage and the regulation of money to Congress as the Constitution demands, I would gladly join them and proudly wear their button of the Libery Bell.

These defenders of property rights, even at the expense of human rights, are seeking a membership of not less than one million persons. Are those who are in opposition to the American Liberty League willing to permit the National Union for Social Justice to be outdone either in number or in moral support? It is yours to decide and yours to act.

To show you more intimately and concretely for what the American Liberty League really stands let me tell you the sordid truth of their General Motors Corporation holdings of which the duPont family, the guardian angel of the American Liberty League, owns and controls 24 per cent. In the year 1933 the duPont family took as profits, in the shape of dividends, out of their General Motors stock enough money to sustain 16,250 families at a living wage of $1,500 a year each.

In the four years of the depression this same duPont family, for whom the Raskobs and Shouses and Smiths are but the dressed-up front-men and spokesmen, took the astronomical amount of $97,780,560 profits out of General Motors from their ownership of 24 per cent of its stock. This was enough money to sustain 16,296 families over a period of four years at $1,500 a family. And this does not count the profits this family took from their many other holdings in various other corporations.

This is the unanswerable argument! One American capitalistic Liberty League family takes out of profits from one of its corporations the equivalent of a living wage for 16,296 families, for 80,000 persons now regimented in the bread lines of destitution. They talk of property rights when human rights have been trampled by their avarice.

This, my friends, indicates the kind of property rights which they wish to preserve. In plainer language they wish to preserve the racketeering by which they concentrate wealth in the hands of the few privileged ones. They wish to preserve the present industrial set-up by which in the years 1930, 1931, 1932 and 1933 the General Motors, with a net income of only $331-million, succeeded in paying dividends of $407-million and more to stockholders! That is embroidered bookkeeping.

Mark ye well then, those who wear the symbol of the cracked Liberty Bell with the letters A.L.L. written across its surface! It is the symbol of those who wish to preserve want in the midst of plenty and the unconstitutional set-up of our present financial system. They are the modern Tories who prefer the racketeering of a George III to the liberty as propounded and fought for by a Washington.

---

# Our Money and How to Use It

THE announcement which I just made, though lengthy, was necessary. May I now proceed with this afternoon's discussion. It will deal with something that is very constitutional, and, as such, with something that should be championed by every American citizen. It will deal with a portion of our third principle which concerns the nationalization of certain public necessities. It is directly associated with the greatest material obstacle which is powerful enough to prevent the laboring man from obtaining a just and living wage. In brief, I am going to talk to you about money and about the necessity of making it our national servant.

## I

As we analyze our economic life we cannot escape the obvious facts of unemployment, of universal poverty and of the ever increasing concentration of wealth in the hands of a few. Three or four years ago we pinched ourselves when we became conscious that there was want in the midst of plenty. Surely, thought we, the editors of the daily press, the experts of business and of banking, as well as the professional economists, could not be wrong. They were the wisemen. We must be the fools! Therefore, one and all, we swallowed the teachings of the financialists as easily as though they were oysters.

But there came a day of rude awakening when the laboring man had ample leisure to sit and think thoughts that were heretical to the theologians of high finance. Gradually there simmered down in the mass mind of America two definite thoughts which expressed the two salient errors of modern finance and business. The conclusions which these laws represented were like a sum in arithmetic which finally had been solved. Here was the sum: There was want in the midst of plenty. There was a superabundance of wealth about us. Money, which is only the receipt of wealth, was lacking. The bookkeepers of our national wealth, otherwise known as bankers, had perverted the true concept of money. (Wheat is wealth, a new motor car is wealth, a new home is wealth, a new suit of clothing is wealth. Whenever the hand of man bestowed its benediction upon field or forest or mine or factory, new wealth had been produced. This we knew positively. But the bankers had been dishonest in their bookkeeping, in their writing of receipts. The books did not balance; the receipts did not equal the real wealth that had been produced. There was a purposeful scarcity of money.)

In our sum of addition, we added up all these and other facts and the answer became clear as crystal. It was the dishonest trick of deceptive bookkeeping that made business operations, agricultural pursuits and industrial labor return to the financiers twice as much as the bankers invested in them. That is "Law number one."

Now the sinister significance of this law arose from its basic association with another assumption of banking which we will call "law number two." This second law, in brief, proclaimed that the banker shall be the sole and only distributor of wealth. He shall have the only right to manufacture money and with it, to issue the receipts of wealth—the credits.

Gradually it dawned upon the laborer and the farmer that if modern private banking is the sole creator of money, it cannot gather into the vaults of its banks the double repayment of its original investment in terms of money because the amount of money in circulation was not equivalent to the wealth produced. Consequently the banker with his policy of gathering more than he invested, was forced to take ownership of the real wealth, of the homes and the farms and the factories. He was forced to exploit the laborer as he compelled him to go without the dollar bills or the receipts that he should have had in his purse. He destroyed purchasing power as he headed himself and his associates together with the entire nation into the ditch of destruction.

Thus, we were surrounded by wealth, but, because of a lack of adequate receipts, of adequate currency, of adequate purchasing power, we were compelled to starve while our fields were heavy wih grain, to go unclad while the spindles in our factories were anxious to work. All this was because the bookkeeping of bankers and their manufactured receipts of money were unsound; all because money, as conceived by them, had been so perverted that it was no longer a receipt for wealth, for labor, for wheat and for homes, but was wealth itself.

Now we began to understand both the nature of bankers' money and the nature of his dishonest receipts. We also began to understand why an industrialist or a home maker who borrowed one thousand dollars from the banker was merely given credit for a thousand dollars but no one thousand dollar bill was created. All that the banker did was to write upon his books a fictitious creation of a thousand dollar bill which he called a deposit and to hand the borrower a check book. But the banker was not content to be paid back by means of the check book. He wanted a thousand dollar bill that had not been created. He did not want to be paid back in credit. He wanted to be paid back in a real receipt for wealth which he alone was permitted, by an unconstitutional law, to create. If the borrower tried to create it, he was called a counterfeiter and his receipt or his thousand dollar bill was regarded as spurious.

As a result of this unsound bookkeeping or banking policy, debts grew to such an enormity that they were unpayable in real money. Individuals searched their pockets for the dime that was not there, each believing himself to be in the debt of the other. In truth, they were only in debt to a system, to a program of racketeering. Every house that was built, every furrow that was plowed, every motor car that was manufactured only added to our debt system.

In the history of ancient Greek mythology, we were told the story where a young man was eternally punished by being forced to roll a stone up-hill which always succeeded in rolling down-hill the moment it neared the top. This young man's stone did not grow bigger as he rolled it. But our stone of debt grows bigger with each generation and rolls further down-hill with every attempt we make to roll it up-hill.

Business man, industrialist, laborer and farmer, in the name of God, how long are you going to subscribe to the heresy that money is wealth, when it is only supposed to be the receipt of wealth? How long do you intend to bear with the practice of permitting the banker to issue credit and then demand from you real money that was never created? How long will your patience dictate to you to suffer privation in the midst of plenty and to pay back the banker with your farm, with your home and with the wails of your hungry children and ill-kept wife because the bankers have purposely failed to issue sufficient receipts for the real wealth of the nation?

## II

Let us pause to study the actual historical facts associated with this questionable right of the banker to coin and regulate the value of money and thereby to issue fewer receipts than the wealth of the nation demands.

The Constitution of the United States provides that our Congress shall have the power to create the army and the navy; to establish and operate the post office system; to levy taxes and to collect them, and *"to coin money and regulate the value thereof."*

Now, what would be your reaction if a group of men proposed that our Government should delegate the power of creating an army to some munitions manufacturer; that it should sublet our post office system to some mail order house; that it should grant a charter to some great public utility, thereby bestowing upon it the power of levying taxes?

Offhand, I dare to express the opinion that the American people would consider this unconstitutional, dangerous and destructive to the welfare of this nation.

The same thought that you have regarding the army, navy and post office is associated with *"the power to coin money and regulate the value thereof."*

It is not a power to be delegated. It is neither a privilege nor a right to sublet to any group of citizens.

My friends, despite your almost unanimous approval of this statement, that very thing has been accomplished in a most questionable and, perhaps, unconstitutional manner.

Here is the history of the case. In the year 1791 Alexander Hamilton, our first Secretary of the Treasury, petitioned George Washington to have Congress grant the right and privilege of coining money to certain of Mr. Hamilton's wealthy associates. He advocated the establishment of a private bank for this very purpose.

As was to be expected, the Father of our Country opposed this nefarious plan on the grounds that it was contrary to the Constitution which provides, as I have just remarked, that Congress shall have the power to coin money and regulate its value.

Supporting our first President were Mr. Edmund Randolph, the Attorney General, and Mr. Thomas Jefferson, the first Secretary of State, who, by the way, had considerable to do with framing the Declaration of Independence. He declared that such a transgression was entirely *"repugnant to the spirit of this democratic republic."*

Eventually, however, Mr. Hamilton succeeded in establishing this so-called Bank of the United States.

What a peculiar name for this first bank! How inappropriate

63

that appellation when only twenty per cent of this bank's stock was held by the United States Treasury and eighty per cent of it by private individuals, the vast majority of whom were foreigners!

Here we have the origin of the privately owned banks—the banks in which you trusted so implicitly; the banks which operated under the colors of our country's name and which failed you in a crisis; the banks over which the government had no management other than that of inspection!

This first bank operated under a charter which permitted its directors and owners to print or coin money by purchasing United States Government Bonds, which Bonds, by the way, were left on deposit in the United States Treasury.

At the present moment may I quote for you the thought which Thomas Jefferson expressed shortly after this private banking business originated:

*"I believe that banking institutions are more dangerous to our liberties than are standing armies. Already they have raised up a money aristocracy that has set the Government at defiance. The issuing power should be taken from the banks, and restored to the Government and the people to whom it properly belongs."*

On the expiration of this bank's charter in 1811, it ceased functioning.

In the year 1816 a twenty-year charter was granted to a second group which wished to establish a second private bank.

Four years before the expiration of this charter Mr. Nicholas Biddle, the president of this new bank, informed Andrew Jackson, then President of this nation, that he would guarantee his re-election if the bank charter would be extended another twenty years. Here we have the banker not only lobbying but practically attempting to bribe our Chief Executive.

To his everlasting honor, Andrew Jackson refused this bribe and declared:

*"If Congress has the right under the Constitution to issue paper money it was given them to be used by themselves, not to be delegated to individuals or corporations."*

On this platform of uncompromising justice Andrew Jackson was re-elected to the presidency despite the opposition of Mr. Biddle and his private corporation of bankers.

To the testimony of Washington, of Jefferson and of Jackson may I add the name of Lincoln's Secretary of the Treasury, Mr. Salmon P. Chase, who wrote the following prophetic words:

*"My agency in procuring the passage of the National Bank Act was the greatest financial mistake of my life. It has built up a*

*monopoly that affects every interest in the country. It should be repealed. But before this can be accomplished, the people will be arrayed on one side and the banks on the other, in a contest such as we have never seen before in this country."*

"If ever in the history of this nation its spirit, its liberty and its Constitution were revered and understood, none surpass in reverence and in intelligence these noble four—Washington, Jefferson, Jackson and Lincoln.

## III

That is the story of the monopolization of coining and regulating money at a precious profit! It was like handing over the ownership of the town pump or of the city's water supply to a group of private individuals. This private right to coin and regulate the value of money, to keep currency inadequate, to call in credit at pleasure, to demand payment of loans with dollar bills when there are not sufficient dollar bills to go around, to reap wheat where they have only sown cockle—these things belong to the heart and soul of modern capitalism, not to Americanism. These principles and the economic system which sustains them are incontestably false if for no other argument than for the proven results. This system produced only an immense number of propertyless wage earners, on the one hand, and a small handful of bankers and banker-controlled industrialists who have concentrated the wealth of the nation within their very grasp.

I know that I shall be regarded as radical and as dangerous for telling you these historical facts and for reminding you of these truths relative to money. But I should prefer to be termed a radical rather than subscribe, like a crack-pot, to the utterances of modern banking as if they came down from some financial Mount Sinai, immutable and eternal!

Yesterday the banker and his philosophy of scarce money, of dishonest receipts, acquired a dignity that paralyzed opposition. But today, in the midst of poverty, in the midst of universal distress, we must look upon his vapid pronouncements as nothing more than the idle incantations of an Indian medicine man.

What has been the history of the banker? Trace his ancestry back far enough and you will find that his professional forebears were dishonest slaves, who kept account of their masters' wealth under the Caesars of Rome and the Pharaohs of Egypt. In biblical days the banker was the unjust steward who throttled the servant while he cheated the master. In modern times, what has he produced to help civilization overcome the handicaps of an untamed nature? Nothing! Of all human technicians, the banker is the most patent and grotesque failure. Especially since the World War, when we placed upon his head the crown of intelligence and in his hand the sceptre of omnipotence, the world has gone from failure to failure. All our material failures are failures in the field of finance.

In no other sphere of human activity has a breakdown occurred in the last decade. The farmer, the laborer, the industrialist and the housewife—all have carried on heroically against the most tremendous odds ever faced by this or any other nation. They have been successful in producing real wealth.

That the banker is a failure is attested by the condition of every country today. He is civilization's tragic comedian. That he is ruining us is bad enough, but it is a little too much that he should demand from us admiration and obedience to his suggestions for doing it.

For generations he has gazed upon a world that, by the common consent of himself, he has made blossom like a rose. He deems himself responsible for all that has turned it into a workshop of marvels.

The truth is that there is not, nor was there ever, in our world, a worthwhile marvel that sprang from a banker's brain. It is a brain that is identified with the non-creative things of this world. It has neither pride of ancestry nor hope for posterity, because its functions are the functions of a sterile mule. The nail, the wheel, the wireless, the airplane, the benedictions of medicine, the artistry of surgery, the devisals of the engineer, the miracles of the chemist—all the steps in that patient progression from the squalor of the primeval swamp are the patient creations of the creators, the workmen of the world, not one of them of a banker.

He has been the parasite that has lived by them and from them and in them.

Thus, the crisis in the world today is, in truth, the battle between labor and science and culture and religion and art on one side, and the banker and the banker-controlled industrialist on the other. It is a battle waged by those who indentify property rights with human rights against those who prefer the dignity of human rights as more sacred than mere property rights.

The challenge has been cast into your very face, my fellow citizens. Those who wish to protect the property right of scarce money are the men who persist in getting themselves heard through the columns of the press and in the corridors of the Capitol. These same men, as they succeed in retaining their unconstitutional privilege of coining and regulating the value of money, will obstruct any living and just wage and any sane hope of prosperity to the farmer and business man. By its very nature, their money system claims that it owns or will own every item of wealth in this nation.

Ask any laborer or any farmer why the former is idle and destitute and why the latter is forced to pursue his calling at a loss, and the answer is identical from Maine to California, from Minnesota to Mississippi. *"There is no money."* This is the common answer to our common economic ills. Because there is no money, because there are too many debts which the bankers will exact payment of either in real money, that has not been created or in the real wealth of homes and farms, confiscations must continue. Want in the midst of plenty must be the order of the day as God's blessings of plenitude are frustrated!

Throughout the generations the human race has been undergoing an absolution from the original curse placed upon Adam, our first parent. In the beginning one ate his bread only by the sweat of his brow. In the beginning thorns and thistles both in the field and in the mind of man obstructed progress. But man's efforts, coupled with God's will, have been working out that curse by making human labor more and more productive. It is the modern banking system of capitalism which has intervened at this auspicious moment to throw us back hundreds of thousands of years to that day of original struggle.

I repeat that there is no hope for a just and living wage as long as this system survives. Money must be coined and regulated by the Congress of this nation. Money must be regarded only as a receipt for wealth.

## IV

Contrary to the view of modern banking, I do not regard the creation of wealth as an evil. We are wealthy. We can become wealthier. I do not subscribe to the doctrine of purposeful poverty because there is a purposeful scarcity of money. With this thought in mind, I would propose that a network of Federal highways shall be built over the face of America—highways amply large, highways electrically lighted. Here, then, is real national wealth! This construction will facilitate distribution of the golden grain of the west to the crowded cities of the east.

I would propose a national plan of vast reforestation almost to the extent of 50-million square miles. The saplings of today will become the cedar and pine, the oak and the hemlock of tomorrow. Within thirty years, 50-million square miles of reforestated land would approximately produce 1,220,000,000 feet of precious timber. This will be a contribution to the coming generation.

I would propose to multiply both power and light distribution for the populous east by harnessing the rapids of the St. Lawrence waters.

Remember how both English and French fought ferociously to gain possession of the plains of this continent! With this thought in mind, I propose to set aside the policy of destructionism and endeavor to reclaim 60-million acres of agricultural land which, though not required by us of this day and age, will be a heritage to future generations—a heritage of real wealth.

Remembering that our citizens are the most valuable asset which we as a nation possess, I propose to marshal an army of idle workmen who, armed with dynamite, will demolish the slums of our cities. In their place I propose to construct habitable homes equipped with the conveniences to which we are entitled. Who can gainsay me that a home is not real wealth?

What would I use for money to realize this dream of American prosperity? If you sincerely inquire of me, I will remind you that Congress has the right to coin money. I will doubly remind you that money is nothing more than a receipt for wealth.

The network of roads—18,000 miles of them at $18,000 a mile —equals $324-million.

Fifty million square miles of reforestation will cost approximately $6,400,000,000.

The harnessing of the St. Lawrence and other rivers so that they will surrender a 7-million horsepower can be achieved for $812-million.

The reclaiming of 60-million acres of agricultural land at $10.00 an acre will require an expenditure of $600-million.

Nine hundred thousand homes at $2,000.00 each will demand of us $1,800,000,000.

Here is a total of government expenditures of approximately $10-billion.

In our treasury we have $9-billion of metallic money—of gold and silver. Against this fabulous hoard there is nothing which prevents our issuing $23-billion worth of currency, if necessary, whereas we ask for the issuance of not more than $5-billion of it. The remaining $5-billion would be in United States credit money.

These public works I would undertake, in opposition to the theories of private banking, which insist that, if we engage in any such projects, it shall be with money borrowed from the bankers and written down upon their books with the dead hand of debt. No more borrowing from the bankers! We have $9-billion of idle gold and silver in our Treasury. For God's sake let it be put to work instead of borrowing bankers' dollars and tying around the necks of future generations the noose of suicide and debt.

I would enter upon this public works program with our own United States money, which Congress and Congress alone has the power to issue and to regulate according to our Constitution, and independent of any banker.

Would this be a permanent program? Most certainly! For it means the permanent end of depressions; the permanent end of production for bankers' profit!

The moment that industry fails to employ a man at an annual wage, that very moment there should be a place for that individual laborer either in road building, in reforestation, in the construction of power plants, in the reclamation of agricultural lands or in the clearing of slums at a salary of not less than $1500.00 a year. Soon the purchasing power of the country would be restored, soon our independence would be gained from the Tory-minded banking fraternity. Soon the wheels of industry would be asked to spin again, supplying the needs of those who are craving for the products of our factories.

At this juncture, when industry requires more men, the permanent public works program can slacken its pace and supply the factories with every necessary laborer.

My friends, this is no Utopia. This is no idle dream. It is within your realization, if you learn to consider money as nothing more than the receipt of wealth, and if you insist that Congress shall restore to itself its Constitutional right to be used, not for the favored few, but for the common good and common wealth of all our citizens. Here is prosperity for all! Prosperity for laborer and farmer, for industrialist and professional man. There is no need of putting up with unnecessary poverty!

---

# Reply to Cardinal O'Connell

As a preface to these last remarks which I am going to make may I inform this audience that they were written only after consultation with His Exellency, Michael James Gallagher, Bishop of Detroit. They are remarks which will cause, perhaps, bitter thoughts and bitter words throughout the length and breadth of America. But the time has come when patience ceases to be a virtue and silence, nothing more than a cowardly subterfuge.

I am going to speak to you about his Eminence, William Cardinal O'Connell, of Boston, who has recently celebrated his birthday by publicly attacking me for the third time in as many years. On the two previous occasions I was content to pass the matter over. This time, and on all future occasions, the matter will not be passed over. Cardinal O'Connell himself has invited this public utterance.

First of all the venerable Cardinal lays down the rule that a priest should talk to his parishioners and a Bishop should confine himself to utterances within his own diocese. Let it be understood that the Cardinal has no jurisdiction over me; that he has no jurisdiction outside his own diocese; that the dignity of the scarlet which he wears as Cardinal confers no more power upon him in his governing the Catholic Church in America than does the purple toga worn by a monsignor give him power within the diocese wherein he resides. Remembering this principle, William Cardinal O'Connell has no authority to speak for the Catholic Church in America and has no business, as a churchman, to impose his thoughts on people living outside his jurisdiction. It is high time that this bubble be bursted. If he spoke as a churchman on the three occasions when he publicly rebuked me he has done nothing more than to usurp the power which belongs to the Apostolic Delegate in America. If he spoke as an individual, which he did, his utterances carry no more weight than they justly deserve. He himself said that he spoke as a layman. Since he prefers to be regarded as a layman I shall speak to him as if he were a layman.

I am criticized by His Eminence as he insinuates that I am doing something contrary to the wishes of my ecclesiastical superiors. As a matter of fact I am simply carrying out the command of my highest ecclesiastical superior, His Holiness Pope Pius XI, in preaching the principles of social justice and the doctrines of the Encyclicals. His predecessor, Leo XIII, said:

*"Every minister of holy Religion must throw into the conflict all the energy of his mind, and all the strength of his endurance."*

Pius XI not only encourages the clergy to bend their every effort to this most important question of the age, but he criticizes those who refuse, either through apathy or ignorance or through some other motive, to stress, in season and out of season, the doctrines predicated by Leo XIII. Of these men he said:

*"There are some who seem to attach little importance to this Encyclical and to the present anniversary celebration. These men either slander a doctrine of which they are entirely ignorant, or if not unacquainted with this teaching, they betray their failure to understand it, or else if they understand it they lay themselves open to the charge of base injustice and ingratitude."*

For forty years William Cardinal O'Connell has had the opportunity to preach and practice social justice and, in fact, has been commanded to do this according to the letters received by him and by every other Bishop from Pope Leo XIII.

For forty years William Cardinal O'Connell has been more notorious for his silence on social justice than for any contribution which he may have given either in practice or in doctrine towards the decentralization of wealth and towards the elimination of those glaring injustices which permitted the plutocrats of this nation to wax fat at the expense of the poor. Now he castigates me for doing what he was ordered to do.

William Cardinal O'Connell practically accuses me of misinterpreting the Encyclicals of both Leo XIII and Pius XI.

Every word that I have written has received the imprimatur of my Right Reverend Bishop. When this is taken into consideration William Cardinal O'Connell practically accuses a brother Bishop, who for years has been famed in Michigan for his defense of the poor and for his opposition to the type of pampered evils which have been so rampant in the textile industries of New England.

May I repeat that the Cardinal of Boston has had forty years in which to carry out the commands of Leo XIII and he now seeks front page publicity by attacking me for attempting to follow out those commands.

He has asked for this reply and he has obtained it.

Since William Cardinal O'Connell has persistently, on three occasions, dragged this matter before the public, instead of discussing it in private with the proper authorities, I invite him on future occasions either to carry the case where it belongs, or else, to be well informed that, despite the dignity of the honors conferred upon him, which I respect, I shall take advantage of the prerogative which he himself invented of distinguishing the Cardinal from a private layman, and treating him as a layman in public.

I repeat that I have had three years in which to consider the voicing of these remarks. They have been voiced only after consultation with my lawful ecclesiastical superior.

I am still a humble priest and I pray Almighty God that, at the end of the long reign of this distinguished prelate, nothing will cause him to echo the words which Shakespeare placed in the mouth of Cardinal Wolsey:

> *"Had I but served my God with half the zeal*
> *I served my king,\* he would not in mine age*
> *Have left me naked to mine enemies."*

\*Plutocrats.

# "MERCHANDISERS OF MURDER"

## (Sunday, December 16th, 1934)

### I

THIS afternoon I plan to address you on another phase of our money situation as related to the program for permanent public works. Also, I shall touch upon a question which is closely allied to money. This second part of my address will explain why I have named this lecture the *"Merchandisers of Murder."*

### II

Last Sunday, if you recollect, I outlined a plan of permanent public works. Conscious of the fact that we have reached that stage in our mass production activities when machines are constantly and increasingly displacing men, I believe that, unless we are willing to wait for the certain revolution which cannot be avoided, profitable work and just wages must be provided for every citizen who is willing to earn his livelihood. Further delay is only inviting disaster.

No one likes the word revolution. No one who has read a chapter of revolutionary history, be it French or Russian, cares to envisage what might happen in placid America.

But on the other hand, no one is so egotistical as to think that five or ten or fifteen million men forced with their families to live in want and below the American standard can be placated by pious preachments ·on patience. Words cannot change the basic elements of human nature.

With this thought in mind I proposed that a permanent plan should be set up immediately to build roads, to plant trees, to harness the St. Lawrence, to reclaim 60-million acres of agricultural land and to construct habitable homes for the millions of our citizens who are forced to live in the pigsty of slums.

The purpose behind my proposition is to give each man who is willing to work an opportunity to use his brain or his brawn to make his own living according to his own ability. This, I conceive to be the duty and the function of a government that deserves to be called a government. For a government merely to guarantee a minimum wage without guaranteeing a job where that minimum living wage can be obtained is just another pious platitude. As a matter of fact, the job should come before the wage.

The advantage to be gained by a permanent public works program is evident. When industry reaches the point of having produced all the clothing, the motor cars, the refrigerators, and

72

other goods which are required or which can be purchased by reason of the ever-decreasing purchasing power resulting from mass productionism, then the laborers can be engaged by the government in this public works program. Instead of being encumbered by an army of idle laborers, the nation will have an army of productive citizens helping to create actual wealth for the next generation. The saplings which they plant will grow to sturdy pine and hemlock, cedar and oak; the acres which they reclaim will be virgin soil from which the children of future years can reap bountiful harvests; the highways and power developments will be real wealth for us to pass on to the future years—as real as the wealth represented by the homes, the farms, the water mills and the highways which our pioneering forefathers coined for us from the savage forests and wind-swept plains one hundred fifty years ago.

*"Real wealth,"* I repeat!

But as logical and as practical as this seems, what is the obstacle which obstructs it? Why the hesitation? I will tell you:

In brief, my friends, it is nothing more than a satanic money system, which is not only incapable of serving the necessities of our modern civilization, but which actually perverts the blessings of God that have come to us through inventions of the scientist and through all the agencies which have tamed a hostile nature or which have wrested her secrets from her. The money question is the obstacle and the hesitation is due to the determination on the part of those in power to preserve that money system.

This age of plenty in which we are living is, from a material standpoint, the closest that fallen man has ever come to the Garden of Eden. But, like grinning devils, there stand at the gates of this Eden of plenty the protectors of privately manufactured money. With the flaming sword of greed in their hands they forbid you people to enter!

What care these men for facts! They realize that the sun never again will dawn upon a day when industry will be able to assimilate the millions of idle laborers. They realize that scientists will continue inventing new machines, new labor-saving devices. Despite this knowledge, they persist in experimenting with piddling policies excogitated for and by the private bankers. Their one ambition is to preserve the lie that money is wealth. Their one determination is to hold fast to their unconstitutional right of coining and regulating the value of money and of controlling the credit, without which not a wheel can turn, not a grain of wheat can grow.

Now the essential thought associated with my proposal of a

permanent public works program demands that we destroy the bankers' lie relative to money.

Money is not wealth. It is only the medium for trading wealth!

Money is not wealth. It is only the ambassador representing wealth!

Money is not wealth. It is only the receipt for wealth!

When real wealth vanishes, then the usefulness of the medium is at an end. All the gold in the world could not buy a glass of water for a thirst-stricken man lost in the sand dunes of the Sahara.

When wealth, the real king dies, his ambassador's pronouncements are idle words.

When real wealth decays and rots, all the receipts for it are as valueless as is a title or deed to a farm which existed on the banks of the Nile in the days of the Pharaohs.

By some satanic method these self-evident truths became so perverted that the high priests of finance succeeded in imprisoning real wealth and binding to the wheel of economic slavery all those who did not share their right of coining and manufacturing money.

Before this permanent public works program can be operated it is necessary that the money to be employed for it be Federal, United States money—not bankers' money. It shall be represented by the roads we build, the trees we plant, the electric power which we create and the homes which we construct.

This $10-billion program must be accomplished with United States money. To attempt it with bankers' money is to attempt the financial murder of the youth of today who, unescapably, will be forced to bear the imponderable burdens of tomorrow's debts.

### III

What is the salient difference between these two types of money—bankers' money and United States money? It is simply this: If $10-billion were borrowed from the bankers at 4 per cent for this public works program, it means that in eighteen years hence the people of this nation would owe these bankers, at compound interest, $20,256,480.00. In eighteen years we would owe more than twice what we borrowed. In eighteen years a great portion of the profits derived from the reclaimed acreage, from the electric power, from the planted trees, from the new homes would be acquired by the bankers and not by the people. In eighteen years hence the bankers, who today would gladly manufacture check book money to the extent of $10-billion, could demand that we repay them with $20-million of legitimate currency which has not and will not be created. In eighteen years hence, it means that, despite the wealth resultant from the public works

74

program, the next generation would be suffering from a depression more terrible than the one which we are experiencing.

If we should enter upon this project of public works with United States money we would be expected to repay no more than $10-billion to the government plus the mere cost of bookkeeping.

In the meantime our nation's workmen would have created $10-billion worth of real wealth.

Now let us pause to get the bankers' viewpoint on this method of producing prosperity by way of bankers' bonds, of bankers' money.

In this way we will learn from their own spokesmen the difference between bankers' money and United States money.

In the year 1862 the armies of the North and South were engaged in mortal conflict. Over battlefields, vultures and buzzards were hovering to prey upon the corpses of slain soldiers.

Closeted in comfort and in safety there were other vultures and buzzards waiting for the opportune moment to profiteer upon the misery of a stricken nation.

Let me read for you a widely distributed pamphlet known as the *"Hazard Circular,"* which was placed upon the desks of bankers and business men in that year of our nation's purgatory. It reads in part as follows:

*"Slavery is likely to be abolished by the war . . . This I and my European friends are in favor of, for slavery is but the owning of labor and carries with it the care of the laborers, while the European plan, led on by England, is that capital shall control labor by controlling wages.*

*"The great debt that capitalists will see to it is made out of the war, must be used to control the volume of money. To accomplish this, bonds must be used as a banking basis. . . . It will not do to allow the greenback, as it is called, to circulate as money any length of time, as we cannot control that.*

*"But we can control the bonds and through them the bank issues."*

What a noble thought excogitated by profit-seeking cowards when their fellowmen lay mained and mangled upon the battlefields of freedom! They will profiteer on bond issues. They will not to be content to permit a nation, bowed down in grief and prostrate by debt, to work out its own salvation. They will set out to control wages and to eliminate national coinage by the substitution of interest-bearing, tax-exempt bonds upon the foundation of which the structure of national banks is erected!

*"Slavery is likely to be abolished by the war,"* so thought the bankers. Well, for this they were really glad. They were glad

because, under slavery, the slave owner was forced to feed and clothe and house the men who worked on his plantation. But here was something better for the banker than the slavery of old! Here was a new system by which the laborer would be paid only while he worked, only while production was in progress. Under this new system the laborer must shift for himself. The responsibility of the slave owner in times of idleness was at an end. The new system, operated by bond issues, was more efficient to exploit the people. Yesterday they placed shackles on the ankles of the slaves. Tomorrow they would place on the shoulders of future generations an unbearable debt which would bow them down under a more wicked kind of slavery—economic slavery.

If it was esteemed profitable for the financiers, represented by the *"Hazard Circular"* in 1862, to issue bonds both to control the the tears of orphans and the poverty of a nation, I presume that fected bond manipulation. We have spent about $8-billion on relief activities during the past two years. These $8-billion are all represented by bankers' bonds. That is good news for the youth of today!

Who can analyze the logic which maintains that the issuance of government currency is unsound inflation while the printing of interest-bearing bonds is sound inflation just because there are little coupons on the end of them? No one but the banker, then, can be opposed to our plan of entering upon a program of permanent public works with United States money.

This permanent program of public works operated by United States' money is the only sound solution for unemployment.

It is good for labor, good for the agriculturist, good for the industrialist who wants products to flow from his factory. But it is terrible for the banker-controlled industrialist and the banker.

American common sense must dictate our future policies on matters of money. The experts and the professionals have proven to be nothing more than bunglers and exploiters. Caesar, advocating freedom to the galley slaves; the barons of feudalism, promising home ownership to the agrarian serf; George III, shedding tears of sympathy for the American patriots—these could be more readily believed in the cause of liberty than can the duPonts, the Mellons, the Morgans, the Baruchs and the Warburgs parading their financial falsehoods under the cloak of justice and truth. They never gave a judgment except for their personal profit. This day belongs to the common sense of the common American people for their common good!

## IV

May I now speak to you about the merchandisers of murder,

76

some of whom happen to be the guardian angels and officers in the American Liberty League.

These are days of tribulation and grief for our nation. Not at Valley Forge with the patriots starving on the hillsides were courage and determination needed as they are on this day.

Not at Gettysburg where it was decided that this nation could not exist half-slave and half-free!

I believe that the spark of patriotism is still burning in your hearts although it has been drenched by untold tears of unnecessary suffering—suffering wrought upon you by your greedy, ignorant fellow citizens. I believe that when you hear this story that spark will burst into the flame of holy indignation and, like the brothers of Christ that you are, you will gird up your loins to drive the money changers and the modern Iscariots from the temple of our national home.

It is a story so repulsive to human intelligence that it makes one hesitate to name its chief characters. *"Merchandisers of murder,"* I call them: cruel men who, with hearts of stone and corroded consciences, have besmirched our nation's fair name; wicked men who, by their greedy treachery, have humbled us before the parliaments of men; unchristly men who, mocking the policies of the Prince of Peace, have won for Benedict Arnold the songs of praise; men who have made it possible by their own infamy for Judas Iscariot to greet his first competitor!

I am deeply stirred by the news which has come from Washington this past week. As I turned it over in my mind, I unconsciously reverted to the inspired words of Pius XI who, having written of the immorality associated with the concentration of wealth, says: *"This concentration of power has led to a threefold struggle for domination. First, there is the struggle for dictatorship in the economic sphere itself; then the fierce battle to acquire control of the state so that its resources and authority may be abused in the economic struggle; finally, the clash between nations."*

The meaning of these words which I have read to you never dawned upon my mind with such clarity until I coupled them with the United States Senate Committee investigating munitions manufacturing. With noon-day clearness the whole scheme unfolded itself in the story associated with the name of duPont.

For weeks we were learning about the Electric Boat Company and the way submarines of American manufacture were sold. We learned that our Department of State promoted the sale of this company's submarines to Spain. Here was control of the State to such an extent that its authority was used in the economic struggle.

We learned that the Electric Boat Company had hired Rear

Admiral Long to represent its interests—not ours—at the Geneva Peace Conference some years ago. We were shocked to discover that this same Electric Boat Company was so influential as to persuade Admiral Niblock, the actual head of our Naval Intelligence Bureau, to send our American submarines around South America as part of a private corporation's sales plan to sell submarines to foreign nations and thereby to start an armament race —thereby to breed war—while the Geneva Conference on Arms Limitation was in session.

+ As the investigation at Washington continued during the past few days we were informed that American battleships sailed down to Rio to demonstrate arms and munitions and that the United States cruiser "*Raleigh*" was sent to Constantinople, at the request of the Driggs Gun Manufacturing Company, to help sell its wares of warfare. Do you not think that the United States Government is controlled by the munition manufacturers? Wait until the end of next week and you will find how the munition manufacturers are controlled by the bankers.

Need I recite this litany of horrible disclosures, of nauseating facts brought to light by this Senate investigation? Behold in Germany, in England and in our own America the munitions and arms manufacturers are so linked together under patent and sales agreements that secret processes for manufacturing are exchanged, sales territories are allotted and profits on death and destruction are divided.

Collusion, bribery of high officials and government corruption were proven to be the elements in making munition sales.

At last the unbelievable truth must be believed. According to sworn testimony it is the practice of our American corporations to arm both warring nations, to arm revolutionary factions in case of peace and to encourage a war for military and naval supremacy between friendly nations.

"*Away with the Prince of Peace! Crucify Him! Crucify Him! Give us the Barabbas of war!*" is the motto of the American munition manufacturers.

The Senate Committee discovered that every effort Congress made to regulate the shipment of arms; every treaty respecting the traffic in arms, in munitions and in powder has been defied by these manufacturers.

## V

Principal in the Senate Investigation of munition manufacturers come those sterling patriots and lovers of our Constitution— the duPonts. Co-founders of the American Liberty League, this family claims residence in Delaware for over a century and a quarter. This family witnessed American liberty in its cradle and is seemingly happy to follow it to its grave.

78

While to this duPont Company, motor manufacturing is only a side issue, their big interest is munitions—powder, powder machinery, explosives, nitroglycerine and chemicals—. Warfare is their game. They have become so wealthy that they dominate their economic sphere.

There is scarcely another powder company in America worth mentioning.

On go the duPonts from fabulous wealth to economic domination. Now the next step must be taken. In the language of Pius XI it is *"the fierce struggle to acquire control of the state so that its resources and authority may be used in the economic struggle."*

On go the duPonts! Do they attempt to gain control of the Government—these lovers of liberty—these co-founders of the American Liberty League?

Let the testimony before the Senate Committee answer that question.

So great was their control and domination over our Government that, when their factory was short of a certain rare explosive, they borrowed 60,000 pounds of it from the Government of the United States out of a total stock of 67,000 pounds to sell to a foreign power. That is point number one.

Point number two: They persuaded General Charles Humphrey to assist them in negotiating a sale through the Polish Embassy. That is using an army officer as a peddler of powder.

Point number three: The War Department and the Navy Department of the United States Government were so placed under the domination of the duPonts that military secrets have been released to foreign powers on condition that the duPonts would obtain the order. Military secrets, that we thought were sacred, were traded as a kick-in and a pay-off so that the orders would go to the duPonts!

Point number four: So vast was the power of the duPonts over both our War and Navy Departments that the officers thereof, along with the officers of the Army and Navy Intelligence Departments, actually supplied the duPont Corporation with military secrets rather than have this private corporation risk failure in its operations.

Point number five: The British firm of Nobels and the British Imperial Chemical, Ltd. are so interlocked with the duPont Corporation that it is hardly possible to keep from England a secret in the economic sphere in which the duPont Company is interested.

Point number six: One of the brothers, Felix A. duPont

"reached" Lieutenant-Colonel J. H. Mackie, member of the Canadian Parliament, who played a major part in the purchase of munitions during the war and whose knowledge of the Far East is impressive.

Mackie's job was simply to sell the Japanese the powder of duPont. He just happened to know Japan needed the duPonts, so the duPonts hired him as their representative, equipped him with the very advantages America had over Japan and rushed to Washington to confirm the arrangement with the Department of War and the Navy Department.

The War Department answered that powder and other munition sales to Japan *"will enable the army to learn how much and what kind of powder Japan was buying and then by deduction the army would then be in a position to obtain a considerable amount of information of military value."*

The Navy Department answered that *"although Japan was a potential enemy, the importance of the information that would reach the military and naval officers would offset this."*

May I comment on this most damnable philosophy? If it means anything it means that the Department of Justice should arm the Dillingers of the country with the latest type of Thompson sub-machine guns so that, in return, the Department may know just what guns kill its agents.

Point number seven: The duPonts never missed a sale because of patriotism. Take as an example the incident of the "mechanical dipper" used in the manufacture of nitrocelulose. Japan wanted the dipper. Although her agents searched England for one, they could not get it there. Imperial Chemical Industries, Ltd. turned the request over to America and the duPonts. The duPonts rushed to Baggaley of the Naval Intelligence Department and received this opinion on the proposed sale:

*"It is not only permissable but desirable for American firms to sell such equipment to the Japanese.*

*"The Japanese will undoubtedly purchase what they desire anyhow. It is desirable for America to secure the business and the Navy to be informed of the amount and nature of the purchases, which information would be lacking if the purchases were made in Europe.*

That is the patriotism of the duPonts and of the particular Navy Intelligence official. They would sell the flag from the top of the Capitol if it would help increase the profits for the duPonts!

Carried to its conclusion, it simply means that the police should sell dope to the children, who will get it anyhow, for then they will know how much the children use.

The "mechanical dipper" will help dip the blood out of our American boys. It used to be ours but now it is common property.

The Army Intelligence Service was approached on this duPont sale to Japan. Major Wilson, Major Marley and Major Froner had no objection.

The Department of State was approached. Here the duPonts were informed that any embargo on the "mechanical dipper" might be regarded by Japan *"as an unfriendly act and tend to render more difficult the already delicate situation in the Orient."*

What comment is necessary! In our infancy America defeated the proudest empire of the world—Brittania.

In our youth we defended our rights to the seven seas successfully against that empire.

Today we actually equip our potential enemies among the world powers and, out of fear of offending Japan, our Navy, our Army and our State Departments all approve a sale of a secret process to Japan.

In those days we had wooden ships and iron men. Today we have ships of steel and the duPonts.

The dollar of duPont capital always seeks its profit. With Japan in the hands of Mackie of Canada, Colonel W. N. Taylor, European sales agent for the duPonts, was ordered to work on Russia in 1928. Poor American Liberty League—sponsored by the identical patriots who sought the communist ruble as they armed the Communist rebel, and, with the same intensity, sought the yen of the Nipponese.

## VI

Let us see how a Liberty Leaguer speaks among his own—not for publication, but *"off the record."* This is a private communication from the lobbyist to the duPonts. I quote from the testimony introduced this past week: *"Congress is too short sighted to see the necessity of appropriating funds to keep private manufacturers of munitions in business. The army and navy would spend money if they could get it, and because they cannot they are doing all they can possibly do, and that is to help us make sales to other nations. But this is our country and not the country of Congress."*

That is the language used in reporting to the duPonts the assistance our War, Navy and State Departments gave to duPont sales abroad.

What wonder then that Pius XI writes: *"The whole economic life has become hard, cruel and relentless in a ghastly measure. Furthermore, the intermingling and scandalous confusing of the duties and officers of civil authority and of economics has gone as far as to degrade the majesty of the State. The State which should be the supreme arbiter, ruling in kingly fashion, far above party contention, intent only on the common good, has become instead a slave—bound over to the service of human passion and greed."*

*"This is our country and not the country of Congress,"* echoes the duPonts.

From mere wealth, to domination of their field; from domination through unchecked competition to dictatorship in the powder, the powder machinery and chemical fields; from this step to the control of the State where the War Department becomes a smart salesman, the Navy a peddler and the Department of State a foreign sales manager! The duPont Corporation has run the gamut. From the control of the state one last step must be taken in its true sequence. That is the clash between states themselves. That is war.

If America is sent into war—war to take us out of the depression—the American submarine already will be in the hands of the enemy. All the world knows just one submarine—ours. Ours, whether made in Germany, England, France, Italy, Japan, Russia or at home. Ours with a profit to the Electric Boat Company. Our submarines challenge our use of the sea.

When our navy meets the navy of any foreign power, mark you, any superiority we have in design or construction was long since sold to our enemies.

When our armies meet on the field of battle, duPont powder will send shot and shell screaming into their ranks. There is no advantage to the American soldiers.

When the new gases developed in laboratories of the United States pour forth death and destruction—even our own civilian population, our women and children will be killed by the self-same gases.

Who will win the next war—communist or capitalist, it matters not. The duPonts will be the real winners.

Yellow or white race—it matters not—the duPonts cannot lose!

Europe or America—they are there as they are here! *"This is our country, not the country of Congress!"*

I ask my audience to pray Almighty God that He cast a protecting arm over the Senate Committee until the end of this week. That must not be disturbed.

Let America have the truth, though the powers of hell, aided and abetted by the duPonts, the steel corporations and the bankers will, in their diabolical wisdom, try to hide the truth—the truth that America harbors traitors to all that is good—the truth that we harbor merchandisers of murder.

These are the men who, at this season of peace, have been consistently perverting the temple of Christ into a brothel of blood. These are the men who have made a mockery of democracy as, step by step, they superimposed their credo of killing upon the various branches of our Government. We have arrived at that point in our national destiny when we are determined to make of the United States of America a real democracy where our Government with its State Department and every other Department will operate not for the welfare of the merchandisers of murder but for the peaceful welfare of those who believe in the policies of the Prince of Peace.

Away with these dictatorships! Give us a real democracy! That is why the National Union for Social Justice was instituted. Choose between it and the American Liberty League with its individualism, its war profiteering, its merchandisers of murder members, its salesmanship of slaughter as represented by the duPonts and their front-men who prate to us about a liberty that is slavery and a prosperity that is death.

# FOLLOWING THE CHRIST-CHILD!

### (Sunday, December 23, 1934)

**M**Y Friends: Within a few hours we will be commemorating the birth of the Prince of Peace. Once more the Christian world will be re-echoing the song which angel voices sounded above a lowly stable more than 1900 years ago—the Christian world with the exceptions of Russia and Mexico, where a handful of atheistic communists regard the Infant Christ as their sworn enemy.

To this thought—the Mexican communism—I shall return. But it is more than expedient that, first, I dwell for a few moments on the more pertinent thoughts associated with the birth of Christ.

### I

Fashioned after the image and likeness of God, man, under the Creator, was appointed master of this world. It was planned that all its creatures should serve him in orderly fashion. Golden grain and fruit-laden orchards were destined to spread their abundance before him. In his vocabulary such words as disease and death were undefined and meaningless. Life, love and a perfect natural happiness were bestowed upon him. His intellect was so fashioned that, easily and without error, it functioned to discover and grasp the multitudinous manifestations of truth which lay hidden in every flower, in the thunder and lightning and beneath every grain of sand. His heart and his will were naturally inclined to love virtue and the beautiful things of life to such a degree that hate, unbridled ambition, greed and war were foreign to man's desires.

If I thus passingly refer to the wondrous days of Eden's garden; if I seem, perchance, to be an impractical poet lost in the dreams of things that might have been, it is only for the purpose of painting a background to the historical facts which eventually made their appearance upon the crimson canvas of life's realities.

Despite his lack of scientific education, even an untutored citizen can read the story of the dim past. He is aware that, from time immemorial, life has been a bitter struggle. Instead of wheat and grapes there grew thorns and thistles. Instead of nature willingly serving man, it buffeted him about with plagues and famines and devastating eruptions. Diseases multiplied. Crime and hatred grew apace. Feuds arose. Intelligence became numbed. And the heart of man, cloaked in ignorance and steeped in selfishness, turned from the God Who created it unto the false gods of its own devisal.

Read the story of the ancient civilizations—of the Medes and the Persians, of the Assyrians and Egyptians, of the Greeks and the Romans! It is a story of slavery and warfare, of famine and poverty. It is a sordid narrative of superstition, of darkness and of social decay.

Man, who had been created to know, to love and to serve, in liberty and in contentment, the God Who created him, eventually was degraded either to the estate of a galley slave or to the base quality of an overtaxed colonist.

Ignorant of the meaning of life, of government and of religion, the dictatorial monarchs of Rome established themselves as owners and proprietors of life. Caesar became a veritable god!

Poor sons of fallen Adam! Though you knew it not—you, whose souls had been immortalized at the touch of the Divinity; you, into whose bodies there had been poured the lustral drop of eternity—you were nothing more than the vassals and serfs of the Prince of Darkness, the Ruler of Death!

Thus, if one fact is crystal clear in all the pages of history, it is man's failure to succeed in life independent of God and God's truths. The further man strayed from Him, the deeper he became mired in slavery!

## II

During the thousands of years of man's degradation one small nation remained more or less faithful to the precepts of the Creator. I refer to the Jewish people. Constantly they prayed that God would send, to the world a Redeemer as He had promised. Constantly they were reminded, through the words of their prophets, of the Messiah's identity. His ancestry was foretold. The place of His birth was designated. The singular fact that He was destined to be conceived by a virgin mother was emphasized! To make sure that the Redeemer would be recognized, not only the outstanding incidents in His life, but His peculiar death and His divine resurrection were specified.

These revelations, most likely, were known to the high priests at Herod's court who, when questioned by the Wise Men from the East as to the place of the Messiah's birth, knew that Bethlehem of Judea was the city where the miracle of miracles was to occur.

My friends, if time permitted I should dwell at length upon this divine birth. But, in the exigencies of our present day, is is more important that I attempt to interpret it for our practical consideration.

First, however, let me pause to make public profession of my Christian faith in the mystery which surrounds this feast of the first Christmas.

I believe that unfortunate man was incapable of redeeming himself from the degraded slavery into which he had fallen.

I believe that out of the depths of His love, Almighty God freely sent to us His Divine Son, the Second Person of the Most Blessed Trinity, to redeem us by His death from eternal punishments and, by His life and doctrines, to teach us how to avoid social and spiritual ruin.

I believe that Jesus Christ, Who was cradled at Bethlehem, was conceived of a virgin mother by the power and operation of the Holy Ghost and not through the agency of natural wedlock.

I believe that Jesus Christ possessed a perfect human nature— intellect, will, memory, imagination—every faculty even as you and I possess them, but in a perfect degree.

I believe that He also possessed the perfect divine nature: All powerful, all wise, all good, all just, all merciful! He was infinite in every respect.

I believe that both His human nature and His divine nature were united miraculously in one Divine Person in such a manner that every human action which He performed was credited to His Divine Personality.

This, at least in part, is my religion. These are my fundamental beliefs as, with you and the shepherds and the Wise Men, I worship in simple faith at the shrine of Bethlehem's manger.

I am so convinced of these basic truths and rely so much upon them that I regard Christmas not only as the feast day of the Saviour's birth but as the birthday of our freedom from darkness, from error, from slavery and from sin. Without Christmas, pagan civilization, which reached both its peaks and its depths under the Caesars, would long since have spent itself. Men, by this time, would have returned to an age of Gothic barbarism but would have carried with them the vices of Rome.

In another sense, Christmas is the beginning of the world's most far-reaching revolution. At the year of our Lord's birth the Roman state finally had arrived at that point of decay where, legally, the last trace of real religion had been destroyed. Briefly, I mean that this was the occasion when Caesar Augustus dared to call himself a god. This was the day when, by imperial decree, he forced the people of his empire to regard him as such. This was the very moment when he was ordering a new census of his citizens, believing that, like so many cattle, they belonged to the state; that children and their parents, robbed of all opportunity to worship the True God, must sacrifice their human rights to him and, like all other state possessions, be identified with this new god's private property rights.

The creature had usurped the throne of the Creator! Despite the fine phrases which have been coined to eulogize Augustus and his golden age, here was the lowest degree to which civilization had fallen.

It was at this moment that Christ was born. It was at this hour when the angels' song of *"Peace on earth to men of good will"* announced the battle cry of the new revolution—a revolution

86

in favor of truth over falsehood, of liberty over slavery, of religion over atheism. Long enough had truth been trodden down. Long enough had slavery ruled. Long enough had wicked men attempted to play the part of God by teaching and practicing that the citizens belonged to the state and that the circlet of divinity belonged to the ruler of the state.

My friends, neither Augustus nor his contemporaries realized that it is the prerogative of God to vanquish those who persecute Him; to conquer at the moment when He appears to be abandoned by all!

These days of the counter-revolution had come to an end. Guided by the star of Bethlehem, the Wise Men from the East desert the foolishness of Pythagoras and the pagans. Shepherds, representing the agricultural class, hasten to the crib to carry away with them a vivid picture of the Truth-Made-Flesh. The laboring class, represented by Joseph, the carpenter, stands guard over the Divine Infant as His mother suckles Him at her virgin breast!

Here is the birthday of a new civilization when its first Royal Family will defy the wiles of a murderous Herod and the pride of a swollen Augustus, preferring to flee into an Egyptian exile rather than submit to a physical death in Palestine or to a spiritual death, if it were possible, at Rome.

### III

After twenty centuries of victory and vicissitudes, through the grace and teachings of Christ, the Saviour, mankind has fought its way back from the valley of state despotism and despair. Civilization did not perish. Faintly at first, then with thunderous acclaim there was preached the sanctity of the family, the brotherhood of man, the Divinity of Christ and the fatherhood of God.

What, though these preachments were interrupted by a Judas and his ecclesiastical successors, or by a Vespasian, a Caesar Borgia, a Cromwell and their political progeny, nevertheless, the torch of truth which was lighted by Bethlehem's star continued to burn!

The winds of human passion never succeeded in extinguishing the re-born doctrines that a human state or government exists for the people; that citizens are not chattels; that men and women are sons and daughters of God!

Hand in hand with the spreading of Bethlehem's story came universities and schools. Science was developed. Culture was extended to all classes.

Christianity was a success, though Christians oftentimes were its greatest foes—Christians who wore the triple tiara of an Alexander the Sixth or who held the gilded sceptre of a Henry VIII. But the revolution born at Bethlehem never faltered. Freedom slowly but surely conquered as long as kings and parliaments, presidents and congresses, together with their people, held fast to the story of Bethlehem.

## IV

From the ancient days of Pythagoras, centuries before the birth of Christ, there was a heresy handed down to posterity. It teaches that *"Man is the measure of all things."* It implies that God has no business interfering in the morals, in the government or in the actions of men.

*"Man is the measure of all things"* is the pagan theory which, followed to its logical conclusion, makes individualists out of all of us and gods out of the most relentless, the most unscrupulous. It is rugged, very rugged individualism.

It is this doctrine that sustained Caesar Augustus. It is this same doctrine that gave the disciples of Karl Marx courage to utter their blasphemy that they would not rest until they dragged the false God from His heaven. It is the doctrine of the present-day counter-revolutionists who pale with anger at the mention of Bethlehem. It is the principle of modern communism and of modern capitalism. It is the beginning and end of the policy which today we are encouraging officially in our relations with Mexico. Of this I shall speak.

I could tell you the story of Mexico. I could rehearse its rise and fall before the white man ever placed foot on her shores. When the Spaniards came with their first missionaries to bring the story of Bethlehem they encountered a pagan people steeped in the grim religious rites that sacrificed thousands of human beings to their pagan gods.

Or I could recall for you the history of Spanish progress in our neighboring southern republic—its university that preceded Harvard by nearly a century, its schools, its hospitals and houses of providence which have bespoken the spiritual and corporal works of mercy. I could unfold for you the story of Mexico as it was before the day of American intrigue. Then slavery was unknown. Then there was Christian peace and civil concord until our own President Polk began to implant the system of human slavery in a sister nation that believed in human brotherhood.

But I hasten down through the years of the Mexican War when we coined the phrase of *"Manifest Destiny"*—a phrase similar to Germany's slogan of *"A Place in the Sun"*—a place in a sun, no matter if it were achieved through the philosophy that might is right. That was the pagan philosophy upon which we Americans rested our only justification for our war of aggression against Mexico. In that day we plotted and planned the so-called independence of Texas. We stooped to steal lower California from the Mexicans. We pillaged and robbed a peaceful people. All these things are hidden facts of history carefully related in text books which are printed beyond our own borders and graphically told in that classic novel *"Ramona"* which was popular when I was a small boy.

In our own time, to the lasting disgrace of his name, came Woodrow Wilson bearing in his heart the same greed for gain which motivated the former Presidents Polk and Buchanan—Woodrow Wilson with his avowals of democratic freedom and his practices of plutocratic plunder.

I associate his name with that of Mexico because of his attitude, because of his policies which were practiced almost at the moment when vast lakes of oil were discovered south of the Rio Grande, in 1912, two years before Wilson's election to the presidency. It was found that the wealth of Mexico was associated not with her silver mines but with her hidden lakes of liquid gold which, because of the trivial barricade of an international boundary line, were barred from the Americans at the minimum price of plunder.

Backed by the elements of intolerance and motivated by men of greed, we Americans, through our President, unloosed in that year of 1912, and the decade to follow, a diabolical propaganda which, through the columns of the press, fired the imagination of the American youth and the gullible American lobarer and agriculturist with the so-called tyranny and absolutism of President Diaz.

Through intrigue, our secret ambassadors chose a Mr. Madero to head a revolution in Mexico. Madero proved to be an honest man—one desirous of honset elections and honest government.

Because of this, Madero offended the Wilson Cabinet. He had refused to promise a lease of Magdalena Bay and its lakes of oil in lower California. At this juncture Huerta, a just and great President for Mexico, took over the reins of government. This gentleman and his Mexican Cabinet were fully recognized by England and Germany. Our own Ambassador to Mexico recommended that the Wilson Government also recognize him.

This was the signal for Woodrow Wilson to go to work. He was determined to secure the oil leases of Mexico at any cost—even at the cost of our national honor. Thus he raised the arms embargo in favor of two of this world's greatest scoundrels —Villa and Carranza—two Dillingers and murderous mobsters who were paid to devastate the peaceful hillsides and contented cities of Mexico.

Fruitless were the warnings sent by our Ambassador Shaunessey to his chief at Washington. The President of the United States was determined to arm these butchers who plundered churches, tortured priests, raped nuns and dismembered Mexico limb from limb with the weapons of war which he, Woodrow Wilson, had sent to them.

Then on April 21, 1914, Josephus Daniels, at that time Secretary of the American Navy for the United States, ordered our Navy, at President Wilson's command, to seize the port of Vera Cruz which was President Huerta's only channel for supplies of defense against the two Dillingers, Villa and Carranza.

Thus, by armed intervention, Woodrow Wilson had placed the butcher Carranza in the President's chair of Mexico. It was Woodrow Wilson who muzzled the press of our own nation. He stopped the entire story of this intrigue from being printed in the columns of *"The New York World."* The same Wilson who, at a later date, was to expound to the world his fourteen points; the same Wilson who was to keep us out of war when, with that campaign slogan still on his lips, he was engineering us into the World War. The same Wilson who prated of people who were too proud to fight while he was in the act of arming and inciting revolutionists across the Mexican border—Wilson, the friend of small nations, who waged battles for the freedom of peoples; the same Wilson who made the world safe for democracy while he was in the act of supporting anarchy and atheism against democracy— all for the greedy commercial dollar!

Personally, I know a story which has not been chronicled in the pages of American history relative to President Wilson and the Mexican situation. Two great and distinguished Catholic Bishops had been sentenced to death by Carranza. Certain of our influential American friends approached President Wilson to intervene and save their lives. President Wilson refused to do this. Then approach was made by these same friends to Cecil Spring Rice, the Ambassador to America from the Court of St. James, England, asking him to befriend us in this hour of need. Cecil Spring Rice walked to his telephone, called the Japanese Embassy, informed the Japanese Ambassador of the necessity for immediate action. In less than six minutes, through the intervention of Japan, a pagan State, at the request of England's Ambassador, the lives of the two Bishops were saved when Wilson had refused to act!

The gangsterism of Carranza was labeled liberalism in our

press by Wilson. His agrarian brigandage was termed peon emancipation. His atheistic educational program was paraded as free teaching. When approached by the late Cardinal Gibbons to discuss his Mexican policy, President Wilson was forced to admit the enormity of Carranza's crimes against life and liberty and property.

This pathological President was so intent on the rape of Mexico that he persuaded Congress to reverse itself on the Panama Canal tolls. He cajoled our Congress into taxing our own American ships for the use of our own Canal to please England in exchange for which England promised recognition of the revolutionary government of Carranza.

Now for the last chapter of American activities in ravaged Mexico. I am telling you these things almost on the eve of Christ's sacred birth because they are more pertinently associated with it than one would surmise.

Coincident with Carranza's rule, or rather misrule of Mexico, there gradually arose to power the supreme dictator of our suffering sister Republic. His name is spelled C-A-L-L-E-S. I shall purposely mispronounce it and call it Calles.

From Wilson to Roosevelt Mexico has fallen the full depth into the slimy cesspool of barbarism. Mexico, with a population of approximately 15-million persons, 95 per cent of whom are Catholics; Mexico, with a population of far less than 1-million organized communists, is today pleading on her knees and asking us in the name of the Infant Christ whom we revere at this moment to have pity on her and cease associating ourselves with her crucifixion.

Never in the heart of Africa could be found the savagery of Mexico's present government. Never in the history of the world, not excepting Russia, has there been a Christian land so despoiled. Word comes to me from France, from England, from every State in our Union that Masonry—Free Masonry—from Presidents Polk and Buchanan down to Presidents Wilson and Roosevelt, is behind the scenes playing its hand to tear down the Catholic Church and destroy the Christian religion.

This I cannot, this I do not believe. There is not an American Mason, free or fettered, who could devise the satanic fury in Mexico today. I have too many staunch friends in Masonry to permit me to believe this. I know that Masonry has, as its fundamental tenet, the belief in a supreme being and I also know that the government of Mexico has as its first principle the tearing of God from the highest heavens.

I will gladly join with the Free Masons of our nation to spike this lie.

They tell me it is the socialists who are to blame for the present Mexican disaster. But I tell you it is not the American socialists, at least, whose political platform has been kind to the downtrodden of this nation.

It is not religious bigotry. It is not partisan politics. It is simply Satan himself, who could have excogitated this persecution, whose only origin could be hell and whose only operator could be Calles.

Let me be specific. Calles is the dictator of Mexico. Cardenas is the recently installed President. A man by the name of Canabal is the governor of the province of Tabasco. It is this latter villain's philosophy of education already in practice in the State over which he is governor that has won for him the distinction under Calles of Director of Education for all Mexico.

Remembering these names and these officers, let us gather our facts. On June 20, 1934, Cardenas, the incumbent President, was placed in office at the command of Calles. On that day Calles, the dictator, began a new phase of his Mexican Revolution which was expounded in a speech he made to the people of all Mexico.

From this speech I shall quote: *"We must enter into the consciences and take possession of them—the consciences of children and the consciences of youth; for the youth and the children must belong to the revolution. . . . It is absolutely necessary to drag the enemy out of his trench. The Conservatives are the enemy and their trench is education; their trench is the school. It would be a grave and cowardly dereliction of duty not to snatch our youth from the claws of the clerics, from the claws of the Conservatives. Unfortunately, the schools in many states and in the Capital are directed by the clerics and reactionary elements. . . . We cannot leave the future of the country, the future of the revolution in enemy hands. . . . With all their trickery, the clerics cry, 'The child belongs to the home, the youth belongs to the family.' What egoistic doctrine! Children and youth I say belong to the community, to the collective body; and it is the inescapable duty of the revolution to attack this section, to dispossess them of conscience, to uproot all prejudices and to form a new national soul. . . . For this end I urge and exhort all the governments of the Republic, all the authorities of the Republic, all the revolutionary elements of the Republic that they give definite battle on whatsoever plane and to whatsoever limit in order that the consciences of the youth shall belong to the revolution."*

My friends, you have lived to hear both Lenin and Stalin outdone. Your ears have just been offended with the philosophical statement that is counter-revolutionary to the revolution instituted at the crib in Bethlehem's manger. Whether you realize it or not, you have learned that Caesar Augustus, without his refinements and culture, has become reincarnated. In the person of one individual, a dozen Cromwells, a score of Neros, a battalion of Machiavellis walk the earth again in this Lucifer-let-loose-from-hell!

Calles lied when he made this speech. As a matter of fact there was not a cleric in all Mexico with freedom, not one Catholic priest for more than fifty thousand lay persons, not a Catholic school open in all Mexico. But Calles was inaugurating the most astounding educational program in all history. To operate it, only teachers dyed red in atheism were admitted.

As the little boys and girls walked daily to their class rooms they saw printed in large type upon the blackboard the sentence, *"There is no God."* That is their first principle. Their second principle is the age old companion of atheism—the satanic, but nevertheless, the psychological fact, that through sins of sexuality even a child can be led away from his God. Therefore, these atheistic communists have adopted the principle that sex knowledge and sex practices must be inculcated early into the hearts and bodies of the virgin boys and girls.

Turn your minds from the manger of Bethlehem! Come, look with me into the Mexican revolutionary school—the same school which Woodrow Wilson fathered when he paved the way for its functioning by lifting the embargo on arms and by making Mexico safe for the communists—the same school which Josephus Daniels helped to establish when he sent the American navy to Vera Cruz.

Blush not! For in your mind's eye you will see little children stripped naked—little children of both sexes, not only taught to examine themselves but taught, by public performance in the class room, how to commit copulation with each other. I could hardly blame you for stopping up your ears when I tell you, upon my word of honor, that in these revolutionary schools, supported today by the Mexican government, sexual perversion is openly practiced and encouraged.

As the little boys and girls leave the schools they are supplied with free tickets with which to gain entrance to lewd and licentious moving pictures.

Object lessons in procreation of the human race are followed by trips to maternity hospitals where the mysteries of child-birth are studied.

But natural and unnatural sins against the flesh are not sufficient for this curriculum. Calles' program is determined to enslave the conscience and the soul of the child. Furthering such enslavement, the governor of Tabasco struck upon a brilliant idea. Canabal, the governor, ran a live-stock exhibition. He summoned all the school teachers and the pupils from the surrounding countryside. He exhibited the bulls, stallions and boars in sexual actions. Then, with his judges, he picked the prize winners. The prize bull was labeled "God." The prize animals of other species he named after the saints of God. This was only in keeping with his policy of naming his own sons—three of them—Lenin, Lucifer and Satan!

That is the man who is the Director of Education for Mexico and those are his practices.

Calles so praised the work of this Director of Education for making brothels of the schools, that he has given him complete charge over all Mexico. To his shame and everlasting dishonor this same Calles openly maintains that this program of bestial education which enslaves the bodies and the minds and the souls of the children; this program which desecrates this Christmas which is the feastday of the Christ Child, is done in the name of Free Masonry and in the name of Socialism.

This, I repeat, is hard for any American to believe. Indeed, every member of the Masonic Orders in America can gladly call upon the members of the National Union for Social Justice to help them choke this lie down Calles' dastardly throat.

Moreover, no socialist who ever followed the honest Debs or the decent and highly intelligent Norman Thomas can suffer the slimy slur cast upon them by this unregenerate beast.

But we do know, my friends, that the crimes against the holy childhood of Mexico, the sodomy that cries to heaven for vengeance, are by his public utterances seconded and praised by no less a character than the former Secretary of the Navy under Woodrow Wilson, now the American Ambassador to Mexico under President Roosevelt. I refer to Josephus Daniels.

We have positive proof that complaints have been sent to the Secretary of State and to the President himself relative to Josephus Daniels seconding and abetting the educational program in Mexico. Up to date we have not had the honor of an answer.

We do know that there is a tradition in this nation known as the Monroe Doctrine which, for a century and more, has specified that, in the spirit of our founder, Washington, we shall refrain from European entanglements and shall expect European nations to refrain from interfering in Central and South America.

Another scrap of paper! For Russia is operating at this hour and on this Christmas Eve south of the Rio Grande, teaching and preaching that Bethlehem's story is a myth.

Moscow is here! The league of the godless is encroaching while we sit idly by with a wicked complacency fearing to offend the dictator Calles lest the American oil operators lose a concession or that the doctrine of neighborliness suffer a setback!

The government of the United States from Wilson down to our President Roosevelt has aided and abetted the rape of Mexico. It was Wilson who ran the guns for the mobsters and it was his man, Josephus Daniels, who won the dirtiest revolution this world has ever known.

As in the days of Herod, the wise men from America were interviewed and asked to seek out the child so that our oil barons could come and adore him. In their hearts the only adoration they knew was the adoration of the dollar.

It is under President Roosevelt that Josephus Daniels who, before the visiting school teachers in Mexico, praised its educational systems which I have been forced, in the name of decency and in the name of a lover of little children, to describe to you today.

Now let me quote Calles again:

*"We must now enter into and take possession of the minds of the children, the minds of the young, because they do belong and should belong to the Revolution."*

Having heard the atheistic dictator of Mexico, let me quote the hero of Vera Cruz, Ambassador Daniels:

*"The spirit of the Mexico of today was clearly and succinctly stated last week in Guadalajara by General Calles in as brief a sentence as that employed by Jefferson decades ago. General Calles, speaking for the ear of all patriotic Mexicans and particularly those entrusted with leadership said: 'We must enter into and take possession of the mind of childhood, the mind of youth! To the carrying out of that aim, which alone can give Mexico the high place envisioned by its statesmen, the Government is making the rural school a social institution.'"*

Here, my friends, you have a Daniels come to judgment. The American Ambassador, in parrot language, repeats the blasphemy of Calles and practically tells the 95 per cent Christian population of Mexico that the Americans are communists and haters of Christ.

It is in the name of social justice, in the name of the little children in Mexico, as well as of the little children in our own nation, that I speak to you today against communistic atheism which in no sense is a real revolution but which in every sense is a counter-revolution leading back to slavery, and to the Neros.

Purposely I have saved the first principle of our sixteen points for this day, which is dedicated to the Christ Child. Freedom of religion, freedom in education because the child does not belong to the state! Its mind and its heart and its soul belong to God, its Creator, and were entrusted by Him to the father and to the mother.

What is happening at our back door can happen in our backyard. Therefore, Protestant, Jew and Catholic have all united in one common saying: *"Remove this blot on our fair name. Remove from office one who aids and abets this atheistic communism."*

We Americans will have no part in the socialization of the children of this nation nor will we participate in the desecration of the sanctity of their innocent consciences.

History is replete with evidence that the world has not succeeded in getting along without God. And history is mindful of the shining star of Bethlehem which illumined the darkest night in this world's life.

We are through with counter-revolutions of communism and atheism. We stand by Christ and the Christ Child. His is the path which leads to progress, to prosperity and to happy eternity. The path of the counter-revolutionist leads to barbarism, to slavery and to a Herod's hell.

Christmas Day is empty and vain unless we resolve to teach and practice the principles advocated by Jesus Christ. It is worse than vain unless we have courage to say to that diabolical fiend, Calles, and to remind those who are responsible for our bungling, compromising Ambassador Daniels, that "whosoever shall scandalize one of these my little ones it were better that a millstone be fastened about his neck and he be cast into the depths of the sea."

Christmas is the feast of these little ones! May God grant that it remain so here in America and that it may become so among the children on the other side of the Rio Grande!

# MONEY IS NO MYSTERY!

*(Sunday, December 30, 1934)*

## I

INCE the year 1929 America has been in a state of transition. Slowly but certainly with every other civilized nation we have been passing from the age of modern capitalism into a new era of communism, of Fascism, of socialism or of Hitlerism. We, in America, have one choice, namely, to follow the course of one of these or else to construct a new system founded upon social justice. Still, withal, those who prospered most and produced least under the old system are battling fiercely to maintain their privileges and their functions of legislation.

Certainly, during this coming year and the years immediately following, we will witness the total dissolution of modern capitalism. It is advisedly that I use the adjective *"modern,"* because capitalism, as we knew it in the past twenty or thirty years, differed almost substantially from the capitalism which was originally conceived. Today it is more renowned for its vices than for its virtues.

Those who are fighting so relentlessly to preserve its poverty-breeding corpse refuse to face the pressing problem of squaring production with distribution. They are those who, during the coming years, will continue to oppose the restoration to Congress of its right to coin and regulate the value of money. They still believe that all wealth should be identified with gold: That is the basic thought behind the gold standard. They still believe that the debts of the farmer, of the merchant, of the municipality, of the state which were incurred through the operation of an insane credit inflation, of manufactured bookkeeping money, should be paid back to them in honest currency which does not exist.

They still labor under the delusion that the factory worker is so ignorant that he is willing to starve or, at least, recede to a lower standard of living, despite the plenitude of capital wealth which surrounds him—factories, fields, mines, forests—all of which are idle, because the banker controls the coinage of money and issues it on the same basis as he did before we underwent an unreal, psychological revaluation of our gold.

They still believe that the American people will become accustomed to bread lines, to forced idleness and to cut wages.

Most important, they will fight fairly and unfairly, scrupulously and unscrupulously, to retain their racket of lending manufactured money to the government for which money the government

97

and we, the taxpayers, print billions of dollars of gold paper bonds which eventually must be redeemed with good currency.

But to this thought of credit—of bonds, of debt—I shall return.

That we will refuse to suffer this financial domination any longer is certain. This form of capitalism, now a corpse, demands, at least, an honorable burial.

It is needless to ask what system of political economy shall replace capitalism. We in America are too religious minded, too devoted to our mothers, our wives and our children to accept the philosophy of the communist. There is a God. There is a heaven. There is a conscience and there is the immutable code of the Ten Commandments. Likewise there is a Christ. There is His Divine Brotherhood. There is His gospel of love in the hearts of His children. These things are too precious to barter for any man-made heaven with its black bread and equality in slavery.

Realizing the distinction, on the one hand, between international socialism, which levels all men down to a standard instead of up to a standard, and, on the other, American socialism, which is an unfortunately named political platform, I cannot envision the American people adopting the philosophy of the former or the proposals of the latter.

International socialism is anti-religious and anti-moral. It not only restrains liberty. It abolishes it. It, too, like communism, cares only for the goods of this world.

But American socialism, as professed by the intelligent Norman Thomas or an honest Debs, while preferable to the capitalism which we have known, goes too far, to my mind, in its program for the nationalization of industry.

Nor does the concept of the Fascist or Nazi dictator appeal to the American liberty loving citizen with his traditional love for democracy and republican institutions which bar both Nazi-ism and Fascism.

Before proceeding further in this discussion I am willing to commit myself to the statement that modern capitalism must go as well as modern democracy. But I hasten to add that while capitalism defended rigorously the right to private property, the main criticism against it was that the operators of capitalism had so concentrated the ownership and control of private property that there was little of it left for the masses of the people. In other words, there was too little private property.

As for modern democracy it degenerated into a system whereby, at least in this country, two political parties, under the leadership of the bankers and the banker-controlled industrialists, so manipulated conventions and elections and so controlled, either directly or indirectly, the majesty of the state that there was too little democracy and too much plutocracy.

Against all these systems—unspeakable communism, philosophic socialism, dictatorial Fascism, decadent capitalism, controlled democracy and modern plutocracy—there stands an economic system known as social justice. Seeking no compromise, enticing no man by vain promises, it writes down a platform for today, with principles of truth, of justice, of humanity as the Jews of old had them in their codes, as Christ taught them on the Mount. Justice to the laborer, justice to the farmer, justice to the property owner, justice to all!

It is a system designed to extend and widen liberty rather than to maim and curtail it.

It aims to free man from the subjugation of unnecessary poverty and from the exploitation of his fellow citizens who are lacking in conscience.

It is a system that is wedded to the belief that man's earthly happiness is identified with the home which he owns, where, in peace and tranquility, he and his beloved ones can know and love and serve their God.

It regards man and his family, not as a chattel of the state, but regards the state as the servant of its citizens.

Finally, the philosophy of social justice teaches us that the earth is the Lord's, to be apportioned for our maintenance, according to our merits, in such a manner that he who gains ownership of any property cannot use that property contrary to the common good.

This program of social justice does not militate against the Constitution of the United States in any degree. It does, however, oppose the misinterpretation given to that Constitution by the international bankers who have written laws for their own selfish purposes.

## II

Today I shall speak of one of the fundamentals of social justice, the nationalization of our money.

The mention of the word money suggests something mysterious. But we, who have mastered the hidden secrets of steam and electricity; we, who have steered our submarines beneath the waves and sent our argosies of freight above the clouds; we, to whom nature has unfolded the secrets of physics and of chemistry and of the applied sciences and arts, certainly are intelligent enough to master the simple problem of distribution. In other words, we are clever enough to evolve a system of finance which will abolish the most tragic phrase that was ever coined by the lips of man—*"Want in the midst of plenty."*

Consider the origin and purpose of money.

Broadly speaking, money is simple. It will require only a little searching into the pages of history to discover its origin.

99

Money is a tool which man invented after the age of barter had passed—after the age of trading a pig for a sheep or a pair of moccasins for a bow and arrow. Eventually, it became necessary to figure out some method of evaluating sheep and pigs and farms and wheat when goods of an unequal value were exchanged between the farmers—when a cow was traded for a dozen of eggs. The owner of the cow had to receive something else plus the eggs. In other words it was necessary for one man to express his debt to his fellowman. He did this by means of money.

Broadly speaking, when one citizen exchanges with another citizen things of an equal value there is no debt, no need of money. But where things of unequal value are exchanged, there is need of money in order to show the difference in the bargain.

At the dawn of history, money was primitive. Iron rings, cattle, wampum, even land itself came to be used as a measure of calculating the debt one man owed his fellowman. Today, when society has grown more complex and when the machine produces the goods of the world, money is needed more than ever in order to distribute the goods from the factory to the family in the home. Money is only the medium of trade. Around it, gravitates our entire problem of distribution. Without it, industry, labor, agriculture, everything comes to a halt.

### III

Pause to consider the history of the use of money in England.

(a)  In the year 1100 when Henry I was King until the year 1694 when the Bank of England was organized England had a peculiar money system known as *"tallies."* These *"tallies"* were simply sticks of wood about 4 feet long and 1 inch square. This stick of wood was notched with a jack-knife to express pounds, shillings and pence. The exact value was printed with ink on the sides of the stick and then it was split lengthwise. It was the government which did the splitting. Half the stick was given to the citizen in exchange for governmental service. The other half remained in the royal treasury.

It was the business of the county sheriffs in England to collect for taxes these sticks which the citizens held. It was the business of the government to match the collected half-stick with the portion already in the royal treasury. When they tallied or matched then the sticks were destroyed.

In 1694, when the Bank of England was founded $70-million of these sticks were gathered together and in their place the new bank issued paper money of a similar amount. Yet the old wooden tallies were legal tender in England until 1783. The accumulation of the centuries was not finally destroyed until the sticks were burned in the House of Parliament in the year 1830. England

100

was not on the gold standard. She was on the "wooden" standard and prospered!

(b)  Before the establishment of the Bank of England in 1694 there were banks in Europe where people could deposit their gold or their silver for safe-keeping. Coins of all nations were brought by the sailors and the merchants to these bank vaults. It was the business of the bankers to place a proper value on these coins and then to credit the owner of the coins with his proper amount of wealth.

Of course it was dangerous to carry gold and silver on one's person. It was better to keep it in the strong bank of deposit. When occasion demanded that one merchant transfer gold to another it was the banker's business, at the request of the two parties concerned, to make the transfer without the gold ever leaving his bank.

Bear in mind, banks did not make loans originally. They did not create credit. They simply transferred credit.

(c)  But with the founding of the Bank of England we begin to find this bank actually creating credit instead of transferring it.

I believe last year I told this audience that the Bank of England received its charter to operate and to create credit, or in other words, to coin money, when the merchants of London approached Parliament and told the members thereof that, if they wanted the merchants to help them put down a revolution, Parliament would have to concede to these merchants the right to coin money. (How similar to the action of the private bankers in the days of Alexander Hamilton and later on in Lincoln's time!)

Thus the Bank of England began to loan what they did not possess. For every dollar, as it were, of gold the bank had, it risked loaning 10 dollars of credit. At least 9 of these dollars did not exist. And more than that, for every dollar's worth of loan money that was extended to a merchant the Bank of England had the audacity to mark on its books that it was a dollar's deposit. Here is the mystery surrounding money.

How can a loan become a deposit?

How can something which you have not be something that you have in your possession?

How can 2 minus 2 equal plus 4?

Never let anybody tell you that these credit notes, or bank notes, manufactured by the Bank of England were backed 100 per cent by gold. This I have explained. The bank notes were seldom, if ever, backed by 40 per cent of gold. The credit money was seldom, if ever, backed by more than 10 per cent of gold.

101

Between the years 1797 and 1822 the Bank of England's paper money was nothing more than paper money and could not be redeemed by gold or silver or anything else. Those were days when there was no gold backing. Yet business and government carried on. That is a good point to remember when the bankers with their tenor voices shriek loudly for sound money.

(How different are we in this country with $9-billion of gold and silver resting peacefully in our Treasury vaults and only $5-billion of paper currency existing against it!)

It is also well to repeat that the Bank of England, even in its prosperous days when its vaults were loaded with gold, always considered it safe to issue two and one-half times as much paper money as she had bullion in her vaults. This historical fact is not open to contradiction. To this thought I shall return.

(d) Let us continue our thumb-nail sketch of money and its history. In the year 1780 the private bankers of London were without the privilege of issuing bank notes, or paper currency. The Bank of England still retained this monopoly. Now these private bankers hit upon a scheme by which they could compete with the Bank of England. It was this: Instead of merely accepting gold and silver for deposit from merchants and transferring this gold on the books of the banks at the will of the merchant, they gave each depositor a check book and permitted the depositor to transfer his own money by writing a check on his deposit. Here is the origin of the check book!

This check book supplied a new currency. The governors of the Bank of England protested to Parliament that this was infringing upon their monopoly. But the Parliament answering said: *"The day of monopoly has gone."*

(e) The system of the London bankers in creating this check book money, together with the system of the Bank of England in issuing bank notes, such as your five and ten dollar bills, and also loans, were both adopted in America when, in the year 1800, the United States chartered a great number of banks which were both banks of deposit like the private banks in England and banks of discount like the Bank of England itself. I need not repeat that the Bank of England was a privately owned corporation with its charter almost forced from the government at the point of a gun.

Thus there grew up in this country a new idea of a bank. It was a place to deposit your coin or your bullion or your currency which you could check out and transfer by using a check book. It was also a place for borrowing money and having your loan marked down on the banker's books as a deposit.

## IV

The above historical sketch is rather dry and uninteresting but it is necessary for the people of this country to know.

Let us now transfer our attention from the past to the present to see if the bankers are true even to their own traditions.

When you read the statement issued by Mr. J. F. T. O'Connor, the Comptroller of our Currency, you will find that there are no more than $5½-billion of real currency money in this whole nation.

(a)   Then read the printed and publicized confession printed by the bankers. The bankers tell us that in 1929 we had $58-billion on deposit and about $30-billion in 1934!

The truth of it is that the banks have no more than $1-billion of currency on deposit. The loans which they extend to industrialists, to merchants and to other citizens make up the difference between the $1-billion which they actually have and the $30-billion which they pretend to have. Bankers are professionals at counting eggs before they are hatched.

If this is so what do bankers really loan if it is not currency money? The truth is they loan credit—stage money, fiction money. They give the citizen who applies for a loan a right to withdraw when that citizen hands them a promissory note, or a mortgage on his house or a chattel mortgage on his farm machinery. When they receive this piece of paper from the citizen they credit the loan which they extended to him as a real deposit. The citizen does not receive a thousand dollars in his hands. He simply receives a check book with the right to check out a thousand dollars.

(b)   With this thought clearly established what then is our modern money? And where is it?

As for the currency—the $5½-billion of real currency money— approximately $1-billion is in the banks. This the bankers keep for till money which they pass over the counter. This is divided among 20,000 odd banks in this nation.

Another billion dollars is in the cash registers and tills of the store-keepers. Certainly the bankers can't loan that billion.

As for the other $3-billion it is in the pockets of the people. It is used in hotels, in restaurants, at railway and bus terminals and for a thousand and one petty transactions. It is also in the homes of the people who use it to pay the butcher and the baker. Much of it is in tin cans and tea-pots, in mattresses and other secret places. That briefly describes where the real currency money is.

What is money? What is the thirty odd billion dollars that the bankers claim to have on deposit? Certainly it is not currency.

It is bankers' money—money manufactured by the bankers; a pure fiction, a figment of the people's imagination, an impenetrable mystery which you can't understand because it is not understandable. It is really what the depositors owe the bankers. It is the amount represented by the people's right to withdraw. If the people ever made up their minds to use their check books on a given date and at a given hour the banks would burst like a bubble!

Yet, my friends, 95 per cent of this nation's transactions are accomplished by the use of this bankers' money, or credit dollars or check book money. It is bankers' printing-press money which the American people are willing to accept!

## V

(a) Now let us examine for a moment how this credit money operates in the functioning of business. Credit, of course, is the life of business. Every banker in the world knows how the extension of a mere $1,000.00 of credit helps keep the wheels of business turning. He himself will tell you that the thousand dollars extended in credit will account for $50,000.00 of real business volume in a single year. A borrower of a thousand dollars purchases goods at retail. The retailer in turn buys from the wholesaler. Soon the jobber is called upon to re-stock the wholesalers inventory. The jobber places an order with the manufacturer, who in turn buys labor and raw materials from the mine or the field or the forest.

In the meantime, many men are employed all down the line where this one thousand dollars has flowed like the stream of a river. Capital prospers and labor prospers as credit flows throughout the nation. Everyone realizes that if the issuance of credit were handled honestly by the private bankers, there would be prosperity.

But, oh! There is the rub! "*If*"—a mountainous word of two letters! At times our bankers extended credit until it became an inflated balloon that could do nothing else but burst. And at all times, with only their billion dollars of real currency on deposit, they loaned this extra twenty or thirty or forty billions of dollars of stage money, of fiction money, at five or six or seven per cent, making a billion dollars profit even in a poor year.

(b) There is another side to this picture. Bankers, as a class, have proven themselves greedy. They can no more escape that qualification than can a tiger escape being called vicious. Their very nature demands that they be greedy.

How is this explained? Well, when the borrower asked for a loan, he handed over the deed to his home or his farm, both of which constitutes real wealth. When the banker has issued a greedy amount of credit, he concludes that it is time to stop issuing further credit and that, moreover, it is time to call in the loans already existing. The thousand dollar loan, of which I spoke, is recalled. It takes $50,000.00 of business out of circulation. The retailer receives no order nor does the wholesaler, the jobber nor the manufacturer. All of them dismiss labor the minute orders cease. The prices of farms and real estates drop and the banker takes them over when the borrowers cannot pay him cash. He takes them over, mind you, although he did not loan real money. A banker loans simply credit, his own monopoly of the printing press. He manufactured this credit and charged interest on it. He created it knowing that there was no bullion or coin behind it. He can make a "run" on the people but the people must not make a "run" on the banker!

(c) ⨯ Now it is very well for the banker to start his printing press. But at the moment a student of banking and of monetary reform brings these facts to his attention, the banker and his kept press yells *"Stop, thief!"* Printing press money is the banker's money. It is his currency. He owns this prerogative. That is why the Baruchs, the Warburgs, the Morgans and the Mellons, the Federal Reserve bankers and every white-carnation-bedecked banker in America sees red if the bankers' racket is interfered with.

That is why they scamper up the steps of the White House and into the cloakrooms of Congress, if anyone dares suggest that the sovereign people of the United States recapture the power over money which originally was placed squarely in the hands of Congress under the Constitution.

A banker is not a producer. He is a leech who lives upon the artistry, the labor and the scientific development of others. He is in business with his prerogative of manufacturing money through an act of Congress and through the grace of a printing press and fountain pen. His business is eventually to get that which he did not create.

Do you wonder, then, that depressions have been decreed by bankers?

⨯ What matters it if fifteen million men be idle, if factories close, if commerce freezes, if dire and abject poverty be the lot of the multitude in this land of plenty! Their racket must continue— a sordid, vicious racket that poisons the very life blood of the nation!

What if there is less banking business to be done in the days of depression—they care not! Because, aside from the ordinary loans which they make to ordinary citizens, they still continue to make money on the interest-bearing government bonds which they possess. At least $20-billion of these bonds are in bankers' vaults. And many of them are bonds which were issued by the government to dress the boys of 1916 in khaki, to pump murder into their hearts, to feed them hardtack and to prepare them to become fodder on the battlefields of France. Bloody bonds which were used for destructive purposes! Criminal bonds which they expect you and me to redeem for the privilege of their having made a slaughter house of this world!

What care they for depressions as long as these bloody bonds continue to drip their malignant poison upon the prosperity of a misunderstanding people!

Six times in the last century and four times already in this century have we been subjected to panics, to man-made panics, the greatest of all occurring after the establishment of the privately owned Federal Reserve Banking system which, in the preamble of its charter, practically guaranteed this nation freedom from panics.

They made their runs on the people and captured the real wealth of the nation!

Shall we permit this system to continue, this system of private banking which creates depressions and cashes in on bloody bonds?

Shall we plot depressions now for our children and grandchildren?

*x* Call the roll in advance as the bankers call it, and plot it and graph it—1940—1950—1970—1990. Listen to the words of *"over expansion of credit," "over production," "speculation"*—words, words that carry every depression back to the cunning mind of the banker who, by his very nature, cannot help but plan to reap where he has not sown.

These facts I present, not only for the consideration of our Congressmen, but also for the consideration of the industrialists and the members of the National Union for Social Justice who are demanding that credit be nationalized and that the prerogative of manufacturing stage money be taken from the bankers.

No longer must the private banker be able to extend credit when credit is over-extended. No longer can he be permitted to call loans when there is no possibility of paying them. No longer can we suffer him to seize our factories, our warehouses, our stores, our farms and our homes. No longer shall we suffer from the whip of insecurity.

If depressions have come and factories have closed, blame not God as if He had failed. It was stupid man who failed! Stupid man who permitted a handful of self-constituted guardians of our prosperity to guide our economic destinies as though we were puppets and pawns! Selfish, greedy men who have devised a simple system of keeping the volume of currency small and the volume of credit flooded so that their little unproductive group can dominate the producing masses.

Members of the Seventh-fourth Congress! I am asked by thousands to attack communism, to join in the drive against radicalism; perhaps to sneak down the alleys and ferret out the agitators who would destroy our institutions.

Members of Congress! You must recall history—radical history! Karl Marx, the founder of socialism, never did an honest day's work in his life, but lived on the generous benefactions of Engel, who, though a German, derived his fortune from the textile mills of England. Wealth, not poverty, paid Marx for his work. Martinez of Portugal was well supplied with this world's goods, yet he is considered by all historians to be one of the profoundest conspirators against the state.

Adam Weishaupt, founder of communistic philosophy, was always amply supplied with funds from the wealthy.

Cagliostro, Sicilian communist, drew huge sums of money from the bankers of Amsterdam, Rotterdam, London, Genoa and Venice.

Adrien duPont, friend of the Duke of Orleans, plotted to hold up the food supply of his countrymen and then block every reform in the National Assembly of France.

Were I plotting the downfall of my country; were I upholding communism or socialism or a dictatorship or anarchy, I would reread the history of all social revolutions and then salute the American banker as comrade and friend.

To create unemployment is the first principle of communism from Adam Weishaupt to Lenin.

To make misery, starvation and dire poverty the lot of the masses is written in large, bold type on the first page of the grammar of anarchy.

To make agriculture so unprofitable as to over-populate our cities with idle rural laborers has been a policy laid down in every catechism of discontent from the *"Illuminati"* of the twelfth century to the red agitator of the twentieth.

To let atheism rise against religion; anarchy against government and famine against the people is taught in the kindergartens of the communists.

Finally, to open wide the gulf between the little group of the very wealthy and the teeming masses of the workers—pitiless, propertyless, but never conscienceless—that is the program of destruction.

Why look in the cellars for the breeding pens of red radicalism? Go into the marble halls of the banker. There you will find practiced what Weishaupt taught—the necessity to spread unemployment—to make misery, dire poverty and starvation the lot of the masses. The bankers' program is reproduced in the grammar of anarchy.

Go into the banks of the nation—into the Federal Reserve Banks, if you will, and find the agricultural loan policy. See if it helps to make farms unproductive and, therefore, send idle rural laborers to over-populate our cities of discontent. I can show you this policy in every radical philosopher's teachings for eight centuries.

Lastly, look at our own dear America, with wealth concentrated into the hands of a little group and fifty millions facing destitution.

Men of Congress! No radical ever succeeded without being endowed by the generosity of a rich patron.

No radical in world history had the ground so well prepared as the American banker has prepared it for him.

Before you drive out the radical and radicalism, you must have courage to drive out the causes which breed radicals and radicalism!

Recover the people's power over money—currency money and credit money—recapture the power our forefathers gave you— *"to coin money and regulate the value thereof"*—whether that money be currency or credit. That is your chief work this year. Unless this is accomplished there is little hope for a just and living wage or for the lifting of the cross of depression from our shoulders!

# PRESIDENT ROOSEVELT AND SOCIAL JUSTICE!

## (Sunday, January 6, 1935)

### I

FRIDAY, January 4th, marked a definite step in the progress of social justice throughout the world. On that day, President Roosevelt appeared before the assembled Congress to enunciate certain principles which, beyond all question, indicate that we are determined to place once and for all the sacredness of human rights above the materialism of property rights.

In clear-cut phrases he delivered an official statement of policy which committed both himself and this Seventy-fourth Congress to the deep, spiritual philosophy of Christian charity and social justice. With a prayer of divine guidance on his lips, with a recognition of God's providence in his mind, he disassociated both himself and the American people from atheistic communism, from Fascism and Hitlerism.

January fourth, 1935, brings to an end the economic principles of individualism hitherto taught, practically in every American university.

It is the date which marks the termination of certain of those principles taught by Adam Smith, by John Stuart Mill and Malthus. Such outworn and impractical economic phrases as "free competition, and "rugged individualism" and "laissez-faire" today are seeking a resting place in the limbo of archaic falsehoods.

Without compromise, without pussyfooting, the President covered the humane philosophical principles which centuries ago were sounded on Sinai's mountain top and of old were echoed on the hillsides where Christ preached His Gospel of brotherhood.

Thus, today, the members of the National Union for Social Justice can rejoice, while the avowed opponents of human rights —the Liberty Leaguers, the United States Chamber of Commerce members, the Manufacturers Association—can find scant consolation as their programs for doles, for balanced budgets, for gold standards, for free rein in the industrial field are indirectly consigned to the wastepaper basket of ancient history.

Let them heed the words of the President that *"we have undertaken a new order of things."* Let them be cautious, henceforth, because only at their own personal peril will they dare obstruct the rising of this sun of social justice which will not set until the new economic system will have been perfected.

To those of you whose misfortune it was neither to have heard nor read this Presidential message, may I quote from it and comment upon its salient passages.

## II

1. In speaking of the new order of things, Mr. Roosevelt said: *"We progress towards it under the framework and in the spirit and intent of the American Constitution."* This means that we are still Americans—in fact, that we will become better Americans than ever—as we will hold fast to our democratic traditions and to our republican institutions. The phrase, *"spirit and intent of the Constitution"* is important—more important than if it read, *"the letter and the legal interpretation of the Constitution."* I need not remind you that *"the letter oftentimes killeth, while the spirit maketh to live,"* as the Scripture says. I need not rehearse for you the deeds and misdeeds perpetrated in the name of the cruel letter of a man-made code of laws which was written primarily for the protection of property rights and only incidentally for the safeguarding of human rights.

2. Well did our President say that: *"Throughout the world, change is the order of the day. In every nation economic problems, long in the making, have brought crises of many kinds for which the masters of old practice and theory were unprepared. In most nations social justice, no longer a distant ideal, has become a definite goal, and ancient governments are beginning to heed the call."*

If, on many past occasions, I was prompted to criticize, to castigate and sometimes to whip with the lash of words these masters of an old practice which was cruel, hard and impossible to bear, I glory in the cause which I espoused. For many years it was evident that social justice should replace the practices of modern capitalism; that the doctrine of exploitation should be relegated to the same graveyard where rots the corpse of feudalism; that the theory of exploitation should take its place with the theory of slavery; and that the teaching of social justice, which distinguishes between the right to own and the right to use, should replace the Bourbon teaching which identified these two rights and thereby permitted the owner to use his goods to suit his own selfish purposes.

At last the day for social justice has had a hearing in the courts of progress. At last we recognize that the God Who created us gave us this earth and the fulness thereof to sustain us; that He intended thereby that what He gave us for our sustenance should not be stolen from us by a little group of individuals who had succeeded in placing a fence of "better-than-thou-ism" around the world, placarding it with the sign "Thou shalt not enter!", thus forcing countless numbers into destitution and into the bondage of economic slavery.

The millions of members of the National Union for Social Justice are deeply indebted to our President for this statement as are the millions of Americans, who long since have learned that there was no justice for the multitudes under the out-worn system of modern capitalism.

3. The President is no optimist. Even his bitterest critics must admit that he is a realist when they meditate upon the following words: *"We find,"* said he, *"our population suffering from old inequalities, little changed by past sporadic remedies. In spite of our efforts and in spite of our talk, we have not weeded out the overprivileged and we have not effectively lifted up the underprivileged. Both of these manifestations of injustice have retarded happiness."*

Here is an honest act of contrition. For two years Mr. Roosevelt was so conservative that he gave ear to those men whose policies were most responsible for effecting the depression. Modern capitalism with its gold standard, its private control of currency and credit, its privately owned Federal Reserve banks and many other trappings, was suffered to continue alongside the emergency relief which was expended upon a down-trodden people. Even this emergency relief was financed by the private bankers.

All this was honest experimentation which resulted in seventeen millions or more citizens becoming recipients of a national dole, in our national debt being increased by billions of dollars, and in our bankers waxing rich as they battened off the interest money resultant from our endeavors of trying to borrow ourselves out of debt with privately manufactured bankers' dollars.

No wonder we did not weed out the overprivileged! No wonder that we did not effectively lift up the underprivileged! The task was impossible as long as the tool for its performance was the system of modern capitalism.

These were two years of bitter verbal conflict. Two years which served as a proving ground, a laboratory. Two years expended in giving a sportman's chance to the corporate body of modern capitalists to rise to the occasion. Two years in which they proved to civilization that their economic system, their financial system, their entire fabric of philosophy were so dissipated and inefficient that the naked facts which confront us today cry out for reform.

4. No wonder Mr. Roosevelt adds that, at this moment, *"We have a clear mandate from the people, that Americans must forswear that conception of the acquisition of wealth which, through excessive profits, creates undue private power over private affairs and, to our misfortune, over public affairs as well."*

What is the conception of the acquisition of wealth to which the people are opposed? In one sense it is related to the practice of industrialists paying their workmen only while they work and starving them while they are idle. In another sense it is related to paying dividends to stockholders all year round whether or not the wheels in the factory are busy; whether or not there is an annual wage for the laborer.

In the more important sense, it is essentially related to the banker who gained control over industry. How did he gain this control over industry? Need I repeat what I have already told you, namely, that in the year 1929, at the peak of prosperity, there were 30 per cent fewer industries in this country than there were ten years before it? This was due to the immorality of our private credit system which permits the banker, who takes your one honest currency dollar deposited with him, to create on his legalized printing press at least nine other fictitious dollars, credit dollars. These credit dollars he loaned to the industrialist who needed money to carry on his business. To secure the loan, the industrialist mortgaged his property with the banker. Billions of such credit dollars were scattered throughout the nation. At least nine times more credit dollars were expected to be paid back to the banker than there was actual currency or real dollars in existence. When the loans became due the currency dollars were non-existent. Consequently the banker took over the property of the industrialist, amalgamated it with other factories and began to build up his monopoly, counter to the best interests of this nation. That is how, as on a former occasion I pointed out to you, the J. P. Morgan and Company control $40-billion of American industry, banking, insurance and other activities in this nation. It was due to this private issuance of credit that such a thing as unjust competition was permitted to run rampant.

All during this period, while the bankers enjoyed the power of issuing credit, they also held control over the actual currency dollars. These they kept scarce. By keeping them scarce they were simply playing the game of a cat watching a mouse—watching the borrower—who eventually would fall into his trap and be forced to surrender his property. Thus, through the existence of an immoral law which is counter to the letter and to the spirit of the American Constitution, Alexander Hamilton and his successors in office were responsible for handing over to a small group of individuals, of parasites who did not produce but who lived upon the labors of others, this control of money which enabled them, in days of prosperity, to grow fat upon interest and, in the days of depression, to grow fatter upon confiscations.

Until a few months ago this mystery of money was a secret which was safeguarded by the international bankers of the world and their hired puppets throughout every nation. But now that the veil has been removed, there goes forth a mandate from the American people calling a halt to this practice.

5. In this nation there is ample room for everyone to profit

according to his merit provided he is willing to work. Henceforth our national motto shall be *"security for all."* Henceforth our laws will be so written and so executed that financial privileges for the few shall disappear. This is what is meant when Mr. Roosevelt said: *"Among our objectives I place the security of the men, women and children of the Nation first."*

These words indicate the philosophy which will guide our President during his tenure of office. It is the philosophy of social justice which is about to vanquish the sophistry of greed and of individualism.

Upon the attainment of this objective Mr. Roosevelt is willing to stand or fall.

6. Let us inspect the proposed policies by which that philosophy of security can be put into practice. First and foremost Mr. Roosevelt plans to develop our natural resources. He said:

*"A study of our National resources more comprehensive than any previously made, shows the vast amount of necessary and practicable work which needs to be done for the development and preservation of our natural wealth, for the enjoyment and advantage of our people in generations to come. The sound use of land and water is far more comprehensive than the mere planting of trees, building of dams, distributing of electricity or retirement of sub-marginal land. It recognizes that stranded populations, either in the country or the city, cannot have security under the conditions that now surround them.*

*"To this end we are ready to begin to meet this problem—the intelligent care of population throughout our Nation, in accordance with an intelligent distribution of the means of livelihood for that population. A definite program for putting people to work, of which I shall speak in a moment, is a component part of this greater program of security of livelihood through the better use of our National resources."*

In my interpretation of this statement there is hereby launched a program for permanent public works. At last we have an official pronouncement that gold is not wealth; that the real wealth of the nation, from a material standpoint, is identified with the homes, the farms, the forests, the developed waterways and highways which we can and will arrange for the benefit of future generations.

This policy is sensible insofar as it is designed to take up the slack of unemployment which necessarily and increasingly results and will continue to result from our development of mass production machinery. It recognizes that stranded populations, either in the country or the city, cannot have security under the conditions that now surround them. Thus a program of public works will be devised by which our hitherto idle population will have an opportunity to earn its livelihood on the basis of a just wage. It dares not be less than a living wage. This wage, however, will not necessarily be commensurate with the wage paid by industry. Henceforth the industrial wage must be predicated upon a new division of the profits, a new share in the goods produced.

As soon as the produced goods of the factory will have been consumed or used, those engaged on the public works program will find a place for their labors in the factories. On the off-season they will return to their road building, to their reforestation, to their slum clearances. This means the end of the unscientific and uncivilized dole system. This means the beginning of a new wealth for the future generations of America.

## III

There is one point which Mr. Roosevelt did not clarify. It is associated with the money to be employed in our permanent public works program. It is associated with the overprivileged banking classes and with either their perpetuation as such or the destruction of their overprivileges as such.

Last Sunday I had occasion to explain to this audience a few facts relative to the nature of money. The only thing mysterious with money was definitely related to the fact that for every valid dollar bill which a depositor places for safe-keeping in a bank, the banker proceeds to lend it ten times. With each loan he marks down on his books that these ten dollars have been deposited when, as a matter of fact, they were never deposited but were loaned. The only thing that was deposited besides the solitary dollar was a mortgage for your home or your farm or your business.

I pointed out that the financial picture which is presented to you in America today shows, on the one hand, no more than 1-billion real dollars deposited in the banks. But the bankers advertise in their statements that they have approximately $30-billion on deposit. This means that when the proper date comes around on the calendar for your mortgage to fall due, or for all the mortgages in the country to fall due, the bankers, who are the manufacturers of money, demand payment in currency, in real dollars. Of course, this is impossible because real dollars to that amount do not exist, there being no more than 5½-billion currency dollars extant in the nation. In this way, through the privilege accorded the bankers, they are lawfully permitted to seize the real wealth of the nation because it is impossible for the citizens of the nation to pay back the bankers in currency when only credit was borrowed.

That is the mystery surrounding money, namely, that bankers reap where they do not sow, or, at least, they reap wheat where they sowed cockle.

All this has a bearing on the point which Mr. Roosevelt failed to incorporate in his message to Congress last Friday.

Here is where it affects you, my fellow citizens. Shall Mr. Roosevelt use bankers' credit money to conduct the program of permanent public works or will he be courageous enough to revert to the Constitution which he loves and which he has sworn to uphold—the Constitution which says plainly and unequivocally, *"Congress has the right to coin and to regulate the value of money?"*

You ask me what difference it makes? May I tell you with emphasis and with clarity what difference it makes.

During the past two years our present Administration has borrowed approximately $8-billion from the bankers. It was used partially for public works, partially for paying men to pick up leaves, partially to sustain a questionable dole system. It was $8-billion of relief which we, the taxpayers, contributed for the sustenance of the destitute. It was $8-billion of credit money, of manufactured money, of fictitious money which never did exist in real currency. Eventually we and our children must pay back to the bankers that $8-billion not with credit money but with real currency money.

Besides paying them back the borrowed $8-billion we are obligated also to pay them back $6,400,000,000 for interest, making a grand total of $14,400,000,000 which the taxpayers must produce in real currency that does not exist when these bonds and notes issued by our present Administration mature. In other words, we have mortgaged the United States to the bankers. We have contracted to pay them $14,400,000,000 on the $8-billion we have borrowed.

It is impossible to fulfill this contract because there are no more than 5½-billion real currency dollars in existence in our country. This means that when the date of maturity arrives for these mortgages and bonds the bankers will own the United States of America, its homes, its farms and forests and fields.

This is their legal right, namely, to confiscate, at least in part, the United States of America. This the present law guarantees.

May I anticipate the objection which the bankers make to this statement—a statement that they cannot deny.

They will tell us that these bonds and notes will be refinanced!

What does this mean? It merely means that we will continue paying interest for generation upon generation. It means that we will keep them living in luxury, in their overprivileged palaces, in their Palm Beach residences, in their Scottish hunting lodges, because, Alexander Hamilton, the first Secretary of the Treasury, and his successors, permitted men of flesh and blood, the same as you and I, to create wealth, to counterfeit money, to manufacture credit, only through the grace of a fountain pen and a piece of gilded paper!

Thus, if our proposed program for permanent public works will be launched through the agency of bankers' money, it means that the five or even ten billion dollars which will be used to reclaim marginal lands, to destroy slums, to build homes, to prevent erosion, to plant trees will sustain the overprivileged banker. It means that, eventually, our generation and the succeeding generations will be working under the fiction of a new deal for the benefit of the privileged classes. The reality of a New Deal will be absent.

Throughout the ages, classes became privileged only because they controlled the wealth of a nation, only because they made either physical or political or economic slaves of their fellow citizens. It was true with the Romans under Caesar Augustus and his millions of slaves. It was true with the baronial lords who lived the lives of leisure while the tenants upon their princely estates lived the lives of serfs. It is still true in America through the grace of an Alexander Hamilton and the plutocrats who followed him. The privileged classes of money manufacturers gained control of the lands, of the homes, of the industries and of the government itself in this country due to no other reason than to the fact that they have controlled the issuance of credit and thereby, the legal right that the borrower pays back in currency when these bankers have kept currency money scarce.

The very heart and soul, the motor of the new deal is the money question. Unless their constitutional privilege is removed from the bankers; unless their purple fountain pens are emptied and it be legislated that it is as illegal for them to create money as it is for you and for me to counterfeit it; unless this Congress has the fortitude and the sagacity to reclaim for itself the right and the duty to coin and regulate our money, the new deal will remain as a noble but unsuccessful experiment on the part of man to destroy the worst brand of slavery that was ever perpetrated!

## IV

What is my suggestion relative to the kind of money which should be used for public works? In plain language it is this. If we borrow $8-billion from the bankers it means that eventually we must repay them $14,400-million including the interest. We have simply created a debt. This debt exists in the nature of bonds, of paper blessed by the printing press!

If the government itself prints $8-billion of greenbacks, differing only in color from the bonds which are yellowbacks and to which coupons are attached, this $8-billion is also a debt. Like the bond, it is born on the bed of a printing press. Like the bond it is headed for the graveyard of maturity.

Need I ask which is the sounder debt? Or, which is more inflationary? There is only one answer to these questions, because most certainly $14,400,000,000 is more inflationary and less sound than the $8-billion backed by the gold in the Treasury.

There is no mystery about this any more than there is a mystery why two and two are four. The only mystery consists in endeavoring to make two and two equal five, or to say that $14,400,-000,000 is less inflationary than $8-billion.

My friends, there is no one who wishes this new deal to succeed more than do I. Thus, more than a year ago I coined the phrase, "Roosevelt or Ruin" because I believed in him when he openly avowed that he would drive the money changers from the temple and hand America back to the Americans.

Today I believe in him as much as ever. Today it is "Roosevelt and Recovery" provided he veers neither to right nor to left; provided he will strike home at the very heart and soul and motor of modern capitalism, namely, the right of the few privileged ones to control the issuance of credit. Through this control they live like lords from the debts which we incur for national public works. Eventually, when these debts fall due, these overprivileged lords will demand payment of their pound of flesh either in currency money, which does not exist, or in the actual wealth of the nation which they will control. Have not the past two years taught us that we can never borrow ourselves out of debt with bankers' bonds and dollars? The National Union for Social Justice answers this question affirmatively. Upon this point, the National Union cannot and will not compromise.

## V

Down the centuries of history two great and sinister stupidities have prevailed—witchcraft and statecraft. Superior and perverted minds have made them the instruments to power. Self-centered brilliant minds have employed them to control the man with the hoe, to exploit the man who stands at the lathe, to subjugate the man who follows the plow, and to rule and pauperize the multitudinous hoary-handed brothers and sisters of toil.

It is nearly a century since witchcraft fell upon evil days. Its stupidities were exposed. Superstition and the black arts were merged in the deeper shadows of oblivion. But its twin brother, the monstrosity of stupid statecraft, still blunders on. Turn back with me the pages of history until you come to the name of Nicholas Machiavelli. His was an inspired genius, which lacked the lustral drop of Christianity's brotherhood. It was he who codified the tenets and systematized the technique of modern statecraft in the most unsocial book ever produced by the mind of man. I refer to "Il Principe." Here is the doctrine contained in that book:

117

*"The masses of men are irreclaimably inferior in intellect, in emotion and in spirit. Left to themselves the only law they will recognize is the law of the jungle. Anarchy is the order of their disordered souls. The masses cannot rule themselves. They cannot be unified and directed by leadership even of an intelligent ruler. Consequently, it is the duty of a superior mind, of a ruler, to deceive them with promises, to circumvent their disorderly impulsiveness by artifice, by oppression and by trickery. And, if necessary, by bloodshed. But always deceive them with promises."*

This Machiavellian theory of statecraft was briefly but accurately expressed in the motto of that Bourbon, Louis XVI of France, "Divide and govern."

It was evidenced in America by the younger spiritual brother of Machiavelli, the brilliant Alexander Hamilton, who said of the people: "I loathe the masses." It was he who taught the powers of plutocracy in America how to divide and rule, how to make a travesty of democracy and a figment of political independence.

My friends, at this juncture I ask your leniency. I am going to speak to a certain group of persons as I have never spoken before. Not to the masses, whom I have defended and whom I will defend, am I addressing these remarks. But to the princes of American industry and finance, to the politicians who still believe in Machiavelli, in Alexander Hamilton and in the doctrines of deceit and of promises unfulfilled.

Bear with me and forgive me if I appear to be a so-called intellectual, speaking to the superior minded intellectuals of our nation.

"Leaders of America, gentlemen of the banking fraternity, members of Congress: Consider with me for a few moments the so-called average man, the man who barters the labor of his hands for the means of his livelihood. As far as all practical purposes are concerned he is your inferior in the intellectual order and in the social order. For the sake of argument let us admit that the great middle class—the laboring class, and the agricultural class of America—are only shadows of your substance in thought, in executive ability and in scientific endeavor as well as in social talent.

"I know how you valuate the common man in the scales of actuality—the actualities of life. You deem him to be the plaything of impulse, the toy of emotion. The demands of his great but foolish brain make profitable your degenerate press, your lascivious moving picture industry and the indecent drama of your burlesque houses.

"Nevertheless the comman man is the man who is the centrifugal force in civilization. He is supposed to be your much talked about purchasing power. He is supposed to wear the textiles which your mills produce. He is supposed to ride in the cars

118

which come embellished and ennobled from your factories. (How pleasing these products are to gaze upon! The common man who produces them comes forth from the same factories broken, disconsolate, and desecrated!)

"In a sense, gentlemen, grant that Machiavelli was right. Grant that Machiavelli revealed his genius when he said that by their very nature the masses require a strong hand and a superior brain to rule them and to exploit them.

"Gentlemen of the intellectual class, now that we have considered the common man and judged him, are you willing to turn the x-ray upon your philosophy with the same objective disinterestedness of the scientific investigator? First may I inquire what were the colossal blunders of statecraft that destroyed the Caesars, the Bourbons, the Hapsburgs, the Hohenzollerns, the Romanoffs?

"Why did the heads of Louis XVI and Marie Antoinette roll from the block of the guillotine?

"Why were Nicholas II and his entire family slaughtered in a Siberian cellar and the nobility of the Russian court scattered throughout the world to be door men and dish washers and menial clerks? All these were your predecessors in practicing the principles so ably taught by Nicholas Machiavelli.

"The answer is simple. Machiavelli forgot that there is one great force that can weld the masses in united and terrible action. That force is common suffering which becomes commonly known. You of the intellectual class, of the ruling class, perhaps forget this. You forget that you are not dealing with a Spartacus and his slaves, with a Condorcet and his rebels, with a Trotsky and his unkempt Moujiks. Today you are dealing with men and women to whom you have advertised the luxury which your factories produce and before whom you have flaunted the illegitimate wealth which your economic system has exploited. You are dealing with an educated common man upon whom you depend in a most intimate manner. You are dealing with the masses whose children are better trained, more virtuous, oftentimes, than your own.

"At this moment there is burning in the hearts of these masses an inextinguishable desire fanned, not by hatred but by justice, to share in the fruits of this nation. They know that these fruits belong to them. They know this despite your policy of deception, despite your broken political promises."

"Gentlemen, I have sat down with members of your intellectual class and have discussed with them the truth of democracy and the truth of finance. They have admitted to me the fiction of their credit system and of their exploitation systems which are in vogue. They shocked me when they said *"To hell with the masses! Every man for himself!"* But they have never argued with me about the

119

facts of the case, being content to tell me that they will scare off the people with the noise which they will make on the drum of inflation.

"Is it not time to appeal to you intellectual people of America who prefer to be disciples of Machiavelli—is it not time to appeal to you to avert the shadow of the Bourbon guillotine that hovers over yourselves and your children? This is the question which I have been trying to arrive at.

"Is it not time to ask you to become fair competitors in the accumulation of wealth either in industry or in agriculture or in the professions and arts rather than attempt to retain this racket of creating it with a fountain pen?

"I cannot argue with you from a spiritual standpoint because this would have no force. You do not believe in Christ's principles. I can, however, appeal to you from your own selfish, material standpoint because I know the pulse of the people better than you will ever know it. If you think yourselves superior, utilize the intelligence you possess, correct the stupidities which your patron saint of intrigue forgot. Permit this Congress without further opposition to restore to themselves the coinage and the regulation of money. Machiavelli is as obsolete as Caesar Borgia for whom he wrote "The Prince."

"The days of Caesar Borgia with his mass murders and mass starvations, with his wars and his robberies have passed. For your own selfish love of life and of terrestial happiness I ask you to be sufficiently intelligent to comprehend the new concept of human liberty and of social justice which was taught to you last Friday.

"Cease, therefore, computing how this program of social justice will be financed for your personal benefit. Look askance upon your overprivileged comrades-in-greed who, at this moment, have not enough intelligence to retreat. They are asking: *Do we get no bloody bonds? How can we loan our fiction of credit at interest to the richest nation in the world which is surely rising to its feet?*"

## VI

And now my underprivileged friends, a word of information for you! To finance our recovery independent of the banker and his privileged greed, we have in our vaults today $8,234,000,000 in gold and $1,229,000,000 in silver. In all $9,472,000,000 of metallic currency against which there has been issued only $5,534,000,000 of greenbacks, of currency.

Shall we suffer while this money remains idle to fatten the wallets of the bankers or shall we employ it to create employment for the underprivileged?

Shall we, the taxpayers, or shall the bankers finance the program of social justice?

I know your answer. The millions of you citizens who have joined the National Union for Social Justice are united on this point.

Thus, may we prosper as a people and not as a privileged class! May God grant that the weeds of the overprivileged be rooted up.

It is your prerogative and duty to uphold the moral arms of our President while he, far removed from the conceits of Machiavelli, attempts to fulfill his program.

It is a program which aims at creating security for the able bodied. In its comprehension it reaches out a kindly hand to protect the aged who have borne life's burdens under a harsh, cruel, financial system.

It has Christian compassion on those poverty-stricken mothers who, when the valley of darkness confronts them, will enter it knowing that the practical sympathy of a grateful nation is extended to them.

It is a program that encompasses within its generous arms the little children, the handicapped and the infirm who henceforth shall not be denied the use of the surplus wealth possessed by their more fortunate fellow citizens.

These thoughts impel us to profess that a new day has dawned in statemanship. The old statecraft has gone to join its twin brother, the old witchcraft, in the tomb of time.

Passing out is the shadow of Machiavelli and coming in is the substance of Roosevelt!

The old order changeth, giving place to new.

The people have given a new mandate for social justice. May our President and our Congress have the grace and the courage to fulfill it careless of criticism, and conscious that God will not fail them!

# THE MENACE OF THE WORLD COURT

### (Sunday, January 27, 1935)

Y FRIENDS: If I am properly informed, Tuesday of this week—Tuesday, January 29th—will be remembered by our offspring as the day which overshadowed July 4th. The one date was associated with our independence. The other with our stupid betrayal.

On Tuesday of this week the United States Senate is about to hand over our national sovereignty to the World Court, a creation of and for the League of Nations. By sovereignty I mean that supreme power by which a free people makes its own laws for its own internal conduct, independent totally from any other law making body in the world; that supreme power by which these laws are judged and interpreted by its own court, supreme in every sense to any other court. Sovereignty also connotes the power to maintain an army and navy, to coin money and regulate its value, all of which are to be adaquate to the needs of the nation independent, in every sense, from foreign interference.

Without sovereignty a nation is but a shadow. With sovereignty it is a substance capable of existing in peace and security, in law and order, free from the dictates of external powers.

I speak to you of these things because there has arisen in our midst a false philosophy which looks askance upon nationalism and disparages the realities of life—its passions of greed and gain, its vices of intrigue and deceit. It prefers to sing the praise of the yellow peril of pacifism while it berates and belittles the vigorous valor of patriotism. It subscribes to the utopian dreams of world peace without resting its arguments therefor upon the undying principles of the Prince of Peace. Forgetful of the word of God which warned us how they who trust their horses and chariots and perverted counsels are doomed to destruction, these advocates of the League of Nations and its World Court propose to pacify a turbulent world through the agency of arms, of battleships and battalions, of dirigibles and airplanes.

My fellow countrymen, no one more than I abhors the crimson ugliness of war. No one more than I desires the benedictions of that peace which the world cannot give. But, conscious of the international conditions which surround us, conscious of the nature of the League of Nations and its functionary, the World Court, I protest against the impending action of those Senators who are about to direct the destinies of the United States along the course which will be mapped for us by the League of Nations, overwhelmingly dominated by the great powers of Europe. I grant that our Senators are sincere. I applaud their desire for peace. But, at this final moment, I appeal to them to reconsider their determination because war and destruction, instead of peace and tranquillity, are the fruits which their action shall reap. I appeal to them by the blood spilled at Valley Forge, by the fatherly admonitions of Washington and Jefferson which still ring in our ears, not to jeopardize our freedom, not to barter our sovereignty, not to entangle us with the religious, the racial, the economic and the martial affairs of the Old World, from which their ancestors and mine escaped to fashion a better land where democratic freedom and the rights to life, to liberty and the pursuit of happiness might flourish.

# I

My friends, this is not rhetoric. It is a calm, plain statement of fact which time alone will vindicate. Perhaps I am out of tune with the tempo of modern events in giving expression to my fears and to my patriotism. Nevertheless, when, on Wednesday morning next, I shall read how our Senators will have voted their approval of America's joining the World Court and therefore its creator, the League of Nations, I shall feel that something sacred has gone out of my life, for I know that these gentlemen will have subscribed to a principle which is not only philosophically unsound but which is contrary to the expressed will of my fellow citizens.

Nevertheless, I glory in upholding a lost cause, rather than crying *"Peace, peace, when there is no peace."* I glory in standing by Washington and Jefferson and their policy of *"no foreign entanglements"* rather than by President Roosevelt and Norman Davis and their modern internationalism. Presidents and Ambassadors may come and go but Washington and Jefferson live forever!

While I disagree fundamentally with the Administration on the World Court issue, yet I shall uphold its principles of social reform insofar as they are consonant with social justice.

The National Union for Social Justice is national and not international. Its ideals and principles are chiefly concerned with obtaining economic peace for my fellow citizens. During this depression they have been so overfed with the stale crumbs of promises that the white blood of cold mistrust is beginning to course through their arteries and veins. They are wondering, questioning how it is possible for this Administration to turn its precious attention to foreign affairs while we are still surrounded with domestic turmoil. They are suspecting, despite our untold wealth, that the paupers' dole of federal paternalism is designed to force them down to the European standard of living now that we are determined to accept the European standard of diplomacy and, in part, at least, the European standard of legislation.

The National Union for Social Justice is opposed to this penurious standard of living. It is more concerned with the prosperity of the minority wealth-holders in America than it is with the minority's political rights abroad. While we sympathize with the Serbian or the Roumanian, with the Jew in Germany or the Christian in Russia, the major portion of our sympathy is extended to our dispossessed farmers, to our disconsolate laborers who have been trampled upon and are being crushed at this very moment while the spirit of internationalism runs rampant in the corridors of the Capitol; while chaos clamors at our doors.

Permit me to be more definite in explaining why the National Union for Social Justice is opposed to the League of Nations and to its World Court. In 1917 came the red revolution of Russia. For centuries the citizens of that nation had been manacled by the chains of serfdom. While wealth was concentrated in the hands of a few the Russian laborer and farmer had been exploited. Seldom if ever had a voice been raised in their defense. Behind the shameful cloak of silence the state-controlled Church hid its head.

No wonder that Karl Marx found fertile soil upon which he sowed his seed of atheism! No wonder that communism grew! Carried on the wings of poverty, it began to take root in France, in Germany, in England and in America—wherever oppression reigned, wherever, even in a modified form, the principles of Czarism were practiced.

Communism is a social disease which is bred in the lurid ulcers of unjust poverty.

International communism was the irrational revolt against the irrational plutocracy of the international banker.

To offset the rapid development of communism, there was organized this League of Nations where, at its secret sessions never published to the world at large, it was planned to build up a counter internationalism whose main purpose was the protection of the international banker, the international plutocrat.

Fellow countrymen, I am opposed to communism as much as I am opposed to a plague. But, thanks be to God, I have sufficient sagacity to realize that if I suffer stinking carcasses to rot on my doorstep, I can rant and rail in vain against the plague until doomsday.

So it is with communism. I can set up my League of Nations to oppose it and my World Court to condemn it. But all this is futile unless the causes which created communism—the unnecessary poverty, the exploitation—are eradicated and removed from our midst.

Thus, the international bankers and those in league with them —they who have guided the destinies of England, of Germany, of France, of Italy and who still hold sway over the destinies

of the United States of America have unfurled their colorless
flag, have organized their own secretive government and established their own international court to dominate the armies and
navies of the world hoping thus to oppose communism and protect
plutocracy.

Between the forceps of these mighty forces the innocent people
of the world and you, the people of America, await to be crushed
by the certain conflict which soon will ensue.

I realize that this thought has not been expressed hitherto in
any publicized document, nor is it commonly known among the
Senators of the United States. But this was taught to me by
men who sat in at the secret sessions when the abortion of the
League of Nations was cradled by those who were determined to,
protect injustice, to bandage the cancer of exploitation, to keep
the carcasses on their doorsteps and to deceive the guileless citizen
and the innocent Senator with their program of peace.

Thus, on Tuesday next, America, instead of rescuing from the
hands of the international bankers the right to coin and regulate
the value of money, instead of limiting the accumulation of wealth
by the favored few, instead of bending her efforts to rescue the
impoverished farmer, instead of guaranteeing a just and living
wage to every laborer who is willing to contribute his honest
work—America is ready to join hands with the Rothchilds and
Lazerre Freres, with the Warburgs and Morgans and Kuhn-
Loebs to keep the world safe for the inevitable slaughter.

In years to come when you young men and young women who
are listening to me this afternoon will have had your economic
lives melted down to the standards of England, of France, of
Spain and of Mexico; when you will be marshaled into an army
to fight the red ruin of communism, I pray that you will still
have faith in the brotherhood of man as preached by Christ; I
pray that you will have the courage to re-echo the words once
spoken from Calvary's pulpit: *"Father forgive them, our Senators, for they know not what they do!"*

Many of these Senators inform us that they have already committed themselves to vote for our entrance into the World Court.
*"Committed themselves to whom,"* may I inquire? Not to the
factory worker, not to the farmer, not to the youth of the nation,
not to the young mother nursing her baby boy at her breast. In
1920 we, the American people, renounced the World Court and
the League of Nations. In 1935 our decision has not been altered
on this point and our Americanism has not rejected Washington
and Jefferson.

With our understanding of political affairs sharpened on the
grinding stone of experience we have doubled our determination
to acquire social justice in all its splendor. Peace cannot smile
upon us until the international banker is despoiled of his unseen

crown and shadowy scepter; until the nations are restored to the people who inhabit them. In that lies our best defense against communism and bloodshed!

## II

But permit me, my friends, to become more specific in advancing a final argument as to why we should refrain from entrusting our destines, in part, to the World Court and to the League of Nations.

Beyond all question of doubt those who are most desirous of peace, those who are most opposed to war and carnage are the veterans who, in the World War, experienced its hell and its misery. More than all the frenzied pacifists and proponents of "Peace-through-the-World-Court" this group of badgered heroes went on record through the official statement of Edward Hayes, the Commander of the American Legion, in 1934, as totally opposed to our entrance into the World Court. This official statement reads as follows: *"Be It Resolved By The American Legion: That it is opposed to the entry of the United States in the League of Nations or to the adherence of the World Court, either with or without reservations."*

These millions of ex-service men, these lovers of peace and haters of war, based their decision not upon the propaganda of idle sentimentality but upon the bitter experience of life's realities; of European hatred and distrust for America; of European rabid nationalism and social enmities.

To bear out this assertion that America need expect no impartial judgment from the throne of the World Court because of its extremely nationalistic personnel, may I cite the comments of the press on a definite World Court case?

A short time ago there was question of Austria's entering into trade relations with Germany. Against this France violently protested. The case was carried to the World Court. An openly unfair decision was handed down by this body of jurists who, despite their learning, could not disentangle themselves from the prejudices of their nationality.

Now what comment had the press of the civilized world to make upon this miscarriage of justice?

*The Memphis (Tennessee) Commercial Appeal* states: *"The decision against Austria's right to enter is clearly a gesture to justify France's position . . . France wins a victory, other nations lose."*

*The Knickerbocker Press* of Albany, New York: *"The decision of the World Court in the Austro-German customs pact controversy has opened the gates for a flood of adverse criticism against the court and the principle for which it stands."*

*The New Orleans Item:* "When the World Court brought in its split verdict on the Austro-German customs union we remarked last week that the plainly political texture of its division would probably revive old doubts and suspicions of the court's judicial disinterestedness. That surmise is superabundantly confirmed by the course of discussion since then. . . . The alignment of the Court in this Austro-German case has evidently been a shock to the strongest advocates of it in our country."

*The Chicago Daily News:* "Many advocates of entry by this Nation into the International Court of Justice, one must think, are deeply disturbed by the inescapable implications growing out of the advisory opinion given by that tribunal in the Austro-German customs union case."

*The Chicago Journal of Commerce:* "The chief victim of the World Court's decision in the Austro-German customs union case is the World Court."

*The Minneapolis Journal:* "The line-up of judges, nevertheless, is assailed as political."

*The Washington (D. C.) Daily News:* "As an advocate of American membership in the Court under the Root protocols, this newspaper is inclined to admit that there probably is some truth in those charges (of impartiality). It looks to us as if political considerations may have influenced some of the judges."

*The Norfolk (Virginia) Virginian-Pilot:* "It is apparent that the majority opinion was colored by grounds which critics of the decision will not hesitate to call political."

*The New York Herald Tribune:* "The reaction in this country to the World Court's advisory opinion on the Austro-German customs union has inevitably been unfavorable. Some of the strongest friends of the Court have expressed the greatest disappointment. It could hardly be otherwise. For the line-up of the Court exhibited a depressingly strong political bias, and its decision by 8-to-7 vote robbed its findings of all weight or pretense to finality. Faced by a major issue, affecting the fundamentals of European organization, the Court failed to function either judicially or effectively."

*The Charleston (S. C.) Evening Post:* "Those under the influence of France, for example, ruled against the union, while those which are disposed to regard as desirable a better balance of power in Europe found the union not in violation of the treaties. . . . And now the Court has materially detracted from its prestige by its own display of political bias, and those who have protested against the United States ever consenting to submit to such a tribunal, issues involving the national interest of this country, have something substantial as an exhibit to fortify their opposition."

127

*The Greensboro Daily News:* "Jurists from the group of nations generally believed to be predominated by French influences voted against the pact."

*The Springfield (Mass.) Republican:* "It is disappointing that the decision was so close, and still more disappointing that it was obviously determined by political rather than legal consideration."

*The Baltimore Evening Sun:* "The product of partisan judges voted like ordinary politicians for the boys back home."

*The Chicago Evening Post:* "Unfortunately for the prestige of the Court, the cleavage was almost wholly on partisan lines, with France and her continental allies swinging the majority votes."

*The Reno (Nev.) Evening Gazette:* "In other words, France through her numerous alliances and by political trading, it is alleged, was able to gather in enough votes to win her case.

"The incident has not strengthened the Court in American eyes."

*The Cincinnati (Ohio) Enquirer:* "Unmistakably, there is evidence here of judges voting in terms of their own nations. . . .

"This cannot fail to be something of a blow to the prestige of the World Court. . . ."

*The New York Times:* "Realistic friends of the World Court are agreed that its prestige has been deeply injured. There can be little doubt that the chances of American adhesion have been badly damaged. In the Senate there has been no particular enthusiasm for the Court. The protocols have been kicked about committee rooms. Presidents, while urging them upon the Senate in grave and lofty terms, have been inclined to let things go at that. No real administration effort to press the issue has been made."

What commentary can be made by you Senators who say that you have committed yourselves to our joining the World Court when practically every honest paper in America has condemned this action of the World Court and every American who knows the inside story of the World Court is standing foursquare against your vote?

Today President Roosevelt is making an administration effort to sell the World Court to the American people, or rather, to sell the American people to the World Court.

Despite the comments of the press which I have read to you and of hundreds of other papers in Europe, in Asia and in South America condemning the partisanship of the World Court; despite the vote of the American people themselves, of the farmers and the laborers of this nation; despite the protests of the American Legion and every soldier organization, all of whom know that the World Court is partisan and, as has been indicated in this one case just cited, Mr. Roosevelt said to the Senate on January 16th: *"I hope that at an early date the Senate will advise and consent to the adherence by the United States to the Protocol of Signature of the Statute of the Permanent Court of International Justice, dated December 16, 1920.*

*"I urge that the Senate's consent be given in such form as not to defeat or to delay the objective of adherence."*

It is difficult for an ordinary person to comprehend how, in the face of this internationally recognized partisanship, such a proposal is psychologically or logically possible.

Even the European papers, hundreds in numbers which I cannot quote because of lack of time, have condemned the World Court for its unfairness, as if through unfairness peace can be propagated.

*The New Statesman* of England says: *"The International Court is not, we fear, likely to add to its prestige by its opinion on the Austro-German Customs Union. Broadly, it may be said that the Latin nations are divided against the Teutonic—Japan aiding with the minority."*

*The Saturday Review* of England: *"There was little in the judgment of the Hague Tribunal on the proposed Austro-German Customs Union to recommend the principle of arbitration in international disputes."*

*The London Spectator: "What really emerges is doubt as to the wisdom of encouraging a Court whose strength lies in its detachment from political entanglements to rule on a question in which politics and law are inextricably intermingled."*

*The "Bund"* of Berne, Switzerland: *"What is the practical use of the ultimate sanction given by the Hague Court by a weak majority of one voice in favor of the French opinions?"*

All this is in keeping with the editorial comment of Germany, of China, of Japan, of the Argentines, of Belgium, of Canada, of every outspoken newspaper in the world. But despite this, we are told by President Roosevelt: *"The movement to make international justice practicable and serviceable is not subject to partisan considerations."*

Now some newspapers who are supporting our entrance into the World Court forget these editorials and forget the partisanship, the favoritism of the World Court jurists who are predominately European, who are nationally opposed to America.

With this knowledge before us, why should we be supercilious idealists, speculating upon the future fairness of the World Court when the past record of the Court proves beyond dispute that it is unfair, that it is political?

I repeat that I take this stand knowing that, while I am expressing the thoughts and the ideals, the hopes and the aspirations of the American people, I am on the losing side and I am subjecting myself to ridicule, to ignominy and perhaps to chastisement. But cost what it may, the American people have a right to know the unvarnished truth of facts. Perchance they have a right to speculate why, with such inordinate hurry, this Presidential message was placed before the Senate for a decision after two years of inordinate delay have elapsed in driving the money changers from the temple!

The President says in his message to the United States Senate: *"For years, Republican and Democratic administrations and party platforms alike have advocated a court of justice to which nations might voluntarily bring their disputes for judicial decision."*

Heartily do we agree with the President. At the present moment, however, do not forget that we have the Hague Tribunal which operates without force of arms and without a threat to annihilate any nation who does not accept its decisions. At the present moment the United States can appeal to the World Court without belonging to it to settle international disputes. Thus, today, if the United States is in dispute with some other nation, if the United States is in dispute with some other nation, it has as much authority and voice in selecting the judges as has the other disputing nation. But after next Tuesday our disputes Nations and not elected by the United States people and their Senate.

The President's message to the Senate did not explain this fact. It did not say that, if today we enter into a dispute with Great Britain, America and England will have an equal number of judges on the bench to decide the dispute. It did not say that after Tuesday of this week the American nation would have two votes—one in the assembly and one in the council of the League of Nations—and that Great Britain would have seven or eight votes against our two.

Is this a practicable and serviceable kind of international justice that we are trading the day after tomorrow for what we possess at this moment?

It appears from the Presidential message to the Senate that America has been hostile, more or less, to arbitration and that now it is desirous to participate in an international court where international disputes can be settled. It appears that it is our duty, as a member of the family of nations, to submit our grievances to *"a court of justice"* (to quote the President) *"to which nations might voluntarily bring their disputes for judicial decision."*

Since the Jay Treaty of 1793 it has been the policy of the United States to address its disputes to an international court of justice. We have arbitrated our boundaries. We have arbitrated the conduct of foreigners and of our own citizens during time of war. We have never once refused arbitration. For a period of over one hundred and fifty years we have been writing a record of arbitration that has never been paralleled in the history of this world. As a practical result of this arbitration the Rush-Bagot treaty of 1818 permits us proudly to point to the three thousand miles of an imaginary boundary line separating Canada from the United States. Not a battleship desecrates the waters of our Great Lakes; not a fortification threatens harm to our neighbor's soil! Shall this record of arbitration and of peacefulness, which has proven so profitable to the continent of America, be thrown into the discard? In the face of these facts we are asked to adopt the European system of the League of Nations which breeds wars and multiplies battleships and fortifications.

More than that, if we have the Hague Tribunal and, I repeat, if we have access to the World Court as non-members, fortified with the guarantee of a fair judicial representation, why, I ask you, is it logical for us to submit our disputes to a new group of judges in whose veins blood is thicker than water and who have already proven themselves to be better politicians than jurists— judges representing nations which have welshed on their debts; nations which have already cost $48-billion to make Europe safe for Hitler, Mussolini, Stalin and the rest of them? How, in the name of God, can jurists from these nations give us justice in their courts?

### III

The next argument advanced by those who are endeavoring to force America into the World Court hinges upon the word *"peace."*

As a matter of fact, since the court was organized, war has been waging almost continually among and between the members of the court. Some of these wars have been waged within the very shadow of the court itself, and yet the World Court has done nothing either to end or to prevent these wars. Thus the World Court has demonstrated that it has no power to keep peace in the world by its decisions.

Those favoring our adhereing to the World Court insinuate that by our remaining aloof we are interfering with world peace. Nothing can be further from the truth.

What did the World Court do in the case of Japan and China other than to investigate the ruins which resulted from the Japanese cannon?

What has the World Court done in the instance of the Chaco

War in South America? Here is the story, my friends, which indicts the World Court as the tool of plutocrats.

In 1878 President Hayes set up a board of mediators to fix the boundaries of Paraguay. Notwithstanding this settlement made by America and which has stood now for nearly sixty years, we find the Standard Oil Company of the United States endeavoring, through the League of Nations, to upset the peaceful agreement arrived at years ago.

Between Bolivia and Paraguay there is a tract of land known as the Chaco. It is fertile in oil fields.

According to the *Congressional Record,* Bolivia received financial help from the Standard Oil Corporation to wage war on Paraguay for the purpose of gaining control of these oil fields.

What action did the League of Nations and, therefore, the World Court take in this war of aggression? (What one does, the other does. They are one!)

It lent its support to curb Paraguay and to further the designs of the Standard Oil Corporation.

Instead of upholding the sixty-year-old decision of President Hayes, the World Court disdained it in favor of a plutocratic oil corporation.

No wonder the Standard Oil Corporation, through its Rockefellers, is circularizing America with literature to join the League of Nations through the back door of its World Court!

No wonder the Standard Oil Corporation, through its Rockefellers, is circularizing America with literature to join the League and the real purpose behind our joining it!

## IV

Last Sunday I had occasion to remark that the Carnegie millions were being spent to realize the dream of inveigling the United States into the World Court and to establish the re-united States of Great Britain and America. To that gentleman, whose heart never left Scotland and whose bones are buried there, the year 1776 was America's disgrace and Washington was a traitor and a blunderer.

I also remarked that according to reports, Norman Davis, our roving ambassador, was associated with the Kreuger-Toll Match Corporation and was interested not only in rehabilitating the stock of that international brigand but of arranging for the sale of Kreuger-Toll products in America. Mr. Davis is most keen for us to enter the World Court. Mr. Davis has contacted the internationalists of Europe. And Mr. Davis now wishes me to retract what I said last Sunday.

I will gladly accommodate him by reading from the *New York Times* of Sunday, January 7, 1934.

Quote: *"Headline: N. H. Davis Heads New Kreuger Body."* *"Norman H. Davis, ambassador at large of the United States has been appointed head of the international committee to compromise the conflicting claims of the companies of the late Ivar Kreuger and to make recommendations for readjustment in order to protect and conserve the assets of these companies.*

*"Mr. Davis accepted the chairmanship of the International Committee on condition that insofar as his work on disarmament may require attention it shall have precedence."*

Mr. Davis said: *"As the Disarmament Conference adjourned last fall until the later part of this month, I decided after consultation with the President to accept the invitation mentioned above upon three conditions: First, that my work as chairman of the American Delegation to the Disarmament Conference shall take precedence. Second: That I shall work on the Kreuger matter only while disarmament does not require my attention and when I am specifically granted leave of absence by the Secretary of State and am receiving no compensation from the government, and Third: That someone be desginated to collaborate with me in the Kreuger work and to act as my alternate if and when necessary."*

This is substantially what I said last Sunday. This is substantially what I repeat because Mr. Norman Davis has asked me to retract.

This is the Mr. Norman Davis working in the interest of the international plutocrats who favors our entrance into the World Court.

It is the same Norman Davis who is a hold-over from the Hoover Administration. The same touchy gentleman who was on the Morgan preferred list.

And behold, when we look into his Cuban record we find that he is well chosen to be our Ambassador-At-Large! Well chosen to represent the plutocrats and advise indirectly the Senators who are about to vote us into the World Court!

Our own United States Supreme Court, in the case of Las Ovas vs. Norman H. Davis, made Davis and one other return the fruits of a $15,000 fraud as well as promoter's stocks which the courts found he forfeited because such stock was intended for honest service and not fraud. Here the court specifically used the word *"fraud."* (See 227 U. S. 80 for said case.)

The same case was more elaborately described in the opinion of the court of appeals of the District of Columbia (Vol. 35 App. D. C. 372) which very pointedly branded the action of Davis as *"fraud."*

Did not Congressman Tinkham show that Davis was a fugitive from Cuban justice?

133

Is this the roving Ambassador whose judgment the United States President and Senate accept?

Is this the plutocratic adviser whose advice we will take to push us into the League of Nations, the man on the Morgan preferred list, the man whose action is tained with fraud?

## V

In the light of these facts which I categorically state and which I will not retract—facts now known to millions of voters; facts which besmear the propaganda of the World Court with plutocracy; facts which indicate the purpose of our entrance into this flagless nation—in the face of these I appeal from the Senators who were ill-informed to the Senators who are better informed not to disparage themselves with the American public and to smear themselves with plutocratic preference.

I appeal to every solid American who loves democracy, who loves the United States, who loves the truth to stand foursquare back of those tried and true Senators of long experience in their hopeless yet honest fight to keep America safe for Americans and not the hunting ground of international plutocrats—Senators Borah and Johnson and Walsh and Thomas and Wheeler and Smith and the rest of them. Today—tomorrow may be too late—today, whether you can afford it or not, send your Senators telegrams telling them to vote *"no"* on our entrance into the World Court with or without reservations. Reservations are innocent and innocuous things. And so are some of the Senators who are of the opinion that a reservation can save us.

What did the great international diplomat and jurist and World Courter say of American reservations?

Listen, gentlemen, to what Viscount Grey of England thinks of your reservations upon which, like a silken thread, you will chance the anchor of our national destiny! He said: *"Let America come in with its reservations. We will construe their reservations."*

In other words, coax the blind mouse into the trap and we will enlighten him afterwards.

My friends, if I remember correctly there are some States which freely entered this Union with certain reservations, if we may call them such. A day came when these States wished to secede. Despite their understanding the Supreme Court of the United States decided they had no right to withdraw from the United States of America. Evenually came the Civil War when judicial decisions gave way to the force of arms. Eventually came Gettysburg and the decision that no State had the right to withdraw from the Union.

This thought was given me by an eminent Englishman who, paraphrasing the words of Viscount Grey, said: *"Once you are in the World Court your Senate will not have the right to judge about American withdrawal. That will be the business of the*

*World Court itself. You Americans have already subscribed to this theory in the days of your Civil War. You can't be welshers now."*

Perhaps that is something for the Senators to think about as innocently they tie the Gordian knot of the World Court around the throat of the American public. It is easy to tie but perhaps it can be severed only by a sword.

*"By a sword say I?"* Most certainly! For it pertains to the constitution of the World Court that its decisions can be enforced by the armies and navies of all its signatories.

This afternoon on a national broadcast, that was donated and not paid for, two advocates of the World Court said that I was totally mistaken in this statement. I sympathize with their ignorance of the eighth plenary session presided over by Woodrow Wilson. Woodrow Wilson definitely stated that, if necessary, America would send her armies and her navies to Serbia and Roumania for the protection of minorities. President Wilson's specific words are: *"We must not close our eyes to the fact, that in the last analysis, the military and naval strength of the great powers will be the final guarantee of the peace of the world. . . . If any covenants of this settlement are not observed the United States will send her armies and her navies to see that they are observed."* This is what President Wilson said before the eighth plenary session (secret) of the peace conference in Paris, held at the Quai d'Orsay, Saturday, May 31, 1919. College professors are sometimes impractical students as has been proven to us during the past two years!

Here we stand today, the creditor nation of the world, hated and detested for our so-called rapacity simply because we had the boldness to ask payment on honest debts.

There stands Europe which has welshed on the post-war debts by more than $12-billion after $14-billion had been contributed to them gratis during the war!

There is not an European judge on the bench of the World Court, save the representative of Finland, who has it not in his heart to uphold his nation's philosophy of welshing when America is the creditor. One of the first things that will be injected into this unholy circus of the World Court will be the question of America's debts and the question of the gold clause!

So this is the kind of a World Court, an European Bully, to which our Senators are about to attach their apron strings.

We make the reservations, and the World Court interprets them. We struggle for peace, and the World Court threatens war. We praise Washington and cheer his compatriot soldiers. But, when the 22nd of February comes upon our calendar, let us bow our heads in shame for desecrating the final words bequeathed to us by the Father of our Country—*"no European entanglements."*

By chance last night I opened my Bible at the Eighty-second Psalm of David which intimates to us the establishment of the first known League of Nations and the first advertised League Court.

This I shall read to you. It is as ancient as the hills. It is a story that has come down through the ages of Palestine, the story that was carried by Peter and Paul to the Romans, by James to Spain, by Thomas to India, by Patrick to Ireland, by Boniface to Germany and by those who first carried the Scriptures to America. It is a story known by every Jewish heart, a story known by everyone who professes Christianity, the story of the first League of Nations, the story of the World Court! It is a prayer to preserve our sovereignty that is about to be lost, our nationality that is about to be jeopardized. It is a prayer to protect us, the seemingly chosen people of this day, from those who are envious of us, from those at home who have raised aloft a noise of propaganda and befouled the air with raucous counsel, from those abroad who have consulted against our national heroes, our Washington and Jefferson.

Therefore, with a humble heart I read this prayerful psalm:

*(1  A canticle of a psalm for Asaph)*

2.  *"O God, who shall be like to thee? Hold not thy peace, neither be thou still, O God.*

3.  *For lo, thy enemies have made a noise: and they that hate thee have lifted up the head.*

4.  *They have taken a malicious counsel against thy people: and have consulted against thy saints.*

5.  *They have said: Come and let us destroy them, so that they be not a nation. And let the name of (America) Israel be remembered no more.*

6.  *For they have contrived with one consent: they have made a covenant together against thee,*

7.  *the tabernacles of the Edomites and the Ismahelites: Moab, and the Agarens,*

8.  *Gebal, and Ammon, and Amalec: the Philistines, with the inhabitants of Tyre.*

9.  *Yea, and the Assyrian also is joined with them: they are come to the aid of the sons of Lot.*

*O God, hold thy peace, neither be thou still!*

# THE FUTURE OF THE NATIONAL UNION

## (Sunday, February 3, 1935)

AM positive that I voice the thought of the majority of persons in this audience when I express our public thanks to Almighty God for having restrained us from identifying our destinies with the World Court. Invested with the humility of the sinful publican rather than with the arrogant pride of the pharisee we are happy that America still belongs, at least in theory, to the Americans. We are doubly happy that we are not to be participants either in the League of Nations or in the World Court both of which were generated, at least indirectly, by the palpably unjust Peace Treaty of Versailles at whose discussions the name of God was intentionally omitted.

This is a day of deserved congratulations to the American people in general and, in particular, to every individual who sent a letter or telegram protesting against involving ourselves in Europe's intrigues. You, my patriotic friends, were the modern minute men whose determination and courageous action turned an apparent defeat into a decisive victory. In sustaining a lost cause, you unquestionably wrote a new page in American history. Do you realize that, according to Senator Hiram Johnson, there were only seven Senators opposed to the World Court when it was submitted for discussion? Do you realize the power of patronage and the prestige of politics which favored its passage? Despite the meager support which its opponents controlled; despite the seemingly insurmountable obstacles which confronted them it was you who rose to the occasion and so magnificently articulated your patriotism, your opposition to dictatorship, to "steam-rollerism," to "rubber-stampism." Well did you indicate to your Senators that, after all, they are your representatives. Well did you exhibit your faith in a democracy which shall not perish in America without a gigantic struggle.

Hitherto you were content to vote for representatives to whose judgment you entrusted the destiny of the nation. That was the scope of your democratic activities. But last week you wrote a new page in the story of democracy, in the long sordid story of man's endeavor to free himself from the bonds of tyrannical minorities. Gone forever is that definition of democracy which confined your activities to the narrow precincts of a polling booth where oftentimes your votes were cast to uphold platitudes and promises, to elect men who were victims of a system which was regulated by an unseen power. Your excursion into the affairs of the World Court politics has demonstrated to you a newer concept of democracy whereby you need not be satisfied with the mere casting of a vote to select a representative. Through the medium of the radio and the telegram you possess the power to override the invisible government; the power, at the risk of their political lives, to direct your representatives on individual matters of legislation.

Hitherto we were suffering from too little democracy. Today it is possible for us to enjoy its benedictions in a more fulsome form. The lesson gained from this victory must neither be underestimated nor forgotten!

I congratulate you, my fellow citizens, in that without preparation, without any concerted attempt to regiment our forces, you were so successful, I repeat, in turning a lost cause into a victory.

If the National Union for Social Justice played a significant part in this achievement, it did so because it is wedded to no political party but rejoices that it is above them, existing only to sustain the rights of the American people regardless of politics, of race and of creed.

Your victory is more pronounced when you weigh the dignity and power of your opponents.

Opposed to you unfortunately was the President's honest yet impractical desire to meddle in foreign politics; to mingle our destinies with nations who had proven themselves dishonest, with nations who have constantly tricked us for their own advantage, with nations who had ganged together to legalize their plunder, with nations who had so formulated the rules and regulations of the World Court and of its creator, the League of Nations, that they could easily out-vote us, with nations who looked askance upon the Monroe Doctrine, with nations who regarded Washington and his *"no foreign entaglements"* as an obstacle to their own conniving.

Opposed to you were the mighty forces of the Rockefeller Foundation and the Carnegie Foundation, the English Speaking Union, the Foreign Policy Association, the Twentieth Century Fund and numerous other subversive organizations which are said to have resources of $900-million at their disposal to accomplish their unholy ends of internationalism.

Opposed to you was the so-called loyalty to party-ism which was used as an argument by those who forgot that Senators were first of all loyal to Americans.

Opposed to you were many news journals which endeavored to blindfold you with the Hauptmann case where one life was at stake and which religiously refrained from advertising the World Court case where the nation's life was at stake.

Opposed to you was the moral influence of others who enjoyed tremendous national prestige. They argued for our entrance into the World Court but did not once quote a substantial part of the constitution of the World Court to sustain their contentions, preferring to base their arguments upon ideals, preferring to cast aside the premises of facts and of history.

Confronted with all this you forcefully demonstrated that this government is of the people and for the people.

Thus, to you individual Americans belongs the credit for preserving in a decent honorable manner the name of Washington, for simply to retain his name and to reject his principles is a betrayal which no logical mind can fathom.

On this occasion it is only fair and just to share the credit for victory with many newspapers, especially the Hearst papers. Over two weeks this news service endeavored to bring to the attention of the American people the World Court case and all its implications. Whether or not you agree with many other principles and policies advocated by the Hearst organization, credit is due it in this instance for its noble and exemplary stand.

Last but not least come those Senators who while preferring principle to patronage and America to partisanship, voted against our entrance into the World Court. It is most fitting that I read this roll of honor. It is a group of names which should live second only to the group of stalwart patriots who signed the Declaration of Independence. This group is composed of twenty Democrats, fourteen Republicans, one Progressive, one Farmer-Laborite.

### The Democrats are

| | | | |
|---|---|---|---|
| Bone | Gore | Murphy | Smith |
| Bulow | Lewis | Murray | Thomas, Okla. |
| Coolidge | Long | Reynolds | Trammell |
| Donahey | McCarran | Russell | Walsh |
| Gerry | McGill | Schwellenbach | Wheeler |

### The Republicans are

| | | | |
|---|---|---|---|
| Borah | Frazier | Norbeck | Townsend |
| Carey | Hastings | Norris | White |
| Davis | Johnson | Nye | |
| Dickinson | Metcalf | Schall | |

The Progressive is Senator LaFollette.

The Farmer-Laborite is Senator Shipstead.

To these names should be added the names of Senators Overton of Louisiana and McAdoo of California who voted in their absence.

These thirty-six immortals are not so selfish as to expect individual praise. The nation knows their leadership. A grateful nation will long revere their momory as a noble group.

## II

Our next goal is to clean out the international bankers now that the international politicians have suffered. For making this statement, my friends and fellow members of the National Union, you can prepare yourselves for reprisals. Why do I say this? The answer is evident when you analyze your nationalism and your ideals, both of which conflict with the internationalism and ideals of your powerful opponents. Your ideals are chiefly concerned with abolishing the depression and the causes which created it. Your nationalism aims at making this country a safer, happier and holier place for your children who, as far as you are concerned, must not be sentenced to live lives of economic slaves in order to satisfy the greedy international money changers.

These latter, beyond all question, are leagued together, careless of national boundaries, careless of your welfare and concerned chiefly with maintaining the questionable right of controlling the money of the world.

You believe that it is possible for us in America to create and maintain a higher standard of living than can be enjoyed elsewhere. At our very doors are untold acres of fertile land, of virgin forest. There are miles of rushing rivers, unmeasurable resources of tumbling waters—all to be used, all prepared to serve us!

What factories and magic machines have we within our borders! What marvelous minds has God bestowed upon our scientists, our engineers! This, according to you, is the land of plenty and we are the most fortunate of all peoples!

This is your land—fought for and bled for by pioneer parents!

This is your land overflowing with benedictions which are withheld from you because the international bankers regard it as a crime if you taste of this plenty; if you laborers and farmers possess the ambition to live in comfort and convenience beyond the degree to which the European people have sunk. They tell you that you must forego your national blessings; that you must starve when food rots in the field; that you must go naked while cotton is plowed under and factories are idle; that you must be forced down to the Old World standard of living—because the money racket controlled by the few will be exposed and lost if America, now retained at least in theory for the Americans, shall become the America which really in practice belongs to the Americans!

In one word you people have expressed your intelligent will to retain the sovereignty of your own nation. Because you are logical minded this sovereignty means that you will not permit the international bankers' money system to forbid you from enjoying the fruits of your fields and the products of your factories. Are you willing to follow in this fight? Are you willing to rid America of the international bankers?

There is no shortage, no famine, no drought oppressing us. Because this is so true, your ideals and your nationalism both demand a just and living annual wage for every citizen who is willing to work.

Because of your righteous hostility to this damnable money system, which encourages and creates poverty in the midst of plenty, and which is being caressed by the present Administration; because of your patriotic belief in retaining the American standard of living instead of leaguing with those who wish to establish an international standard of living, because of these things, you will be referred to as nit-wits and morons. Your program will be disparaged as the brain-child of a demagogic crackpot and your organization will be listed among the so-called radicals.

If in the new vocabulary of modern exploitation social justice is translated by radicalism; if patriotism is referred to as bigoted isolation, we will gladly accept these charges with the same philosophic attitude in which our forebears were trade marked with the name of rebel and revolutionist. I would rather be a rebel with Washington than a patriot with George III. I would rather be a crack-pot for social justice than a hired "yes-man" and an internationalist for the present monetary policies of this Administration. I would rather subscribe to the name of inflationist, which was coined in Wall Street to intimidate you people, than I would rejoice in being called a sound money man for supporting the policy of keeping more than $9-billion of gold and silver sterile in our Treasury, while the depression rages on in all its fury simply because there is a lack of money!

Because a patient in a pathological institution calls himself Napoleon and illusions himself that his physicians and nurses and fellow shut-ins are marshals and generals and privates in his armies, such names matter little when reduced to fact because facts are always more eloquent than words. The facts which confront us after two years of refusing to abolish the financial plutocracy and industrial tyranny which are strangulating our nation are unemployment and poverty, sterilized gold and silver, borrowing ourselves out of debt with bankers' manufactured money, the evils of mass production, unburdenable and unpayable debts, loans made for destructive and non-productive purposes, proposals to maintain the unemployed at no more than $30.00 a month, an unfair system of taxation. These are the things which concentrate wealth in the hands of a few.

141

The words of so-called economists who predicate their conclusions on a financial theory similar to the one that the world is still flat—words which criticize us for expressing such thoughts—matter little except insofar as they betray the mentality of those who employ them.

Thus with your support the National Union for Social Justice will forge ahead determined to rid America of the financial philosophy so dear to the heart of the international banker now that we have been so successful in impeding the progress of the international politicians. We are willing to accept honest criticism but we refuse to be deterred from its main objectives or to be victimized by fine phrases and broken promises.

## III

If from a political angle the practical purpose of the National Union for Social Justice has been demonstrated by our participation in the World Court victory, there is another serious practical side to our activities and to our future usefulness which I must mention.

Until the present moment I had no right to discuss with you this phase of our organization. It was logical that first we prove our worth, at least in a small degree.

Thus the remainder of this hour will be devoted to a brief summary of the sixteen points in the program for social justice prefaced by a few remarks on our financial standing. I believe that you have a right to this information both as actual and potential members in the National Union.

According to an Associated Press dispatch the American Liberty League, our rival, has issued a financial report of its contributions and expenditures since its formation last August. This organization received $104,830 in contributions. It spent $95,062 leaving a favorable balance of $9,768.

Now the total income of the National Union for Social Justice since November 11, 1934, was $97,269.71. Our total expenditures were $138,239.50. One item of purchase was a bottle of red ink because at the present moment, including the cost of today's broadcast, which must be paid in advance, we are short exactly $40,968.79.

This money I have borrowed. This debt in excess of $40,000 must be repaid within the next month. It is a personal obligation I contracted upon my own authority and therefore am personally responsible for it. Even though I were forced to spend the rest of my life in endeavoring to accumulate that sum I feel that it has been money well spent in arousing the American public to the facts which confront them; money well spent in teaching the American people what they can do once they are organized.

142

Never before in the history of this broadcast have I once asked for funds. Today I appear before you to notify you that it is impossible for me to carry on unless the members of the National Union for Social Justice are willing not only to support this movement with their moral backing but also with their financial aid which is required immediately. At present the propaganda is being circulated that the National Union for Social Justice is rolling in wealth. This propaganda will increase as the fear on the part of our opponents increases.

Thus the question revolves itself into this, namely, despite our more than 5-million members who have signed the sixteen point program; despite the fact that when acting in unison we can accomplish something; despite the fact that personally I received no salary whatsoever from the National Union and am most happy to contribute my time gratis to help realize its principles, this work cannot carry on without your financial support.

Today I appear before you as a beggar in your own behalf. If your membership in this organization means anything it is worth a small sacrifice. If you are content to permit this organization to vanish or if you think that my services are no longer required, I shall bow to your will and immediately suspend further activities. I have carried on as long as it is possible through my own initiative and with the financial assistance of a very small percentage of our members.

Perhaps the majority of you failed to realize the cost of broadcasting, of printing, of postage. Perhaps you failed to realize the financial sacrifices and burdens freely borne by the League of the Little Flower. The National Union was spared many expenses, such as rental for a huge office space, dozens upon dozens of typewriters, mailing machines, printing machines, heat, light and power —all of which were donated to the National Union by the League of the Little Flower.

But the fact still remains that the necessary expenses to conduct this organization must be borne by those of us who care to see it survive.

While I thank the National Broadcasting Company for the ten minutes which they donated to me on Monday night last I wish to call to your attention that our two Sunday broadcasts, costing in excess of $20,000, was the only paid time in the course of the whole battle against the World Court. These two broadcasts, with the assistance of others, helped to bring us victory.

As for the future I dare not prophesy. But I surmise that if we fail to function the obsolete money system and the money changers will still continue to call America their own. We will retain sovereignty in theory but they will retain it in practice.

# IV

As much as I dislike to burden you with unpleasant news, I feel it my duty as your spokesman to inform you that the present Administration together with the majority of the members of Congress apparently are opposed to making any substantial change in the financial system. This Administration, while professing and expressing fine ideas relative to our national security and to our individual happiness, is wedded basically to the philosophy of the money changers. No serious attempt has been made on its part to rescue the coinage and the regulation of money from the hands of the private manufacturers of money. No serious attempt has been made on the part of the Government to issue United States currency. No serious attempt has been made to explain the $9-billion of sterile gold and silver which mocks us from the vaults of the United States Treasury. On the contrary, the Administration is still engaged in borrowing money—credit money—from those who create it with their purple fountain pens. The Administration is still engaged in keeping America safe for the plutocrats!

This determination is so deeply entrenched in the minds of those at Washington that it is rumored how an amalgamation of the liberal Republicans and liberal Democrats will be launched in 1936 to further the activities of those who are sick and tired of international finance and plutocratic control.

While the World Court issue touched upon such abstract things as our sovereignty, upon such probable but not absolutely certain exigencies as war, nevertheless, the World Court was not so plain nor so pressing a problem as the one which is related to the scarcity of money and to the distribution of wealth. This latter problem the American people fully understand ten thousand times better than they did the World Court problem.

If, therefore, the people can be aroused to democratic action over an abstract foreign policy which was steeped in probabilities, is it not more logical to say that, when united in a solid organization, these same people can be doubly aroused to fight democratically for their simple human rights of bread and butter, of clothing and of shelter and of the right to coin and regulate their own money, a right which our Constitution bestows upon us?

No argumentation on the part of economists of the old school or the politicians who attempt to serve the old capitalism has any force against the logic of bread and butter, of decent shelter and of respectable Americanism. These economists and politicians can purchase editorial space and dominate propaganda. They can spar for time, hoping that things will right themselves. Nevertheless, their arguments and their propaganda are of no avail simply because they are contrary to the natural laws of life which are supported by a well organized group.

The most obvious thing about democracy is that our representatives should represent the common demands of the people—of the majority of the people. Politicians can exist only upon the sufferance of your votes. Politicians can remain in office provided they fulfil the will of the voters. Ten or fifteen or twenty years ago it was possible to circumvent the voters. Today that is becoming more and more impossible, provided the majority of the people unite upon a single platform of definite principles which will be enacted into concrete laws.

Thus, from this day forward, the die-hard Democrats and the die-hard Republicans can amalgamate and form their conservative party, if they please, for the purpose of conserving the financial and, therefore, the major industrial abuses of the past together with its privileges for the few and its exploitation of the many. On the other hand, the liberal Democrats and Republicans and Progressives, the liberal Labor leaders, who are not tied up to Wall Street, the liberal minded farmers, who have made up their minds to produce their wheat and their cotton, their corn and their pork only at a profit—these men and women will stabilize themselves in a liberal party where the duly elected representatives will be democratic enough to subscribe to the will of the people. This is the trend of the times against which we must prepare. This is the crucial political battle in which all must participate if we wish to give America back to the Americans.

It is just as well to be truthful and direct about this thing. We are satisfied that, if we take into account modern machinery and modern science, it is impossible for the average working man to be employed profitably more than eight months in a year. We are satisfied that wealth has been concentrated in the hands of a few because we have permitted these few to own and operate both finance and industry for their own benefit and at the expense of the many. We are satisfied that those who control finance and industry will never relinquish this control without a bitter struggle. And we are satisfied that those who are suffering, because they cannot control finance and regulate industry, will never be pacified until there is restored to their own Congress the right to coin, to issue, to regulate both currency and credit and to guarantee a just and living wage.

The conservatives, be they labeled Democrat or Republican, are commonly known as plutocrats, which is the Greek word for "the rule by the wealthy." Those who have been robbed of the control and who wish to regain the control of money are true democrats, which is the Greek word for "rule by the people."

In its choice between plutocracy and democracy the National Union for Social Justice stands absolutely for the latter. In its concept of money it differs absolutely from the concept entertained indirectly by the present Administration and directly by

Wall Street. We believe that factories, farms, homes, forests, motor cars, universities, schools, churches, and the products thereof constitute the real wealth of this nation. Wall Street believes that money is wealth. We believe that this national domain of ours which has been bestowed upon us by a beneficent Creator belongs, under God, to the American people and not to any small group of these people. The plutocrat cherishes the belief that this nation belongs to him, the rest of us participating in its fruitfulness only insofar as we can gather the crumbs which fall from the banquet table of plenitude. To the plutocrat money is not only wealth, it is control. When he issues credit through the grace of his fountain pen, factories are built, business is created, prosperity is resplendent. When he contracts his fictitious money by calling for payment, he demands that the borrower pay him back in currency money which is non-existent. Because it is non-existent, then the borrower is obliged to pay him back with his factory, his farm, his home and with his property.

It is true that the plutocrat in Wall Street and in Washington recognizes that the age of scarcity is past, that the age of plenitude is at hand. He recognizes that, if our laborers and farmers work assiduously every month in the year, of necessity they cannot help but produce too many motor cars, too many shoes, too many refrigerators, too many sheets and pillow cases simply because modern machinery and the inventiveness of man's intellignce have brought about the age of plenty.

Everything is plentiful except money!

Because of this recognition he will suggest his old age pension, his unemployment insurance, both of which are not designed to retain the American standard of living and neither of which entertains even the slightest hope of guaranteeing to the American man the standard of living to which he is entitled.

He will set about to tax the employed laborer to support, at least in the major part, the unemployed laborer. He will connive to tax the youth for the support of the aged—but at all times his purpose is to preserve the present financial philosophy of private money control, of inadequate currency, of super-imposed interest-bearing bond issues. This is the program which salves the plutocratic conscience as it bestows a niggardly $30.00 a month to the unemployed and a miserly $15.00 a month to the aged. Is that a just and living wage? Is that a decentralization of wealth in a nation that is overflowing with wealth?

Again I ask you, why are such penurious proposals proffered to the unemployed and to the aged? Why are the factories closed when millions of citizens are anxious to purchase their products? Why are cotton and grain and pork destroyed when millions of others are hungry? Why is a dishonest dollar containing approximately 129 pennies still in vogue today? Why do we persist in trying to borrow ourselves out of debt with bankers' bonds? Why are we piling unbearable burdens on the back of the next generation? Why are we striving to avoid the obvious—a plenitude of everything except money?

There is only one answer and that answer is, "because we will not relinquish the false concept of money which characterized the age of scarcity." With these thoughts in mind, that is why the National Union incorporated as its second principle the following words: *"I believe that every citizen willing to work and capable of working shall receive a just and living annual wage which will enable him to maintain and educate his family according to the standards of American decency."*

## V

Permit me to touch upon the other principles advocated by the National Union for Social Justice.

The third principle in the National Union for Social Justice reads as follows: *"I believe in nationalizing those public necessities which by their very nature are too important to be held in the control of private individuals. By these I mean banking, credit and currency, power, light, oil and natural gas and our God-given natural resources."*

By banking I simply mean the coinage, the printing, the regulation and the issuance of all money. I do not mean the destruction of the small local bank which, to the best of its ability, has served its community, an ability that was harnessed and hobbled by the dictators of a great central bank. In a moment I shall expand on this thought.

By the nationalization of power, light, oil and natural gas I mean that the time has arrived when these natural resources as represented by the waters of Niagara and the rapids of the St. Lawrence, by the Tennessee Valley Power Project and by the Coulee Dam—I mean the time has arrived when America shall put its own resources to work for its people and cease farming them out to private individuals for their private profit. I do not subscribe to the theory that we should nationalize public utilities. They should be permitted to operate under government control so that their rates and their profits will be scrutinized and rationalized. But, on the other hand, there is nothing to prevent our government, be it Federal, State or municipal, from building its own power plant and from operating in competition with the privately owned utilities which, through their lobbies and their wealth and their influence, have dominated State and municipal governments and, until a short time ago, exerted their malevolent influence on the Federal government.

There are millions of homes unlighted because of excessive

utility rates. In our rivers there are wasted tens of millions of horse power that easily could be distributed to, at least, three-fifths of our population at half the cost which is being charged today. As important as is our post office system, which is nationally owned and controlled, I hold in equal, if not in superior importance, our natural resources of power and water, of banking, of credit and of currency.

We permit express companies to compete with our post office. We will still permit privately owned public utilities to compete with our nationally or state or municipally owned public utilities. It is our program, if you will, to put the government into the banking business insofar as it will own and control the Central Bank, but it is not our purpose to put the individual banker out of business provided he wishes to loan real United States money instead of manufactured money.

More than that, according to the third point in our program, it is our plan for the government to finance its own public works, to pay its own public servants not with money borrowed from the local bank at interest, but with money borrowed from the nation and secured by the wealth of the nation at no interest. This is a program which demands the recall of certain government bonds now extant. As they come due, their holders should be paid off in redeemable bonds which bears little or no interest. By this procedure almost $1-billion a year would be saved in interest money to you, the taxpayers—interest money that is now supporting bankers, who, instead of loaning their manufactured money to private industry, prefer to wax fat by loaning it to you people of the United States to keep them in their luxury.

Point number six in the program for the National Union reads as follows: *"I believe in the abolition of the privately owned Federal Reserve Banking system and in the establishing of a Government owned Central Bank."*

Every person knows that the Federal Reserve banking system is a privately owned corporation. The stock in it is owned and controlled by a handful of wealthy American bankers. Everyone knows that this privately owned Federal Reserve Bank, through its domination and power and influence, actually controls the policy of practically every little private bank in the country. It is this gigantic bank that sends out the word to extend credit and create a so-called prosperity. It is this great bank which sends out, through its subterranean channels, another word to contract credit and thus bring about a panic, or, as they call it, a seasonal depression. It is this bank which refuses to issue any credit that is worthwhile mentioning and thereby practically prohibits every bank in the nation from extending credit because it is satisfied to loan money to the government at interest or, in other words,

148

to purchase government bonds which are designed to borrow us out of the depression. The only ones being borrowed out of the depression are the bankers!

While business is stagnant, while unemployment is still rampant, the owners of this bank are still profiteering upon the misery of the people—even loaning money to the government for federal emergency relief at interest; loaning money to the government for its Tennessee Valley project at interest; loaning money at interest to the government for the PWA and CWA workers who gathered leaves. This program is so prosperous that for $8,600,000,000 of emergency relief money expended upon the indigent American citizens, the government will have paid the bankers approximately $6-billion interest within the next eighteen years.

Thus, it is the proposal of the National Union to nationalize this organization which exists under the name of the Federal Reserve Bank. It was established in 1913 to prevent depressions. Since its birth we have suffered the depression of 1920 and the fury of the present break-down.

It was established to keep the American dollar honest, or, in other words, to keep 100 pennies in the dollar. It was established to help a man who borrowed 100 bushels of wheat to repay his creditor with 100 bushels of wheat and not with 150. The Federal Reserve Bank is the Gibraltar of the plutocrats. It is their last stand. To destroy it, the very powers of hell must be moved. To destroy it, there must be a perfect amalgamation of the agricultural and the laboring classes of America together with the small industrialists, the professional men and the merchants. As long as it exists; as long as the policy exists of our borrowing money from it at interest to dig ourselves out of the depression there is only the semblance of democracy in America.

The ninth point in the National Union reads as follows: *"I believe in the cost of production plus a fair profit for the farmer."*

My friends, there is scarcely a farmer's organization in the United States which has not gone on official record against the present monetary system. Today there is a bill before Congress known as the "Frazier-Lemke Bill" which proposes direct relief to the farmers and the immediate addition of $3-billion of currency. The Farmers' Union, which is perhaps the largest and most active of all the farm organizations, has had this Frazier-Lemke Bill endorsed by twenty-five State legislatures. At present the bill is in the limbo of the Committee room and cannot be called to the floor of Congress for a vote because of the "gag rule" in vogue at Washington unless well over two hundred representatives will petition that it be brought out for their consideration.

Of course, the National Union for Social Justice supports this Frazier-Lemke Bill because we realize, while doles of various and slaughtering his pigs, that the American farmer has been forced, over a period of ten years and more, to become a slave to a financial system which has unremittingly compelled him to produce at a loss instead of at a profit.

There are approximately 60-million farmers in this nation, including their wives and their children. These people form the backbone of our purchasing power. If they cannot produce at a profit, it is impossible for the laboring man in the city to make motor cars or clothing or other commodities whose sale is dependent upon the farmer's pocketbook. Speculative wheat will sell, perchance, at $1.00 per bushel, but the farmers have been paid forty to sixty cents a bushel for it when it did not profit them to operate. These are the same farmers who in 1929 contracted to buy their homes for ten thousand bushels of wheat, as it were. These are the same farmers who in 1935 are expected to pay anywhere from 15-thousand to 20-thousand bushels of wheat to retain their homes.

In conjunction with the tenth point of the National Union for Social Justice, we will support the farmers who should organize against this outrage of being victimized by a privately owned central bank. Just as much as it is the business of the Department of Labor to protect the laborer and his union, so it is the business of the Department of Agriculture to protect the farmer and his union.

The eleventh and twelfth points of the National Union for Social Justice read as follows: *"I believe in the recall of all non-productive bonds and thereby in the alleviation of taxation. "I believe in the abolition of tax exempt bonds."*

I have often spoken to you about non-productive bonds—Liberty Bonds—bonds by which the bankers profited and are still profiting upon the wounds of our veterans, upon the shell holes in France,—bonds which permit the favored few to profit while the veterans who served in the World War are denied the pittance of a just debt which we recognize as their due. In one sense they are bonds which the bankers wish to increase instead of decrease because, according to the Vinson Bill, they say to the American war veteran: *"If you get your pay it will be through another bond issue."*

Now that as a nation we have notified the world of our determination to remain aloof from foreign entanglements, the question of preparedness arises more acutely than ever.

The fifteenth point in our program advocates that the burdens of war be shared equally and proportionately by all—by rich and poor, by soldier and citizen.

We are not a militaristic state. Nevertheless, let us lock our doors against the possibility of foreign intrusion. Let us build ten thousand airplanes to guard our coasts, to secure our liberties and to keep America safe for Americans from without. It is our business to make America safe for Americans within by recapturing, first of all, the sovereignty of our money from the unholy hands of the international banker and by learning to use our national credit for the guarantee of a just and honest annual wage for the laborer and for the farmer. Until this objective will have been attained there is no prosperity and little contentment for the United States of America.

Today these are ideals. Tomorrow you, ladies and gentlemen, can realize these ideals. If you determine that the National Union for Social Justice will continue to function, I shall be happy, independent of partisan politics, independent of creed and of race, to be your servant with the provision in mind that I shall never seek and that I shall never accept a public office. No matter what the future holds in store, I shall always be conscious of the happy memory that, whatsoever I have accomplished in the past, was motivated by the love of God and by the love of my inarticulate fellow men who are the sons of God and who have inherited this earth that has been unjustly kept from them!

# SOVIETIZING OR SAVING
AMERICA?

*(Sunday, February 10, 1935)*

**M**Y FRIENDS and fellow members in the National Union for Social Justice; Adequate words fail me to express my sincere indebtedness to you for the magnificent response which you made to my appeal for financial assistance. During the past week there have been placed on my desk thousands of letters each containing, perchance, a contribution for the purpose of carrying on the work which we set out to perform.

To report to you at this moment in a definite manner or to acknowledge your communications before ten or fifteen days will have elapsed is not physically possible. I ask that you patiently await my reply which will not be possible until these letters have been carefully read. In the meantime, however, our financial emergency most likely will vanish. And in the future, even more than in the past, you can truthfully consider that this broadcast belongs entirely to you. As for myself, rest assured I shall be no slacker but shall attempt to double my perseverance in your behalf. We dare not falter until through our mutual co-operation we shall gain our total, uncompromising economic liberty.

Together we will carry on! The National Union for Social Justice and its principles will live! Some day, through our combined efforts, the ambitions which we cherish will be realized if the events of the past week are an indication of what the future holds.

## I

This afternoon two principles with which the National Union for Social Justice is concerned will be discussed jointly. The first is related to our defense of private ownership. The second is identified with our advocacy of nationalizing, in the full sense of the word, the Federal Reserve Banks. As you are aware, Mr. Roosevelt tacitly and at least indirectly opposes the restoration of the coinage and regulation of money to Congress. According to the Administration Bill commonly known as *"The Banking Act of 1935"* he directly opposes the full nationalization of the Federal Reserve Banks, being content to give his benediction to a measure which permits the present private owners to continue profiteering upon bonds and the manufacture of money under a firmer federal control. To us this is most disappointing.

According to Professor Irving Fisher of Yale University: *"The new bill gives the Federal Reserve Board more power at the expense of the banks and gives the President more power at the expense of the Board. It comes nearer to making the President an economic dictator than all previous legislation put together."*

Whether or not Mr. Roosevelt assumes through this bill the title of a financial dictator, he cannot escape the charge, either now or in the future, of protecting the bankers' questionable privilege of manufacturing money, of loaning credit and exacting in return their pound of currency flesh. Here, as I shall explain, is capitalism at its worst.

On the other hand, through the agency of his appointed high officers, Mr. Roosevelt also shares the responsibility of having endorsed a most radical leaning towards international socialism or sovietism in relation to the rights to private property ownership. This I shall also amplify with reference to documentary evidence. Combine this adherence to obsolete capitalism with the decided though, perhaps, unintentional tendency towards sovietism and the result is that we stand confronted with the latest, the most unique creation of an impossible economic system!

Let me become more explicit.

I fully realize that industry, as we have experienced it, has been cruel, harsh, selfish and careless of the common good. Although I am aware that a strong governmental hand must establish a just and living annual wage for every laborer who has dedicated his life to industry; although, I fully appreciate that it is the business of good government to destroy the unholy alliance now existing between industry and finance and to assist in formulating a union between industry and labor, yet, in no sense, do I subscribe to any doctrine which permits the government, even in theory, to become the chief industrialist of the nation while, at the same time, it persists in preserving the fundamental cause of our economic disaster, namely, the private ownership of money, of credit, of finance by a group of privileged counterfeiters and financialists.

If these two tendencies are indicative of our future policies and practices, namely, the continued opposition to the full and complete nationalization of our money system on the one hand, and, on the other, the radical leaning towards industrial socialism or sovietism, I fear that this Administration will sooner succeed in driving the industrialist from America before the money changers will have been driven from the temple!

For a moment, at least, let us analyze the basic economic errors of sovietism and of capitalism so as to better understand this statement.

For more than five years we have been attempting to find a way out of this depression. The financialist, refusing to recognize that this system of capitalism had suffered a complete collapse, obstructed every effort to rescue from his hands the coinage and regulation of money by which he was enabled to control the wealth of the nation. What cared he if we had passed from the age of scarcity into the age of plenty? What cared he if his financially controlled industries paid men only while they actually worked—paid them less than a living wage? What cared he if thereby the purchasing power of the nation was destroyed, if money became scarce, if prices were slaughtered, if agricultural pursuits were unprofitable? At least he retained his control over money and the power to amass profits acquired through the purchases of debt bonds and the foreclosures on mortgages.

Nature pleaded with him in vain when she loaded the fields with golden grain and snow-white cotton! Still people must starve and go naked because the financialist, refusing to supply us with an adequate money which would enable us to enjoy the plenitude of God's blessings, destroyed this plenitude to create a scarcity equivalent to the scarce money.

So did science plead in vain. Wondrous factories, miraculous inventions stood like ghostly sentinels of disaster to mock us. The lathe, the loom, the power press, the dynamo—all must cease multiplying wealth because, to protect the bankers' plutocracy, a false scarcity of production must be created to equal the manipulated scarcity of money.

O God forgive us who have said: *"Give us this day our daily bread!"* Forgive us for the sacrileges we have committed against Thy children, Thy brothers in Christ—all in the name of sound money, in the name of unholy modern capitalism and its scarce money!

Who, then, has the effrontery to acclaim the villainous role played by capitalistic money in the tragic story of our depression? The very essence of that system of capitalism was identified with the private manufacture and control of money. Therefore, we are told by this Administration Banking Bill of 1935, "This system must be preserved even though the common people should be misled into believing that capitalism means the right of private ownership; even though we shall take the old Federal Reserve Act and dress its wolfish substance in the sheep's clothing of compromise."

Thus, proclaiming vociferously the sanctity of private ownership as the essence of capitalism those of us are damned as international socialists or communists or radicals if we question the presumed right to own and control the money of the nation. For, according to capitalism, all things, including the sovereign right of coining money, must be privately owned!

On the other hand the communist, whom the practices of capitalism generated, went to the other extreme in maintaining that all things must be publicly owned. To him private ownership was as illogical and immoral as was public ownership to the capitalist.

Both the communist and capitalist, while expert at figures and statistics and propaganda, proved themselves to be very unintelligent and inexpert when faced with the reality of morals, of history and of experience. As a matter of fact the capitalist was seriously in error when he upheld the doctrine that all things must be owned privately. Equally in error was the communist who maintained that all things must be owned nationally. The truth evidenced both by nature, by reason and by the pages of history, clearly indicates that some things, because of their common importance, should be owned in common but that the majority of things such as your home, your farm, your factory and other things too numerous to mention should be owned in private.

Thus the vast population of America, caught between the two forces of unintelligent capitalism and equally unintelligent communism, continued to suffer the unnecessary evils of this depression. Money, which is the common denominator of all economic life is, therefore, by its very nature the commonest necessity in our prosperous existence. Without it in some shape or form not a wheel can turn in our factories, our hospitals are handicapped, our schools are closed, business becomes paralyzed while poverty stalks the land to mock us who have solved the riddle of production.

These thoughts which single out the predominant errors of capitalism and of economic communism are a necessary preface to the remarks which I am about to make. When you consider them you will find that certain agents of our present Administration at Washington are, to say the least, theoretic communists, while the Administration itself is in practice still wedded to the chief error of capitalism.

## II

Bearing in mind that economic communism is hostile to all private ownership and reserves for itself the right to acquire by any means any private property, let us see how communistic certain agencies created by the Administration have proven themselves.

In the autumn of 1934 an investigator was sent to the State Capitol of Delaware to inspect the charters of five new government corporations whose names had appeared in the *New York Times* under the date of March 25, 1934.

These, the investigator discovered, together with the charter of a sixth government corporation known as "The Public Works Emergency Leasing Corporation," the existence of which had been carefully concealed. Photostatic copies of the papers legalizing these corporations were made and from them I submit the following facts:

⊥ First: There was "The Commodity Credit Corporation." It was established on October 17, 1933, by Executive Order 6340.

The incorporators were the Honorable Henry A. Wallace, Secretary of Agriculture, the Honorable Henry Morgenthau, Jr., Secretary of the Treasury, and the Honorable Oscar Johnston, a third Government official. The corporation was granted $3,000,000 to operate but there already has been allocated to it more than $756,000,000.

Second: There is listed "The Public Works Emergency Housing Corporation." It was chartered October 27, 1933, by the Honorable Harold L. Ickes, Secretary of the Interior, the Honorable Frances Perkins, Secretary of Labor, and by the Honorable Robert D. Kohn. This Emergency Corporation was amended by Executive Order 6470. Despite the fact that it exists for an emergency the sixth section says: *"The Corporation is to have perpetual existence."* In other words the emergency of the depression is supposed to last forever.

Third: There is "The Federal Surplus Relief Corporation" which was chartered October 4, 1933, by Honorable Henry A. Wallace, the Honorable Harold L. Ickes and the Honorable Harry L. Hopkins. In its sixth section there is the following sentence: *"This Corporation is to have perpetual existence."* In other words it is a consolation for all of us to know that surplus relief is supposed to be perpetual in this nation.

Fourth: There is "The Federal Subsistence Homesteads Corporation" which was chartered November 21, 1933, by the Honorable Harold L. Ickes, Oscar L. Chapman and M. L. Wilson and it likewise is to have perpetual existence.

Fifth: There is "The Electric Home and Farm Authority" which was created on January 13, 1934, by Executive Order 6514 by the Honorable Arthur E. Morgan, by the Honorable Harcourt A. Morgan and the Honorable David E. Lilienthal, the chief executive of the Tennessee Valley Authority.

There is nothing whatsoever alarming in what I have said relative to these five corporations except the fact that certain emergencies are foreseen to be perpetual.

We might inquire, however, why the United States Government, through its agencies, went into the State of Delaware to establish these corporations. Delaware has long been notorious for the laxity of its corporation laws and for its subservience to the duPonts. A Delaware corporation is one that is accountable to the State of Delaware and not to the United States of America. A Delaware corporation is not answerable for its functions to any Federal law, according to Senator Schall. Incorporation under the laws of Delaware, perchance, was not an accident but evidently a cold blooded intention. As it was pointed out on the floor of the Senate on February 6th by Senator Schall: *"Under Federal Law every Government official is answerable for every dollar of property entrusted to him. To avoid answerability, the*

*schemers behind these corporations evade opinion as to legality
that might properly be expressed by the Attorney General, and
have removed their projects from the jurisdiction of Federal
Courts."*

So far I have not demonstrated any sovietistic tendency on the
part of the Administration. These five corporations are, at the
most, nothing more than flattering attempts to emulate Benito
Mussolini and his ideas of a corporate State. But let us hasten
to the inspection of the sixth corporation which bears the name
of "The Public Works Emergency Leasing Corporation."

At the present moment our Congress is occupying itself with
debate relative to allocating approximately $5-billion for relief
purposes, all of which money is to be used in the discretion and under the sole directive power of the President of the United States.
It is in this connection that I shall mention the sixth and vitally important corporation. First, however, let me be as clear as possible
in stating that no sane man is opposed to relief and to its rational
activities. No one would attempt to uphold the sophistry that in
this land of plenty, nakedness, starvation and disease should not
be fought with the last ounce of energy and the last penny of
finance which we possess. No one would stultify himself in this
age of perfected mass production to deny that a program of permanent public works is necessary for the purpose of creating
national wealth and of guaranteeing constant employment. But
the question which is pertinent at the moment hinges on the danger of this vast sum of money being committed to some radical
corporation chartered in Delaware and smacking of sovietism.
Shall not our Congress be unfaithful to the American traditions
of democracy, if it allocates this money without assuring itself
and its constituents that it will be spent in a democratic manner
and through a democratic non-partisan, non-soviet agency?

I am referring to the "Public Works Emergency Leasing Corporation" which was chartered January 2, 1934, but which was
withdrawn just the day previous to the meeting of our Seventy-
fourth Congress last month. While the word *"emergency"* appears in the title of this Delaware Corporation, those who chartered it evidently were hiding behind a smoke-screen of intrigue,
of double-dealing, because in the Articles of Incorporation we discover that it is to have perpetual existence.

I associate this appropriation of approximately $5-billion which
our Congress is about to allocate for emergency relief measures
with the Corporation to which I have just referred because it is
stated that the $5-billion can be expended possibly through the
agency of this or of a similar Corporation which can be chartered
by the State of Delaware.

Let us, therefore, inspect the photostatic copies of this "Public
Works Emergency Leasing Corporation" to which the names of

157

Harold Ickes, Oscar Chapman and Theodore Walters are signed as incorporators.

Paragraph (2) gives the power *"to undertake . . . any project eligible to be included in the comprehensive program of Public Works to be prepared pursuant to the provisions of the Recovery Act."* This paragraph identifies the Public Works program to be undertaken with a Corporation similar to the one which I am about to dissect.

Paragraph (3) gives authority *"to collect fees, tolls, and other charges in the construction of"* public works.

Paragraph (5) gives power to this Corporation over the *"maintenance and operations of edifices, structures, and buildings of every kind, nature, or description."* I may be simple minded enough to be of the opinion that privileges and rights should be specific and limited. But here we discover illimitable privileges and rights to maintain and operate every type of edifice, structure and building which includes departmental stores, churches, schools, factories, dairies, buildings and businesses of every description.

The ordinary citizen could never hope to compete with the State which has so sovietized its powers as to condemn at its own price and at its own bargain the best site of land and then operate it, not with money begged from a banker, but with money borrowed from the illimitable funds controlled by a State soviet.

Paragraph (11) endows this Corporation with the legal right *"to furnish, equip, operate, manage and maintain projects and structures of every kind, nature, or description, and to do any and all things necessary, suitable, or convenient in connection therewith, including without limitation the supplying of heat, steam, water, gas and electricity and transportation, telephone, and any other facilities or utilities necessary, suitable, or convenient."*

Paragraph (12) gives this Corporation power to carry on its functions *"in the State of Delaware or in any other State, Territory, or locality . . . without restriction or limitation as to amount."* Here the veil of the internationalists was removed for a moment. That one phrase *"in any locality"* betrays its internationalism because it was not satisfied to operate within the domain of the Stars and Stripes. For fear that it would lack the qualifications of infinity that phrase, *"in any locality,"* was added as was the following phrase respecting the money placed at its disposal—money *"without restriction or limitation as to amount."*

Paragraphs (13) and (14) give it the right *"to acquire personal property of every kind, nature, or description"* and *"in any manner to acquire, hold, use, or dispose of any franchises, licenses, grants, concessions, patents, trade marks, trade names, copyrights, or inventions granted by or existing under the laws of any government or subdivision thereof."*

Read the histories of the first or second and third international conventions of the Communists. Scrutinize the economic laws or edicts which have emanated from Moscow since 1917, and I challenge you to discover a more comprehensive theoretic onslaught against private property than was expressed in this paragraph which I have just read—a paragraph that was conceived in Washington and executed in Delaware; a paragraph which legalizes the theoretic confiscation of any private property; a paragraph which prepares the way for the Commissars of Communism to acquire in *"any manner"* any industry and trade name which exists in America!

Associate what I have just read with paragraph (16) of this Corporation which reads as follows: *"To acquire, by purchase, exchange or otherwise, all or any part of or any interest in the properties, assets, business, and good will of any one or more persons, firms, associations, or corporations engaged in any business for which a corporation may now or hereafter be organized under the laws of the State of Delaware; to pay for the same in any lawful manner; to hold, operate, reorganize, liquidate, sell, donate, or in any manner dispose of the whole of any part thereof; and, in connection therewith, to assume or guarantee performance of any liabilities, obligations, or contracts of such persons, firms, associations, or corporations, and to conduct in any lawful manner the whole or part of any business thus acquired."*

I do not pretend to be a judge of the mental activities of those who composed this blanket power of confiscation and acquisition, but in opposition to the spirit of communism which militates against the possession of any private property I protest most vehemently; against those who have sanctioned the existence of such a threat to a nation which, up to the present date, has no desire to erase the blue and the white from our national emblem I raise my voice; against any government going into business—into any and every business—with illimitable funds, with illimitable political backing, I protest in the name of liberty, in the name of America!

This, then, is the partial publication of the Corporation's charter which had marked upon it *"Do not publish."* This is the attitude at least once expressed by this Administration's agents towards private property and industry. This is the attempt, at least theoretically made, to uphold the worst error in communism which is identified with the denial of the right to possess undisturbed one's private property. This, then, is the Administration's tendency towards sovietism of which I spoke.

## III

Now let us approach the chief error of capitalism—the private money control—which not only in theory but in practice is upheld by our Federal Government.

Because our most necessary public necessity is money, the National Union for Social Justice upholds the principle that it should be owned, coined, regulated and controlled by the people of this democratic country. Because, at the present moment, our money is coined and owned by a few private individuals that is no argument for them to defend their ownership and possession of it on the basis of a private property. Possession is not nine-tenths of the law. I will not admit, because a stick-up man has my watch in his pocket, that he owns it.

These private money coiners obtained a property to which they had no right either by the Constitution of the United States or by the very nature of money itself.

Now to refresh our memories on the nature of money and how it is abused consider these twelve vital facts:

(1) Money is merely the medium of trade. It is not wealth. It is only the transportation system, as it were, by which wealth is carried from one person to another.

(2) For more than one hundred years the people of this nation have permitted a small group of men to possess the privilege of making money and thereby of controlling the flow of wealth to such a degree that many of us began to believe that money was the real wealth instead of the truck, as it were, whose only reason for existence is to carry the precious freight of food, of clothing, of shelter, of human beings and their labor from one point to another—from the producer to the consumer—. There are many kinds of transportation, such as the railway, the truck, the steamboat. There are three kinds of capitalistic money all monopolized for use by the banker—metal, paper currency and credit. In round figures there are $9-billion of idle metal in the Treasury, $5½-billion of paper currency throughout the nation and at least $250-billion of credit or of debt money such as mortgages, loans, bonds, etc. Credit money or "pen and ink plus check book" money is really the major portion of all our money by 90 per cent.

(3) How is this check book money created in this nation? First a group of wealthy men petition the Government for a bank charter or, in other words, for the right to counterfeit legally.

(4) These men deposit, for example, $100-thousand with the Treasury. In return the Treasury gives them $100-thousand worth of interest-bearing bonds which are kept at Washington as security. But the interest on the bonds belongs to these new bankers.

(5) These men return to their home town after they have the Government print for them, at scarcely no cost, $100-thousand worth of paper dollars which they deposit in their new bank.

(6) John Smith comes to these bankers for a loan of $10-thousand which he obtains at 6 per cent on depositing as security the deed for his $20-thousand farm.

(7)   Then the banker gives John a check book—no actual cash, mind you—and immediately writes on his own books that $10-thousand has been deposited whereas in truth it was simply loaned.

(8)   Fifty, eighty, one hundred John Smiths go through the same process until the bank, which started with only $100-thousand of printed money, has loaned $1-million at 6 per cent. That was their rule to lend ten times what they actually had. Therefore, the first year in business grossed the bank $60-thousand interest profit on an investment of $100-thousand which, all this time, was bearing interest for them through the bonds which they deposited originally at Washington at 4 per cent.

(9)   Of course, Jim Jones and one thousand other neighbors of Jim Jones placed their savings in the town bank. They thought that this money was safe and that the bank would surrender it on demand.   But Jim did not read the fine print in his bank book. Had he done so, he would discover that he actually loaned his money to the bankers; that he had become a creditor and, therefore, had to take his chance of getting his money back with all the other creditors and patrons of the bank.

(10)   Meanwhile from the bankers' bank, the Federal Reserve Bank, word went out that too much credit money had been loaned by the affiliated banks. It was time to call in the loans. It was time to cut down on credit. Thus Henry Doe, the manufacturer, John Smith, the farmer, and Peter Adams, the merchant, all of whom borrowed from the bank, were ordered to pay back in currency money, mind you, what they obtained in check book money. Simultaneously this happened all over the nation. Ten, twenty, thirty billion dollars of loans were called. There were only five billions of dollars of currency money in existence. It was an impossible situation. Therefore, a depression arose. The deeds and mortgages were claimed by the bankers and homes and farms and industries were confiscated by him because there was no currency money.

(11)   Did the banker close up shop? He did not. At least the big bankers did not. They liquidated the homes and farms and industries which they confiscated when the borrowers had no currency money to save them. They sold them for what they could obtain on a depressed market. Then they turned around with this new fresh currency money and bought government bonds at 4 per cent or less.

(12)   Meanwhile bread lines were established. Unemployment increased. Poverty stalked through the nation. Of necessity the government must obtain money to feed the poor and must undertake public work to salvage the unemployed. Therefore, it borrowed $8-billion from the bankers who, playing their game even in the face of a national distress, loaned the government a fat

161

check book and perhaps, for good measure, a bottle of ink and a fountain pen. Still there were only $5-billion dollars of actual currency in the nation. But through a banker's magic and a gambler's instinct they loaned the $8-billion because they knew that, in eighteen years hence, $6-billion in interest would be returned by the government for the privilege of using a banker's check book— $14-billion in all!

Need I explain the chief error of capitalism any further? Need I ask you if you favor the principle which our government advocates of permitting bankers to manufacture their own money, to expand and contract currency at will, to issue and recall credit at will, to live like leeches on the people of this nation by lending, for example, $8-billion of check book money and demanding that we repay them, even in times of distress, with $14-billion of currency?

Is that social justice to permit this ungodly profit to accrue to the Federal Reserve banks and their affiliates, while a nation is still stricken? Is that the heritage of debt to be passed on to future generations?

We speak in ignominious terms of the foreign nations who have welshed on us. Dare we apply some of that ignominy to ourselves who are welshing on our children?

Dare we for a moment, once we understand these incontrovertible facts, uphold the hands of those who are supporting the Banking Act of 1935 or, like cowards, dare we make compromise with them?

My friends, I shall not desert the position which I have taken despite the Administration's "Banking Act Bill of 1935" which, with platitudes and promises, veils over these facts. I shall not compromise with our 1935 Banking Act which still permits the private bankers to create check book money and demand in repayment currency money or your home or your farm or your business.

Since 1913 the President of this nation, as every Senator and Congressman knows, had control, through appointment, both of the Governors of the Federal Reserve Banks and therefore of the credit. What did it amount to?

We demand more than control of the credit situation. We demand ownership of the Central Bank. We demand that having obtained ownership, we shall keep 100 pennies in the present fluctuating dollar. We demand that this government owned bank shall be the fiscal agent to refinance our national debt free from the present unjust interest racket. We demand that this Central Bank shall refinance the billions of dollars of bloody bonds, of non-productive bonds, and re-issue them with fresh bonds bearing a minimum of interest. We demand that this bank shall issue adequate currency of one kind instead of the eight different kinds in circulation today. We demand that all deposits made by customers be held in trust and in no way be jeopardized. We demand that some consideration be taken of those mulcted bank depositors who lost their money through trickery; that this bank shall restore and maintain the production of goods and services in the nation, substantially at the maximum of production capacity, so that the laborers and farmers and citizens of America may be fully employed at wages and prices which will insure a high and increasing elevation in the general standard of living.

In one word we demand that the counterfeit money manufactured by the banker shall be called out of circulation—his counterfeit currency, his counterfeit check book money and his counterfeit privilege of regulating it to the detriment of a country whose Constitution says that Congress has the right to coin and regulate the value of money; whose Constitution does not say that Congress can delegate this right or that privateers can capture it. In its place we want United States money predicated upon the wealth of the nation and the need for its use by the people.

There, my friends, are the major articles of a bill which has been drawn up legally and constitutionally for the National Union for Social Justice. This bill is in harmony with the pledge I publicly made to you on November 11, 1934. I dare not, I cannot compromise with any person or with any principles on this matter without breaking faith with the millions of members of the National Union for Social Justice. Some of my friends have pleaded with me to compromise, to betray you who have put trust in me! Friendship or not, justice predominates! There is only one right way and ten million wrong ways. I will not compromise.

No compromise with the chief error of capitalism!

No compromise with the hypocritical, false-face Banking Act of 1935 which is about to be passed in a few days!

If we are honest; if we are lovers of the principle of "America for the Americans," we will drive out the international bankers from their stronghold of Federal Bank ownership.

The reign of plutocracy must pass!

The age of want in the midst of plenty must be destroyed! This can never be done by flirting with sovietism or by clinging to modern capitalism! It can never be done by compromise with error!

If we uphold the right to private property, let us be logical and permit private property possessors to breathe freely without threatening them with the whip of soviet governmental competition.

If we uphold the right to public property of those things which, either by nature or by convention, are fundamental common necessities, let us again be logical and restore money, the life blood of trade, of clothing, of food, of shelter, of prosperity, to the hands of the people's government!

Unquestionably, the nationalization of the Federal Reserve Bank together with the other articles incorporated in the bill which we have prepared and which will be introduced in Congress next week—unquestionably, this is the first step towards real prosperity —towards a permanent prosperity, unless the hand of God shall punish this entire nation for this cruelty which it is about to be imposed upon the children of next generation.

I do not pretend that this proposed bill, of which I have made mention, is a cure-all which will eradicate every ill to which human nature is heir, but I do affirm that it is not a hypodermic palliative merely to increase a flow of currency today, a spasmodic prosperity tomorrow and the inevitable depression to follow. I do affirm, however, that it is the answer to low wages, to unprofitable agricultural pursuits, to unbearable and unpayable debts, to unjust plutocratic profits, to the concentration of wealth in the hands of a few and to the periodic stagnation of business. I further affirm that this new bill answers once and for all the question in the perturbed minds of the industrialists as to whether or not their factories will remain idle or, perchance, be confiscated by sovietized measures.

Why compromise? Why deal with the devil's agents whose only ambassadorial mission is to bind tighter, by subterfuge and platitudes, the shackles of economic tyranny which hold a civilized and liberty loving people bound to the rock of unnecessary poverty?

Once more I affirm that, with the passage of this bill and its future proper execution, there will be little need for the children of the next generation to agitate, either in leaderless mobs or in regimented armies, for the purpose of securing, as did the Roman slaves of old, their crust of bread, their unemployment pension, their old age pension, all of which things characterize the age in which we live and the policies which we practice as totally inefficient and totally unjust.

Why compromise? Did Christ compromise when His hands were outstretched on the cross? When His enemies said to Him: *"If Thou be the Son of the Living God come down from the cross,"* did He unfasten the nails, destroy His principles of sacrifice and walk in the midst of those who had spat upon Him and derided Him?

Nor shall we American citizens come down from the living cross of poverty until those who have crucified us with its nails and crowned us with the thorns of its worry agree to end its social inequalities.

As members of the National Union for Social Justice I ask you to carry on. Be not like those who stood in the highway as the Innocent Christ was led to slaughter. Rather be ye like the one courageous Simon of Cyrene who stood out from the mob and declared himself immortally on the side of Christ. Rather be ye like the Veronica, ye patriotic women of America—the Veronica who bathed the face of the thorn-crowned Christ—because today is your day to rescue your impoverished, down-trodden, persecuted, deluded and deceived fellow citizens.

In the meantime stand by! Prepare to suffer just a little longer. Prepare to rise glorious from the tomb in which the schemers of international finance hope to bury you for evermore.

# THE BANKING AND MONETARY CONTROL ACT OF 1935

*(Sunday, February 17, 1935)*

## I

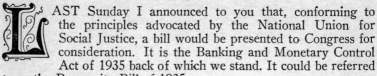 AST Sunday I announced to you that, conforming to the principles advocated by the National Union for Social Justice, a bill would be presented to Congress for consideration. It is the Banking and Monetary Control Act of 1935 back of which we stand. It could be referred to as the Prosperity Bill of 1935.

Today I shall read its nineteen articles and briefly comment upon some of them.

In its present form, which of course will be subject to constructive suggestions and amendments, the bill reads as follows:

"A BILL TO DESTROY WANT IN THE MIDST OF PLENTY; TO ENABLE THE PEOPLE OF THIS NATION TO ENJOY ITS WEALTH WITHOUT RESORTING TO UNCONSTITUTIONAL METHODS; TO PROVIDE FOR THE ORDERLY DISTRIBUTION OF THE ABUNDANCE WITH WHICH A BENEFICENT CREATOR HAS BLESSED US; TO RESTORE THE PRICES OF PROPERTY TO JUST AND EQUITABLE LEVELS; TO INCREASE THE PRICES OF AGRICULTURAL PRODUCTS TO A POINT WHERE THEY WILL YIELD THE COST OF PRODUCTION PLUS A FAIR PROFIT TO THE FARMER; TO ENABLE THE CONGRESS TO PROVIDE THROUGH LEGISLATION A LIVING AND JUST ANNUAL WAGE TO EVERY LABORER WILLING AND CAPABLE OF WORKING; TO REPAY DEBTS WITH DOLLARS OF EQUAL VALUE; TO LIFT IN PART THE BURDEN OF TAXATION; AND FOR OTHER PURPOSES.

"WHEREAS THE CONSTITUTION OF THE UNITED STATES IN ARTICLE 1 SECTION 8 CLAUSE 5, PROVIDES THAT CONGRESS SHALL HAVE THE RIGHT TO COIN MONEY AND REGULATE THE VALUE THEREOF AND OF FOREIGN COINS, AND

"WHEREAS THE PRESENT PRACTICE OF ISSUING BOOK CREDITS BY COMMERCIAL BANKS, AND TRANSFERRING THE TITLE OF SAID CREDITS BY CHECK, PROVIDE A SUPPLEMENTARY MEDIUM OF EXCHANGE, ABROGATING THE SAID CONSTITUTIONAL PROVISION AND ESTABLISHING A SEPA-

RATE, PRIVATE AND INDEPENDENT MONETARY SYSTEM, AND

"WHEREAS THE PERMANENT WELFARE OF THE PEOPLE AND THE PROTECTION OF THE ECONOMIC LIFE OF THE NATION RESTS IN PART ON A MONETARY SYSTEM WHOLLY SUBJECT TO THE CONTROL OF CONGRESS WHICH WILL PROMOTE THE INTERESTS OF AGRICULTURE AND LABOR, OF INDUSTRY, TRADE, COMMERCE AND FINANCE FOR THE ECONOMIC WELL BEING OF ALL CITIZENS BY THE MAINTENANCE OF PRICE LEVELS WHICH WILL AVOID EXCESSIVE INFLATION OR DISASTROUS DEFLATION AND WHICH WILL PROTECT THE NATIONAL CREDIT AND CURRENCY IN THE WORLD'S MARKETS;

"NOW THEREFORE:

"BE IT ENACTED BY THE SENATE AND THE HOUSE OF REPRESENTATIVES OF THE UNITED STATES IN CONGRESS ASSEMBLED

"Sec. 1. That there is hereby created a central bank, which shall be known as the Bank of the United States of America, which may be abbreviated as the Bank of the U.S.A.

"Sec. 2. The Bank of the U.S.A., so created, shall be the agency of the Congress of the United States to issue the money of the United States, to control the value thereof, and the value of foreign monies, and it shall be the custodian of all monetary stocks and of all monies, and of all the public credit of the United States. It shall be the custodian of the reserve funds of all banks, banking institutions and banking firms of the United States and Territories. It shall be the fiscal agent of the United States Government."

(Those two sections just read provide for the legal creation of a central government bank to control the issuance and regulation of all money and to care for the debt of the United States.)

"Sec. 3 (a). There is hereby created a governing board of the Bank of the U.S.A. which shall be known as the Board of Directors of the Bank of the U.S.A. which shall be the monetary authority of the Government of the United States. The Board of Directors of the Bank of the U.S.A. shall be composed of one representative from each State, chosen by the people thereof for a period of 12 years. Immediately after they shall be assembled in consequence of the first election, they shall be divided by lot equally into six classes; the seats of the directors of the first class shall be vacated at the expiration of the second year; the seats of the second class at the expiration of the fourth year; the third class at the expiration of the sixth year; the fourth class at the expiration of the eighth year; the fifth class at the expiration of the tenth year; the sixth class at the expiration of the twelfth year; so that one sixth may be chosen every second year; and if vacancies happen by resignation or otherwise the chief executive of the State affected may make the temporary appointments until the next general election to fill the vacancy. The board of directors shall choose from among their own number an executive committee consisting of seven members and including a governor and a vice governor selected by a majority of the forty-eight directors. The salary of each director shall be the same salary as that of an associate justice of the Supreme Court of the United States. They shall not during their term of office hold any direct or indirect financial interest in any bank, banking institution, banking firm, financial institution, or in any firm or corporation as stockholder, director, or officer either in the United States or in any foreign country. The board of directors shall assemble on the first Monday in December and remain on duty for at least 9 months out of each year; a majority shall constitute a quorum to do business; it may determine the rules for its proceedings; and Congress may, with a concurrency of two-thirds, expel a member. No director shall, during the term for which he is elected, be appointed to any civil office under the authority of the United States or of the States or territorial possessions, nor shall he be a member of either house of Congress. Upon attaining the age of seventy years, each director must retire, but with an annual pension equal to two-thirds of the annual salary granted him for the rest of his natural life. Any director shall be eligible for re-election."

(Here, my friends, is financial democracy. Forty-eight directors to manage this government owned bank, one director elected from each State!

What a contrast with the present privately owned Federal Reserve bank dominated by a small group of banker-minded men who have proven by the most eloquent testimony of facts—unemployment, industrial stagnation, poverty, concentrated wealth, frozen credit, inadequate currency, wholesale bankruptcy, sinful want and many others—that all their so-called knowledge of banking and political economy has been inefficient, unsound and hostile to the best interest of the people at large!

Hitherto bankers operated the Federal Reserve Banks solely for the profit of bankers. Hereafter this central bank shall be operated democratically for the profit of the American people; operated by men of your choice, operated so that the financial district of a nation can no longer take advantage of the industrial or agricultural sections of the nation. This article of the bill sounds the death-knell of plutocratic exploitation and the beginning of democratic financial liberty.)

"Sec. 3 (b). The Secretary of the Treasury and the Comptroller of the Currency shall be ex-officio members of the Board of Governors of the Bank of the U.S.A.

"Sec. 3 (c). The members of the Federal Reserve Bank Board at the time of the passage of this Act, shall serve as members of the Board of Governors of the Bank of the U.S.A. until their successors are elected and qualify, as herein specified.

"Sec. 4 (a). The Board of Governors of the Bank of the U.S.A. is authorized to appoint and fix the compensation of such executive officers, examiners, economists and other experts as may be necessary to carry out its functions under this Act, without regard to provisions of other laws applicable to the employment and compensation of officers and employees of the United States; and, in addition thereto, the Board may, subject to the civil service laws, appoint such further officers and employees as in their judgment may be necessary, and fix their salaries in accordance with the Classification Act of 1923, as amended.

"(b). The Board of Directors of the Bank of the U.S.A. shall have its office in Washington, District of Columbia, but it shall establish branch offices in each State of the United States and in its Territories and possessions, and may establish branches and appoint agents elsewhere than in the United States as may be necessary or convenient for the purpose of this Act, and shall formulate policies and regulations for the management of the branch offices and agencies. Branch offices shall be designated by States, as New York Branch, Bank of the U.S.A., Illinois Branch, Bank of the U.S.A. and so forth.

"Sec. 5 (a). After the passage of this Act, all currency to be issued shall be United States Bank notes of similar form, size and denomination to the present Federal Reserve Bank notes or such other denominations as may be determined by the Board of Governors of the Bank of the U.S.A. which said Bank notes shall be in all respects the obligations of the United States and shall be full legal tender at face value for all debts and dues, public and private.

"(b). Within one year from the passage of this Act, all present Federal Reserve notes, Federal Reserve Bank notes, National Bank notes, gold certificates, silver certificates, treasury notes of 1890, and United States notes issued and outstanding, shall be recalled, and those turned in for redemption shall be retired and destroyed, and the United States Bank notes herein provided shall be issued in exchange, it being the purpose of this law to substitute the United States Bank notes herein provided for all other forms of paper currency of the United States.

"Sec. 6. In the exercise of its jurisdiction as agent of the Congress of the United States to issue money and to control the value thereof, the Executive Board of the Bank of the U.S.A. may from time to time order and direct the Treasurer of the United States to engrave or cause to be engraved, and to print or cause to be printed, United States Bank notes as provided in this Act, in such quantities and denominations as the said Board may deem necessary, and to hold the said United States Bank notes subject to further order of the said Board.

"Sec. 7. Upon receipt of directions or instructions or orders from the Executive Board, duly authenticated in such manner as may be prescribed by the Board of Directors, the Treasurer of the United States shall execute the said directions, instructions, or orders forthwith, by engraving, printing and disposing of the United States Bank notes as specified in said duly authenticated directions, instructions, or orders, and the said duly authenticated directions, instructions, or orders, shall at all times be considered and construed to be the direct acts of the Congress of the United States, through its duly authorized agent, the Bank of the U.S.A.

"Sec. 8 (a). Immediately upon the passage of this Act, the Bank of the U.S.A. is hereby authorized and directed forthwith to purchase the capital stock of the twelve Federal Reserve banks and branches, and agencies thereof, and to pay to the owners thereof in the United States Bank notes, as hereinafter provided, the paid-in value of said stock with all lawful increments to the date of purchase.

"(b). All member banks of the Federal Reserve System are hereby required and directed to deliver forthwith to the Bank of the U.S.A. all the stock of the said Federal Reserve Banks owned or controlled by them, together with any and all claims of any kind or nature in and to the capital assets of the said Federal Reserve Banks, it being the intention of this Act to vest in the Government of the United States the absolute and unconditional ownership of the said Federal Reserve banks."

(This section just read provides for the termination of the privately owned Federal Reserve Banks, their present owners to be paid for their holdings at par in United States money.)

"Sec. 9. Immediately upon the purchase of the stock of any Federal Reserve bank by the Bank of the U.S.A. as herein provided, the said Federal Reserve bank shall immediately become a branch of the Bank of the U.S.A. and subject in every respect to the jurisdiction of the Board of Directors of the Bank of the U.S.A. herein provided for, and the terms of the officers of the Board of Governors of the said Federal Reserve Bank shall immediately cease and terminate; provided, however, that the Chairman of the Board of Governors of the said Federal Reserve bank and all the executive officers or employees, shall continue to perform their customary duties and obligations in the operation of said Federal Reserve bank until their successors shall be appointed by the elected Board of Directors of the Bank of the U.S.A.

"Sec. 10 (a). All individuals, firms, associations, or corporations engaged in the business of banking as defined by law and among other things receiving deposits of money or credit from the citizens or firms, corporations, or associations of any State and transferring or transporting said money or credit or the title thereto to other banks or individuals, firms, associations, or corporations of any other State or States or Territories of the United States, are hereby declared to be engaged in interstate commerce, and as such are subject to Federal jurisdiction and to the jurisdiction of the Bank of the U.S.A. and all the provisions of this Act."

(This brings to a close a tragic chapter in American finance: Hitherto private banks like the J. P. Morgan & Company were more or less independent of Federal authority. Henceforth, in all their financial dealings these private banks will fall under the jurisdiction of our central government owned bank.)

"(b). Within one year after the passage of this Act, all banking institutions under the jurisdiction of the Bank of the U.S.A. shall be required to keep on deposit with the Bank of the U.S.A., United States Bank notes herein provided for ten percentum of its deposits which are subject to check and payable on demand, and shall be required to keep on hand and in its vaults an additional twenty percentum of its deposits subject to check and on demand; and, in addition thereto, it shall keep within its vaults the further sum equal to five percentum upon all savings or investment deposits commonly known as 'time' deposits.

"(c). Each year after the passage of this Act the Board of Directors of the Bank of the United States shall raise the percentage of reserves behind the demand deposits of all banks under its jurisdiction to a point deemed practical; provided that gradually and reasonably in the course of years the total reserves shall equal one hundred percent of all demand deposits."

(Formerly, when you deposited money in a demand account, you did not know whether or not you would receive it on demand. This section of the bill provides that after a reasonable number of years banks must retain demand deposits up to 100 per cent of their value.)

"(d). For the purpose of creating the lawful money reserve hereinabove required, the Bank of the U.S.A. shall purchase from banks, and from individuals in the United States, bonds of the United States Government.

"Sec. 11. The Bank of the United States shall purchase or sell gold, silver, foreign exchange instrumentalities, or the obligations of foreign governments, in the financial markets of the United States, at such times and in such quantities as in its discretion may appear to be necessary to carry out the purposes of this Act, namely, to regulate the value of money of the United States and of foreign nations."

✝(Formerly the regulation of our money was conducted either directly or indirectly by the Federal Reserve Bank that was privately owned. At the present moment there is the tendency for the Chief Executive of the nation to be made the dictator of finance in the nation. Both the former private control and the present tendency of dictatorial control are hereby abrogated by your electing the board of directors who will be the sole judges in this entire matter.)

"Sec. 12 (a). The Bank of the U.S.A. shall have jurisdiction over and shall control and supervise all banking institutions whatsoever of the United States and Territories thereof and possessions, subject to law, and shall have the power to prescribe such rules and regulations not inconsistent with the law as it may deem desirable for the safe and proper conduct of the banks and banking institutions within its jurisdiction.

"(b). The Comptroller of the Currency and all officers of the Government of the United States, exercising any supervisory powers or duties over the banks of the United States, or any of them, shall carry out and perform such rules and regulations for the conduct of banks and banking institutions in the United States or Territories thereof or possessions as may, from time to time, be prescribed by the Bank of the U.S.A. through its duly designated officers.

"Sec. 13. Directly upon the passage of this Act, the Bureau of Labor Statistics of the Department of Labor shall be transferred to the Bank of the U.S.A., and such bureau shall thereafter be under the supervision of the Board of Directors of the Bank of the U.S.A. The Statistical department of the present Federal Reserve Board, together with the Statistical department of the Comptroller of the Currency, and together with the Statistical department of the Secretary of the Treasury and of the Treasurer of the United States, shall all be consolidated with the Bureau of Labor Statistics, and the name of the consolidated bureau and departments shall be the Bureau of United States Statistics. The duties of said Bureau, in addition to all those now prescribed by law, shall be to collect, assemble and analyze authentic data, for the purpose of determining the true and correct relation of the total amount of money in actual criculation, including both currency and credit money commonly called demand deposits, to prices, wages, industry and commerce, the standard of living, employment and unemployment, to the end that the Board of Directors of the Bank of the U.S.A. and the Executive Board thereof may scientifically and accurately determine the rate at which progressive additions to the stock of circulating money, both currency and credit, must be made to maintain an even and stable purchasing power, and to promote a constantly rising standard of living for the people of this nation, unlimited except by the extent of natural resources and the willingness of the people to work."

(You realize, my fellow members of the National Union, that correct and scientific statistics can be obtained by this United States Bureau. It will tell us definitely how many bushels of wheat are grown, how many acres of land under cultivation, how many men employed, how many pairs of shoes manufactured, how much money in circulation—a million and more facts from which it will not be difficult to ascertain how many dollars of currency should be in circulation as well as how much credit should be issued. This Bureau will know also how many pennies are in a dollar at any given time.

(Through this agency the Board of Directors of our Central Banks will be able to keep 100 cents in the dollar. Through this agency it will be possible to keep money as our servant and prevent its becoming our master.

(Through this agency our nation, its natural resources, its factories and farms and fields and mines will be recognized together with our labor and science as the real wealth. Through this agency we will be enabled to distribute this wealth and to rise to higher standards of living.

(Heretofore the facts and data supplied by the Bureau were disregarded by the privately owned Central Banks which regarded money as wealth and the making of more money as its chief objective.)

"Sec. 14. It shall be mandatory upon the Board of Directors of the Bank of the U.S.A. and the Executive Board thereof to provide such stable purchasing power of money and such equitable price levels, first, by the progressive purchase of the bonds of the United States and the building of the reserves behind demand deposits, and further, if necessary, by increasing the money in circulation by paying the extraordinary and then the ordinary expenses of government by currency issue until the average commodity price level reaches the index of the Bureau of Labor Statistics for 1926 and until the Board of Directors of the Bank of the U.S.A. may determine a true and equitable price level to succeed that of 1926, which price level should be not less than to enable agriculture to operate at a reasonable profit."

(For years we have justly complained about the impractical and asinine foolishness of trying to borrow ourselves out of debt with bankers' bonds and of forcing agriculture and labor and small industry to operate at a loss because of dishonest dollars. To correct this error, this section of the bill just read provides that the Central Bank is empowered to do three things:

(1) Purchase United States Bonds from those now holding them.

(2) Purchase mortgages and secured notes from financial institutions holding them.

(3) To print and issue, if necessary, additional currency and to circulate it by paying it to the laborers and civil servants engaged in government works.

(These three powers are to be employed in the order mentioned to maintain the average price of iron, lumber, butter, meat, coffee and other commodities at the price level where a profit can be gained. As prices sink below this level, then the bonds will be retired and more currency put in circulation in order to raise prices to a controlled profitable level. The bondholders will be paid off in legal tender currency to which no interest-bearing coupon is attached. No longer will it be economically necessary for a person who borrowed 100 bushels of wheat to satisfy his creditor with 200 bushels of wheat.)

"Sec. 15. The Board of Directors of the Bank of the United States shall recommend to Congress the retirement through taxation of such excesses of currency as may be necessary.

"Sec. 16. All laws or parts of laws in conflict with this Act are hereby repealed.

"Sec. 17. If any provision of this Act or the application of such provision to any person or circumstance shall be held invalid, the remainder of this Act or the application of such provisions to persons or circumstances other than those as to which it is held invalid shall not be affected thereby.

"Sec. 18. This Act shall take effect July 1st, 1935, or sooner by proclamation of the President.

"Sec. 19. This Act may be cited as the BANKING AND MONETARY CONTROL ACT OF 1935."

The bill which I have read to you, my friends, is entirely within the scope of your understanding. Despite many warnings which I have received to refrain from attempting to read and explain it because it was said that the American people are too dense to comprehend such language, I have disregarded such an insulting appreciation of your ability. I know better than my critics realize that the silken veil of deceitful mystery has been torn from the ugly face of banking. I know from thousands upon thousands of your letters that you fully understand that a banker manufactures money through the agency of a fountain pen. You well understand that this credit of check book money is loaned to the borrower and that the borrower is expected to repay the legalized counterfeiter with currency money which does not exist. You well appreciate that this check book money controlled by the bankers has been substituted for our national currency to such an

174

extent that at least 90 per cent of all business is transacted with it. You are not ignorant that you, the taxpayers, through your Federal Government have been borrowing this fiction of money at interest to feed the poor, to stabilize the bread lines, to borrow ourselves out of debt in an emergency which was profitable for the bankers who always loaned ten times more than they possessed. You will never forget what happened to so-called demand deposits which, when the veil of secrecy was lifted, proved to be nothing more than loans which you had made to the bankers— loans which millions of depositors are still seeking to regain. This knowledge can never be taken from you despite every effort being made today to gloss over these facts and persuade you to support a system of finance which more than all things else is responsible for the plight in which our nation finds itself. You know that no matter how virtuous the bankers may be in their personal lives, modern banking must necessarily be vicious because it is conceived upon an immoral principle of exploitation. These facts were hidden from you before and yet were known by our Federal Administration which evidently did not have the courage to restore to you your constitutional right of coining and regulating your own money but which preferred to lean towards the radical expedient of sovietizing industry.

Thus, I present to you a constitutional bill which I am asking you to support with all your courage, your virility, your determination. If this fails, so do we all—except the bankers. If this program for social justice fails, then the program of the radicals will succeed, monopoly will rule, small businessmen will be eliminated from the field of competition, labor and agriculture will be left to the tender mercies of cold blooded finance which will march on its unmolested way to continue its policies of concentrating wealth in the hands of a few at the expense of the exploited masses, who eventually will be forced to rise in revolution. Need I encourage you to support this bill? Need I warn you to stand by fully prepared to act at the critical moment?

## II

Last Sunday I unfolded to you the existence and the nature of certain Federal Government Delaware Corporations so stinking of sovietism that they were buried in the cellar of secrecy.

Today I shall tell you of another government document which has been suppressed and which bears directly on the continuation of the depression.

On October 29th, 1934, the United States Bureau of Census released a mimeographed report known as the "Credit Requirements of Small Industry for Recovery."

Now by "Small Industries" I mean those concerns which employ between 21 and 250 wage earners each. It is astounding to

175

realize that these represent 97 per cent of all our industries; that they employ 48.1 per cent of all the wage earners of this nation.

In other words, small industry, so described, is the backbone of our nation's prosperity. The 3 per cent of the remaining industries are mostly banker-controlled and secure the necessary funds to operate by the sale of stocks and securities.

Now the facts pertaining to the point in question are the following:

(1) On November 10, 1934, Mr. Roper's United States Department of Commerce released officially this report on "Small Industry" to which I just referred.

(2) According to the report these small industries were almost totally paralyzed because from no source—not from the bankers, not from the government's agents—could they borrow money with which to operate.

(3) Here are the direct words of the report:
"In many cases the urgency of immediate credit aid is so great that some firms with large, unfilled orders already on hand face complete shutdown of their plants with consequent unemployment and bankruptcy.

"Their criticisms are leveled against the sudden changes in bank policy, the attitude of bank examiners, the failure of the Federal Reserve system to meet the situation, and the utter collapse of the Reconstruction Finance Corporation as a means of direct aid to industry.

"They contend that the mania for liquidity on the part of the many bankers, and fostered by federal bank examiners, is largely responsible for the failure of other heroic efforts on the part of the present administration to bring prosperity out of chaos."

(4) Now this was and still is political dynamite. The small industrialists of the nation are fully conscious that both the banks and the government have deserted them. On the other hand, the government, fully realizing that the publication of this report would cause unfavorable repercussions, simply smothered it. The 16,000 men, all owners or representatives of small industry, who made this report knew more about practical economies than did all the soviet-minded theorists or self-confessed economists put together. Was this report suppressed because it was unscientific? This suppression was accomplished by John Dickinson, the Acting Secretary of the Department of Commerce, who said that the report was only a preliminary draft prepared by Doctor Beckman; that it represented nothing but the views of Doctor Beckman; that it was not an official publication nor that it represented the views either of the Department of Commerce or of the Bureau of Census. It did, however, represent the views of industry.

Every businessman and small industrialist in the nation fully appreciates that it is impossible to borrow money to any extent from the private bankers who, evidently in this case, were powerful enough to get this report suppressed, although it was issued, according to its front page, by the United States Department of Commerce and compiled by Doctor Theodore Beckman, chief economist in charge of research.

I make mention of this to indicate to the small industrialist and to the 48.1 per cent of the American laborers whom he normally employs that he is the victim of the present banking system and the lending agencies of the United States government—a government still wedded to the monstrosity which has stolen from the American people—the farmer, the laborer and the industrialist—their right to coin and regulate the value of money; a system that is so strong and mighty that it can and does suppress the known and published truth; a system that prefers to sovietize American industry rather than surrender its unconstitutional privilege of coining and regulating the nation's money!

In conclusion permit me to recall a traditional story which is found in the annals of ancient Scotland: This happened in the days of the real crusaders when kings and knights, artisans and farmers vowed to redeem the tomb of Christ which had fallen into the hands of the Saracens.

Let me recall this heroic incident because our America, in fact, practically the entire world, has fallen into the hands of the Saracens of greed—into the hands of the privileged counterfeiters whose system of finance more than all other causes has created want in the midst of plenty, has made idlers out of laborers, paupers out of farmers and has permitted the sovietization of America to make progress.

Bruce of Scotland and his Captain Robert are the heroes around whom the story is woven.

King Bruce, so we are told, assembled his soldiers and sailed with them to the coast of Spain. Eventually they arrived at the foothills of the olive-sandaled Pyrenees. To his consternation Bruce discovered that the Saracens held the mountain tops and guarded every pass. There seemed to be no possible strategy which could be employed for the Scottish leader to break through the ranks of the enemy. Undismayed, however, this brave soldier ordered his followers to advance. Amidst a shower of stones and arrows, amidst the clashing of battle axes and the moans of the wounded, the army of Bruce was repulsed and driven in disorder down the steep mountain paths!

Alas! Bruce himself was mortally wounded. Kneeling by his side was young Robert, the captain. To him the brave King whispered: "My boy, take out my heart and carry it with you—carry it to the tomb of Christ."

According to military tradition the corpse of Bruce was burned on a funeral pyre. But his heart was placed in a small, silver casket which Robert clasped close to his bosom. Meanwhile, the Scottish troops were re-assembled. Robert was now in command. With grim determination he ordered another attack to be launched against the Saracens. Up the hill he led his soldiers. Down came a new shower of arrows and stones and boulders. Once again the Scotsmen were about to turn in defeat when suddenly young Robert, taking the silver casket from his bosom and holding it high in view of his entire army, turned and plunged with it into the midst of the Saracen host. That heroic action electrified his troops. With one sudden onslaught they pushed aside the weapons of their enemies! They stormed the heights! They won the day!

My friends and fellow members in the National Union, the spirit of Bruce and of Robert must not perish!

I mean the spirit of liberty in America must not be overcome by the Saracens of greed and of destruction. Turn then, with me from the pages of Scottish history to those of America. Read the story of our founders who gave this nation its Constitution. The very heart of that document which bestows upon our delegated representatives the right to coin and regulate the value of money has passed into the ranks of the enemy who occupy the mountain tops of power, of prestige, of publicity, of wealth.

+Every effort in the past one hunderd years to rescue this right from their Saracen hands has been met by a shower of verbal arrows, by a barrage of lying propaganda which time after time has driven us back to the valleys of depression.

I ask you if either selfishness or carelessness will be the cause of your compromising with the enemy, or if, in the spirit of Bruce and Robert and their followers, you will follow liberty? Think of your children! Think of your country! Think of the possibility of its being sovietized!

I ask you if we will not reform our ranks, and move forward to recapture that heart of our Constitution which is so imperiled?

Today each member of the National Union is, as it were, another Robert, another captain in our army!

We have something worthwhile to fight for. Alone we are lost! Together we cannot fail!

# PROSPERITY AND TAXATION

*(Sunday, February 24, 1935)*

## I

FOUR weeks ago this afternoon I had occasion to address this audience on the "gold clause" case. At that time I maintained that Congress had the right to coin and regulate the value of money and that there is no unconstitutionality related to the exercise of that right if, at any time, Congress so decides to regulate the number of dollars contained in an ounce of gold or in a bushel of wheat. In other words, Congress can change the price of an ounce of gold from $20.67 to $35.00 or to as many dollars as it reasonably sees fit. In due time the Supreme Court rendered its decision, upholding the constitutional right of Congress. And in due time there arose a clamor of criticism which caustically condemned both the Congress and the Chief Executive for refusing to honor the gold clause which existed in many contracts. Because many of our public debts, such as Liberty Bonds, contained a clause that the holders thereof should receive at a given date either so many dollars or else so many ounces of gold, Americans, according to these critics, are now classified as prime defaulters because they refuse to pay the gold as stipulated despite their willingness and readiness to pay the dollars.

Now this afternoon I have a few passing remarks to address to you relative to these omniscient critics. But first, may I refresh your memories with a few pertinent facts on gold and on contracts.

1. For many years it was held as a matter of convenience and not of necessity that gold was worth $20.67.

2. Moreover, under capitalism it was generally believed, but erroneously, that gold was the basis of all money.

3. Because of the fluctuating value of currency dollars, creditors often arranged for debtors to pay them in gold which most people erroneously thought was of a fixed value.

This is simple. It is veiled by no mystery of ethics or of jurisprudence.

Now the fallacy at the bottom of the whole "gold clause" case happens to be twofold. First, it was erroneous to consider that gold, by nature or by capitalistic logic, had a fixed value. Supposing half of the gold of the world was lost, would not the law of supply enhance the value of the remaining gold? Or, supposing that a new Yukon, or California or South Africa development doubled or tripled the amount of gold in the world, would not that cheapen the price of gold in the world? These suppositions are not preposterous. As a matter of fact the amount of gold in the world was doubled about the beginning of our present century.

Morever, an ounce of gold was never in reality the "yardstick" of value as it was held. There is only one standard yardstick. All others are imitations. There are millions of ounces of gold, each an absolute duplicate of the other.

Second: The contracting parties who signed "gold clause" contracts should have realized that if gold is money, Congress has the constitutional right at any time to regulate its value. If it was not money, Congress has the constitutional right to declare how many dollars are contained in an ounce of gold.

Keeping these thoughts clearly in mind; keeping the related thought equally in mind that a creditor-debtor contract means to give back equal value for value received, let us approach the critics who are casting ignominy upon the American people as they classify us with the welshers of the world.

The chief critic happens to be Senator Carter Glass.

Senator Carter Glass is quoted in the Congressional Record of February 21st as saying: *"I wish to make one observation, and that is to express wonder at what our foreign debtors will think of the measure of our sincerity in reproaching them for repudiating their indebtedness to us when the Congress itself has repudiated the most sacred indebtedness that any nation on earth ever incurred—the indebtedness which was incurred with which to fight the last World War."*

This is the same eloquent Senator who assumes the responsibility for conceiving the Federal Reserve Bank Act by which coinage and regulation of money were handed to Paul Warburg and to his successors and cooperators whom we classify as international bankers.

This is the same Carter Glass who, believing in the propaganda paid for by the $900-million World Court slush fund of the Rockefellers, of the Carnegies and of a dozen or more minor contributors, voted to sell America short by identifying our interests directly with the World Court and indirectly with the League of Nations.

This is the widely advertised philosopher of finance, Carter Glass, who through some secret process of induction, is certain that the world depression, its poverty in the midst of plenty, is in nowise related to the breakdown of the financial dogmas which he places on a par with the most sacred obligations in life.

Now he insinuates that we should hang our heads in shame

for even approaching the European debtors who have repudiated their financial obligations because Congress itself *"has repudiated,"* so he says, *"the most sacred indebtedness which any nation on earth ever incurred."*

These are his words. They are not mine.

These words prove what we have long suspected. Carter Glass is the champion exponent of financial gymnastics. His logic simply annihilates us as, like the man on the flying trapeze, he moves through his arguments with the greatest of ease.

England, France, Russia—every foreign nation is hereby indirectly justified in repudiating their total indebtedness to us because the American citizens refuse to pay 169 pennies on every dollar which the gold clause bondholders were demanding!

As a matter of fact, my friends, we are willing to pay not only what is just and equitable. More than that, we are willing to pay 127 pennies on every dollar which, by the way, is the actual purchasing power of the American dollar today. Carter Glass should apologize to the American public.

Do not be misled by the slanderous attacks against Congress and therefore against the American people which have been trumped up in reference to the gold clause decision. The simple truth is this: Debtors contracted to pay creditors either in so many dollars or in so many ounces of gold valuated at $20.67 an ounce, this to be left to the discretion of the creditor. This gold clause was inserted in all contracts simply to guarantee the creditor that he would obtain equal value for what he loaned. If gold had not been revaluated, and if our dollars had a 200 penny purchasing power, every European bondholder would have chosen dollars in preference to gold. Congress has not violated our contract. It did not repudiate our debts.

Moreover, the entire world recognizes that gold is now at least $35.00 an ounce. We are willing to pay in dollars which are backed by gold worth $35.00 an ounce. That is more than England can do; more than France or Germany or Russia or the rest of them can do.

In the future when Senator Carter Glass swings with the greatest of ease through the arguments of his esoteric financialism, you will be able to appreciate his dazzling speed and startling conclusions if you follow him through the binoculars of this conclusion, namely, *"England, France and the foreign nations are therefore not to be censored because they have repudiated their debts in their entirety."*

Once more I shall measure for you his gigantic dimensions by reading his recorded confession:

*"I wish to make one observation, and that is to express wonder at what our foreign debtors will think of the measure of our sincerity in reproaching them for repudiating their indebtedness to us when the Congress itself has repudiated the most sacred indebtedness that any nation on earth ever incurred."*

By the way, I almost overlooked mentioning that when Senator Joseph Robinson exhausted his ability in trying to persuade Congress to legislate a slave wage instead of a living wage for those about to be employed on the Public Works Activities, it was Carter Glass who rescued the torch of serfdom from the falling hands of the Democratic leader. It was he who tried to persuade the United States Senate to pay these future government laborers less than the prevailing wage, less than a living wage. This doughty representative of Wall Street, while so eloquently defending the financial rights of the bondholders, with equal logic and equal vehemence repudiated the rights, the human rights, of the laborers. President Roosevelt, Joseph Robinson and Carter Glass upheld that the wages paid to public contractors and professional men should be according to the prevailing NRA code. But the public workmen on PWA should be treated like scavengers. Oh, yes! Let the government pay the prevailing price for the bag of cement, but for the sweat that drips upon it from the laborer's brow, pay for that with the blood-dripping dollars of discontent!

Fortunately for the Democratic Party, if it can ever survive this Administration's onslaught against the laboring people of this nation, it will thank Senator McCarran of Nevada who successfully cushioned this crude blow by humanely amending it to pay the public works laborers a minimum living wage. His amendment, however, will be defeated.

I tell you these things, my friends, because Carter Glass will be our chief opponent as we struggle to rescue the right for Congress to coin and regulate the value of money—Carter Glass whose gymnastic brain claims to have conceived the Federal Reserve Bank Act as it is, Carter Glass, the World Courter and internationalist, Carter Glass, the pro-repudiationist in behalf of foreign nations, Carter Glass, the advocate of slave wages for the laborer, Carter Glass the man on the flying trapeze!

The nation seems to be seriously upset over the allocation of approximately $5-billion for a public works program. At the present moment the United States Senate has not committed itself either for or against this program. It has simply gone on record that if and when this money is turned over to the President it will not be spent through the agency of a Delaware Corporation.

Every person who is acquainted with the real problem behind unemployment readily realizes that it is almost impossible for industry, which is privately owned, to assimilate the ten or eleven million idle laborers in this nation. We have been singularly blessed by God with the inventions of our scientists. It seems that the primeval curse placed upon man is gradually being lifted through the fatherly solicitude of a benevolent Creator. In other words, the age of want and of necessary privation has passed. The age of plenty with its needless privation is present.

It is evident to any observer who is willing to be honest with himself as well as with his fellowmen that, after all, money is not real wealth. Real wealth is identified with our bounteous farms and fields, with our far-flung forests, with the silver and gold and copper and tin and zinc hidden in the bowels of the earth. More than that, our real wealth is identified with our dwellings and institutions of learning, with our hospitals and churches, our paved roads and tumbling streams and rushing rapids which carry the waters of the mighty rivers to the oceans where our fishermen practice their calling. If these things, then, be the real wealth; if money be nothing more than the receipt for wealth which either actually exists or is morally certain of existing, why in the name of God, Who has blessed us so abundantly, do we hesitate and stammer and stutter over five billion or ten billion or fifteen billion dollars to be used in a permanent public works program for the actual creation of almost illimitable wealth?

Have we not the muscle, the virility and the perseverance resident within the body and soul of the finest group of laboring men within all this world? Have we not the engineering and scientific ability to plot and plan and chart this dream of today which by tomorrow will become a veritable reality for our children and their children?

Have we not the confidence in the co-operation of God Whose only motive in giving us this vast resource of raw material was that we should use it to praise Him and to make this world a better habitation for our brothers in Christ?

Why do we hesitate? The answer is simple. It is because we still believe in the worship of the golden calf. It is because we still believe in permitting the ownership and the control of money to be held captive in the hands of a small group of profit-loving, greedy-minded men.

Why are slums still permitted to house our fellow citizens? Why are the rushing rapids of the St. Lawrence hourly wasting their millions of gallons of water power? Is it because, once we have turned our backs on the past and have faced the rising sun of a new day, we cannot stand the golden glare of its blessed light in our eyes; we cannot move ahead with a song in our hearts and a prayer on our lips, conscious that the new deal will not fail if there is but confidence in our fellowmen and confidence in God?

My fellow citizens, there is not a Senator who would hesitate a moment to set aside an ample fund of United States money for the purpose of erecting a permanent public works program. But if we persist in attempting to borrow ourselves out of debt with bankers' bonds, I prophesy that the new deal will crash and will deserve to crash; the new hopes will be dissipated; the new leaders will become lost leaders and the new day will be either postponed or perverted into a red day.

At this moment those who have dedicated their lives to the philosophy of bankers' loans have sent their ambassadors to Warm Springs to excogitate some plan for the perpetuation of a dole and the continuation of the bankers' bond racket. But, if heed be taken of them, if deaf ears are turned to the voice of an awakened people, rest assured that it becomes a most critical and unfortunate situation.

Our people are not paupers and they do not plan to remain paupers. Our people want no dole. We want honest work where we become part of those factors which mingle in the production of wealth. We want a just and living annual wage based upon our national abundance, our national leadership and our nationally owned and controlled money.

With these thoughts in mind there is no need to appeal either to the people or to the Senate for the institution of a program of permanent public works and for the allocation of a niggardly $5-billion. But without these thoughts in mind $5-billion of bankers' money, which over a period of twenty years mean $10-billion of currency or of assets to be returned to them, is becoming an unthinkable and unbearable proposition.

Blame not the Senate if they debate upon this allocation of money. The thought which is troubling their hearts is what kind of money shall be used. Shall it be the kind of money that casts us deeper, together with our children, into the chasm of debt and death or shall it be the kind of money which, like a guardian angel, will lift us aloft upon its wings to newer heights, to newer conquests, to undreamed of prosperity?

There can be no prosperity forthcoming until the immoral mania of borrowing this nation out of debt with bankers' bonds is destroyed. There can be no prosperity until Congress recaptures its right to coin and regulate the value of money. There can be no prosperity until our national credit is predicated upon our national wealth!

## II

Today I plan to speak to you on the thirteenth point of our program for social justice. It reads as follows: *"I believe in the broadening of the base of taxation founded upon the ownership of wealth and the capacity to pay."*

It is both impossible and impractical to discuss the whole tax situation. I am content to confine my remarks chiefly to one phase of taxation, namely, to the taxation of the bigness of industry. When approaching this subject, therefore, I emphasize the bigness of industry. Thus, I desire that my remarks be interpreted in the light of an effort to save small industry, to protect to a degree the medium size industry and to eliminate the danger of America's becoming a nation where all industrial wealth will be concentrated in the hands of a very definite minority.

As I remarked last Sunday, 97 per cent of the industrial activities of America are conducted by small industries. Nevertheless, the remaining 3 per cent which represents big industry, commonly so-called, employs 51.9 per cent of all labor engaged in industrial pursuits. Thus, it is evident that the development of mass production has had a tendency not only to eliminate labor but a corresponding tendency to eliminate small industry and thus concentrate all industrial activities in fewer hands. It is not necessary at the moment to cite arithmetical facts when every person is aware that the motor industry, which a few years ago was widely distributed among many corporations, is now concentrated among six or seven corporations. The same process tending towards monopolization of industry has manifested itself in the textile industry, in the steel industry, in practically every mass producing industry in our nation.

These are preliminary statements to define, if possible, the one single phase of taxation with which I am concerned this afternoon. As I approach the subject I wish to acknowledge that I am deeply indebted to Senator Burton K. Wheeler of Montana who has compiled valuable information on this topic and whose illuminating address before the Senate last week has opened the door for wide discussion.

His remarks evidenced that, while we have had various laws enacted to prevent the monopolization of industry, nevertheless, every law contained some loophole and thus proved to be inefficient at stopping the steady growth of big industry. The small industrialist has been bought out or has been destroyed by questionable competition. The big industrialist has been nursed along by his banker associates. The small industrialist in these depression days has been denied both governmental and banking loans. The big industrialist has been the recipient of ample loans because of his intimate relation with Wall Street. The small industrialist was forced, because of his financial stringency, to discharge his millions of laborers. The big industrialist, generally smiling at the innocuous requirements of the NRA, either cheated on living up to the code statutes or proceeded to step up production and thus, indirectly, evade the letter of the law. This meant that in reality his profits increased at the expense of the laborer's pay envelope.

✛All these things I have specifically stated on former occasions when I presented accurate, official facts to bear out these conclusions. All our previous legislative efforts to correct these abuses either through The Sherman Anti-Trust laws, which forbade monopolies, or the NRA which attempted to regulate industry, or the RFC which proposed to lend money to small industry have proven abortive and more or less idealistic.

We are faced, therefore, with the problem of still preserving small industry and of preventing the future formation of more monopolies if we are really desirous of keeping our laborers employed. We are faced with the problem of destroying monopolies for the preservation of our national security. We are faced with the problem of divorcing industry from finance in the sense that a banker should be a banker and not the controller of a motor industry.

The solution of these problems is related to taxation.

But I have not fairly sketched the entire picture of big industry as I approach the proposition of taxing it into submission. It is only fair to explain that big industry properly so-called is ordinarily owned by a vast group of stockholders. For example there are approximately 300,000 owners of the General Motors Corporation. It is equally fair to mention, however, that one family—the duPonts—practically own 23 per cent of that entire stock and thereby acquire 23 per cent of the $96-million profits gained by that Corporation last year.

It is also fair to recognize that when I propose to tax this and similar giant corporations into submission I am necessarily including the much talked of "widow and orphan" who hold perhaps one or two or three shares of stock. But for the preservation of the other widows and orphans and laborers who have been innocently victimized by the growth and establishment of mammoth monopolies, it is in harmony with the tenets of social justice that the welfare of the majority must be preferred to that of the small minority when there is a necessity to choose between them.

Nor is it fair to include all big industry under the classification of the big industries which we propose to tax into submission. Necessarily some public utilities such as the American Telegraph and Telephone must be big or they cannot exist. While these industries can be controlled as to their activities and profits, nevertheless, the size of our nation, the density of its population and the nature of the service rendered necessitate that a national telegraph company be large if it exists at all. However, lest I be misinterpreted, I am neither affirming nor denying the right of the government to build, own and operate public utilities to compete with those which are privately owned.

With this clarifying preface I think you understand the preliminaries of our specific tax question.

The National Union, therefore, is ready to support legislation which will institute a system of taxation based upon the ownership of wealth and capacity to pay. That is its general principle. The application of this principle for practical purposes impels us to support legislation which will tax monopolistic industries into submission for this twofold purpose; first, to acquire tax money for the maintenance of government; and second, to provide fair competition and thus protect small industry from being forced out of business.

To my mind, therefore, there is no necessity for defining big industry at the present moment in terms other than which I have pictured it. Our position is sufficiently stated in the present manner in this one sentence: *"There should be a graduated tax imposed upon industrial profits."* For example the United States Steel Corporation practically monopolizes 50 per cent of the steel industry. Their stockholders' profits are immense in the aggregate. Thus I suggest a tax of 2 per cent upon their first million dollars annual profit, 3 per cent upon the second million, 4 per cent on the third and so forth up to a given point. When ten million dollars profits had accrued I would levy against it a profit-tax so large that it would not be profitable for the United States Steel to operate much beyond that point.

Of course this taxation levied against the bigness of business means the decentralization of monopolistic industry. It is a step towards preserving small industry. It is a theory of taxation which is predicated upon the necessity of securing employment for our idle engineers, for millions of our idle laborers. It is a theory which aims towards preserving honest competition.

It is a theory which I willingly submit to public criticism both constructive and destructive because I am firmly convinced that we must tax monopolies into submission if we wish to approach sanely the problem of preserving private ownership.

Before proceeding further let us pause to consider passingly the statement which I just made about preserving private ownership.

It is only a mad man who endeavors to deceive himself or others with the belief that wealth is not concentrated in the hands of a few. A multitude of facts—both arithmetical and human facts—have proven indisputably the opposite. Wealth itself is becoming monopolized. The opportunity to work at a living and profitable annual wage has not been afforded to the masses of our people simply because the problem of supplying that opportunity has been artfully dodged or purposely avoided. The evils of capitalism have been religiously suckled at the breasts of greed. Bond issue has followed bond issue with a forlorn presumption that this is the way out of our financial difficulties. Less currency money, believe it or not, is in circulation today than when Mr. Roosevelt went into office. Less credit money was loaned to industry this year, believe it or not, than was loaned last year. The confiscation of farms and homes still continues. Annual wages are far below the standard of living. Taxes are becoming more and more an unbearable burden.

And what are the facts of industrial ownership itself?

In 1930 there were over 300,000 non-financial corporations in the United States with assets of approximately $165-billion. Of these 300,000 corporations the 200 largest including 42 railroads, 52 public utilities and 106 industrials had assets of over $81-billion. Now here is the point: These 200 corporations representing less than 7/100 of 1 per cent of the number of all American non-financial corporations controlled practically half of the corporate wealth of the nation.

When you consider that 78 per cent of all American business wealth is corporate wealth it is estimated that these 200 corporations control more than 38 per cent of all the business wealth of this nation. And when you consider that the national wealth, as distinguished from the corporate wealth and business wealth, is on an average, estimated to be $367-billion, then these 200 corporations control 22 per cent of the national wealth. As astounding as these figures are, they are correct.

For a moment regard the rapid rate at which the concentration of industrial power is increasing. If in the next 20 years the monopoly of industrial power and industrial wealth increases in the same proportion as it increased between 1909 and 1929 then we are forced to conclude that by the year 1950, unless salutary laws are introduced in the meantime, 70 per cent of all the corporate industrial activities in the nation will be carried on by 200 concerns. By that year they will possess half the national wealth and by 1970 they will own all industrial activity and practically all the national wealth. In other words, the children seated by your side at the radio will be forced to live in a state of industrial feudalism unless this monopolistic tendency is checked through a process of taxation. This conclusion is certain provided the facts of the past 20 years are accepted as truths. This conclusion forces us to accept the thesis that wealth is gradually being monopolized and that this monopolization can be stemmed only through profit-taxation.

From the foregoing arguments the National Union, firmly believing that private property should be maintained and that private ownership should be protected, is opposed to this concentration of power and of wealth because it is hostile to social justice. Whether or not the monopolistic industrialists are aware of it they are actively, decisively preparing the way for the nationalization of all industry. They are the bakers who are mixing the cake. The communist will eat it for them!

To multiply private ownership and not impede it; to protect small industry and not assimilate it—these are sensible, socially just and American methods of eliminating the causes which produce communistic effects.

Thus I offer to you one phase of the plan to institute a system of taxation based on the theory of one's capacity to pay; based on the theory of taxing the excessive wealth-profits; based on the theory of so taxing huge monopolistic industries into submission that the smaller industries will have an opportunity to breathe, to survive and to operate.

I fully recognize the existence of so-called income taxes and other forms of taxation directly effecting profits. But this present suggestion which I propose is intended to aim beyond all these forms of taxation and directly to attack the profits of the corporation in question for the purposes which I previously mentioned.

By no means is this a complete exposition of the theory of taxing monopolies into submission. For example I have barely suggested that some monopolistic industries are banker-controlled to such a degree that they are operated primarily for satisfying the profit making instinct of the banker. I have not spoken either of the loss or gain in national efficiency should monopolistic industries be taxed to a point where it was no longer profitable to expand. I have not even intimated the dangers to labor resultant from ill-managed monopolistic industries. There are many important questions either so directly or indirectly related to the existence of monopolies that they deserve specific examination.

As there are a few minutes still remaining, permit me to discuss briefly some of their salient points.

At one time there appeared a statement in the authentic records of our Federal Government to the effect that the J. P. Morgan and Company controlled, either directly or indirectly, approximately $40-billion of business—motor corporations, steel industries, banks, insurance companies and so forth. I am citing this to give you the glaring example of banker controlled industry.

Speaking of the United States Steel Corporation—a Morgan controlled interest—Senator Shipstead informs us that this steel corporation purchased several other plants. Eventually they bought out their largest competitor, the Carnegie Steel Corporation. Previous to the time of sale, the Carnegie Steel Corporation manufactured rails for approximately $21.00 a ton. But after the United States Steel Corporation purchased this institution the price of steel rails was immediately raised to $28.00 a ton. The increased cost of production, so the Senator informs us, caused an increased capitalism. If they had an honest capitalization, Mr. Shipstead affirms that they could produce steel rails as cheaply now as did Andrew Carnegie. The pertinent point which everyone understands is that when the competitor was out of the way the price of the product was raised. Does this not suggest that banker controlled monopolies are primarily interested in profits?

Relative to the efficiency boasted of by giant corporations, Senator Wheeler opens for us the pages of the judicial record in the dissolution suit against the United States Steel. This court record shows that the smaller independent competitors were just as technically efficient as that mammoth monopoly. This bubble about giant corporate efficiency again is punctured according to the Senator by a fact finding survey made by a Mr. F. A. Fetter, one-time president of the American Economic Association. ("The Masquerade of Monopoly" is the name of the book to which I refer.)

Mr. Justice Brandeis of the Supreme Court is quoted on that same subject as follows:

"(a)   No American Trust owes its existence to the desire for increasing efficiency.

"(b)   No profitable trust owes its profits to superior efficiency.

"(c)   No trust is efficient enough to maintain its proportion of business without buying up successful competitors.

"(d)   No trust except an absolute monopoly can show comparable efficiency to independents."

Finally, after these devastating remarks relative to the so-called efficiency of big business, Senator Wheeler informs us that giant monopolies, which are desirous of making profits primarily, so own and control the patents for devices which permit progress that they purposely suppress these patents rather than risk the expense of fashioning new tools or destroying old patterns and dies.

As for the proximate and ultimate injury done to the laborer by giant corporation mistakes in policy and in technical decision, there is plenty of evidence. We who live in the midst of the motor industry are well acquainted with this misfortune.

One motor manufacturer postponed beyond good judgment the changing of a certain model design. Practically 90,000 laborers were thrown out of work for weeks due to this error.

But I chance to be more interested in another phase of this giant corporation activity. It is manifested in the case of Mr.

Henry Ford. Whether or not you agree with his industrial policies is beside the point at this moment. The fact is he is considered to be the greatest genius in the entire motor industry. He thoroughly understands the mechanics of his motor product. He lives with the car constantly developing in his sub-conscious brain. His talent for business and corporation management is supreme. But the question in Detroit today is similar to the question in Italy: *"After Mussolini, what? After Henry Ford, what?"*

We sincerely doubt if another brain or group of brains can sustain this gigantic octupus of the Ford Motor Corporation once Henry Ford passes out of the picture.

Here then, if this doubt is valid, is a real argument against giant industries. Can 100,000 laborers rest secure, even in prosperous times, so dependent upon the health, the life, the wizardy of this one individual? Is it not more conservative, more prudent, to tax into submission such giant corporations and thus multiply other industries by dividing the giant into parts, thereby eliminating at least in part, the contingency of shut-downs due to single judgment-error?

I have not referred to many other phases of taxation as interpreted by social justice. Our principles are definitely related to the taxation of wealth and to taxation according to one's capacity to pay.

To complete our picture, at least in outline, social justice is not satisfied with the mere taxing of corporation profits. Capital wealth should not go untaxed, whether it is the capital wealth of a corporation or of an individual; whether it is idle capital wealth or invested capital wealth.

I mean that if, as an individual, I own 1-million dollars of securities—bonds, stocks, real estate, diamonds—wealth that is both tangible and intangible—I should certainly pay a tax on all of it at its present value. In this connection, our wealth tax is certainly halting and inefficient. Social justice would likewise graduate this tax, practically eliminating the first five thousand dollars worth of an individual's wealth from any Federal tax or State tax and then gradually progressing until the man whose wealth is estimated at one or two or three or four or five million dollars is obliged to pay an increasingly higher rate of taxation —so high that when the $10-million mark has been reached, he is subjected to a tax which renders it impossible for him, even through his investments, to proceed further in amassing wealth.

Certainly there must be something radically erroneous with our modern system of taxation which permits any individual to amass 100 or 200 or even 1000-million dollars worth of material wealth.

There is something iniquitous with such a haphazard system which permits monopolization of industry and the concentration of wealth in the hands of a few!

Almighty God did not make us equal as the communist preaches when he deigns to speak of God. But on the other hand God did not make us so unequal that such a tremendous distance must separate the paupers in the valley from the princes on the mountain top.

There is plenty for all!

This is God's world. We are His children who profess our belief in Christian charity, in Christian brotherhood and still, despite it all, "do as the pagans do."

At least, my friends and fellow members in the National Union for Social Justice, I have afforded you food for thought. Upon these things I ask you to think, to ponder. It is our destiny to solve the problem of want in the midst of plenty. From performing our duty, we will not shirk!

There is no cowardly necessity which impels us to legislate for starvation wages. Our Senators will have the courage to stand opposed today and tomorrow against starvation wages. Eventually our Senators and our Representatives will have the courage to give America back to the Americans and rescue it from the hands of the international bankers.

There is no fallacious faith which binds us to the fetish of gold worship, of privately owned money manipulation, for you are not the deluded followers and worshippers of the golden calf. Yours is a faith that inspires you to love God above all things and your neighbor as yourself.

There is no high command so imperious and powerful that binds your intellects with promises or with flattery to the errors and superstitions of the past. Yours is a trust that has set you free—free from ignorance, free from tyranny, free from the domination of exploitation.

Courage, my friends!

Carry on—today, tomorrow, forever as should true soldiers of the living God!

Social justice shall not be preached in vain! Social justice, because it is consistent with Christianity, shall prevail!

# TWO YEARS OF THE NEW DEAL

*(Sunday, March 3, 1935)*

THE fourth day of March 1932 will long be remembered as the birthday of the New Deal. For twenty-eight months prior to that date the entire nation had been living in the hope of better days to come. For twenty-eight months our people had been suffering from the ravages of a so-called depression.

In the wake of a litany of injustice there were the inevitable consequences of unemployment and destitution, confiscation and foreclosure, mass poverty and mass unrest. Want reigned in the midst of plenty not because the social life of America had become totally vitiated but because the economic theories of our leaders had proven to be fallacious. Entirely forgetful that civilization had solved the problem of production, our captains of industry and princes of finance were mentally and philosophically unprepared and unfit to face the new problem of distribution.

Every laborer and farmer, every housewife and merchant and small industrialist recognized that an immediate economic change was necessary for the survival of our ideals, of our form of government, of our cherished standard of living. Every honest citizen realized that the day had arrived when Wall Street must surrender to Main Street, when the mass good must be preferred to that of the class good.

With what uncontrolled joy, therefore, was our nation electrified on March 4th, 1933! The money changers were given notice to withdraw! President Hoover and his property rights must surrender to President Roosevelt and his human rights! A free people had voted the old deal out of existence and given a mandate to enthrone in its stead the principles of a new deal.

Today I shall occupy your attention with the new deal as we find it summarized in *"The Economic Consequences of the New Deal."* In the face of the facts which surround us, I shall try to be just although my criticisms may appear to be caustic.

## I

+Desiring to preserve the continuity of thought expressed last Sunday, may I first recall to your attention that today America is dominated by 200 corporations which not only control our industrial wealth but which, if allowed to proceed as they have during the past two years, will eventually force our nation into a state of industrial feudalism. This thought was a development of a previous thesis in which I relied upon a suppressed but authentic government document to prove that small industry which employs more than 48 per cent of our laboring class is being relentlessly destroyed because both our private banking institutions and our Federal Government steadfastly refuse to loan these small corporations a minimum of working capital.

At the beginning of the century there was a rugged Roosevelt, who became famous for being a trust-buster. In our day, the new deal Roosevelt has inadvertently characterized the first two years of his office by setting aside the Sherman Anti-trust laws which were designed to curtail the growth of monopolies and trusts.

This is the first indictment of the new deal which is drawn from the addresses which I delivered during the last two broadcasts.

I mention this unpleasant reality simply for the purpose of employing it as a peg upon which I can hang a homely observation. Our well-intentioned President has endeavored to be eminently fair in his experimentations and decisions. As he launched forth upon his new program he desired not to be known as an iconoclast. "To perfect and not to destroy, to build and not to lay waste"—this appeared to be his guiding star.

But there are times when strong men and leaders are faced with irreconcilable issues. There are times when the compass of counsel points so steadfastly north that there is no sanity in turning south.

In 1776 Washington was faced with a clear cut issue. He closed his mind definitely to one side of a question although for the moment he jeopardized his fortune and his life.

In 1861 Abraham Lincoln was confronted with the making of an irreconcilable choice. Because he could not think of a nation half slave and half free, he cast his lot with the bloody sword rather than with the procrastinator's weapon of compromise.

Those first two years of the New Deal have failed to appreciate this immortal mark of leadership which, disdaining to compromise, turns not back, once it has set its hand to the plow, nor pauses to conciliate with tyranny or slavery once the battle cry of freedom has sounded.

President Roosevelt not only compromised with the money changers and conciliated with monopolistic industry but he did not refrain from holding out the olive branch to those whose policies are crimsoned with the theories of sovietism and international socialism.

If I interpret correctly the tenor of American thought, our people are unalterably opposed to make any compromise with the economic theories of the old deal and are steadfastly opposed to cast our destinies into the unhallowed hands of the international communist. We cannot applaud a new deal which, with all its chaotic implications, submits either to the supremacy of a financial lord more obnoxious than was George III or to the red slavery of an economic Simon Legree more ruthless than the one confronted by a Lincoln.

The American concept of a new deal was cradled in a revolution and nursed at the tortured breasts of a Civil War. In the past there has been no compromise! In the present there can be no compromise, if a new liberty and a fresher freedom shall be born!

✝ The first two years of the new deal will long be remembered as the years which enunciated a new philosophy for future years to practice. However, they were years which, despite its gracious pronouncements, are still wedded to the basic evils of capitalism, to the fundamental errors of the old deal. The money changers have not been driven from the temple. The financial system which crashed on the eve of the new deal's birth has been revived and handed back to the care and ownership of those gentlemen of exploitation who, more than any other group, were responsible for our misery. Big industry has grown unimpeded to an abnormal size, pregnant with the profits of monopoly. Eleven million unemployed bread winners—500,000 more than last year—, 18-million dole fed citizens, and 20-million industrial workers are wondering how low the ever-dipping scales of inequality will sink below the American standard of living. One hundred and twenty-five-million Americans are puzzling their minds to determine when and in what manner courageous action will be taken to decentralize wealth, and to permit the bounteous products of our fields and our factories to flow unhampered by the undemocratic and unsocial private control of money.

Although the new deal has recognized what should be done, nevertheless it is evident that it could not set up a just insurance rate against unemployment and old age and sickness without taxing big ownership to pay the cost. It was likewise evident that economic independence and financial freedom were idle dreams unless, despite all trivial consequences, President Roosevelt would break the chains of financial bondage by handing over to Congress the constitutional right to coin and regulate the value of money.

I might interpose and tell you that this very thing was accomplished by the Argentine Republic only yesterday despite the opposition which the socialists and the communists bestirred. Sometimes I wonder if this communistic and socialistic opposition is impeding Congress from rescuing the control of our finance.

These things, nevertheless, our Administration has not done. This compromising with the old deal is the basic reason for the continuance of our misfortunes.

## II

↖Although proven obsolete by a multiplicity of glaring facts, the old economic deal still reigns supreme with its bankers and bonds and protected monopolies. Instead of attacking the problem of instituting a new deal in this respect, our present Administration has spent its best efforts in attempting to establish a new social system. Is it not evident that our government has been captured by a group of scientific social workers who preach to us that big, bad bankers and good, little laborers shall submit to a multiplicity of conventional regulations, each class retaining what it had under the old economy, as they learn to habituate themselves to a strange admixture of fascism, of capitalism, of communism and a modicum of Americanism?

I refer to a new social system where, by intent if not by practice, the federal government reserves for itself the right to enter into every phase of business—business which not only respects the development of public resources, with which no fault is found, but business of the most private nature, which is described in the Delaware federal government corporations.

I refer to the tendency to substitute undemocratic methods of government for the democratic usages and legally established institutions to which we have dedicated our political destinies.

I refer to the establishment of unnecessary bureaucracies which inordinately have transgressed the fundamental rights of state government.

I refer to the indomitable determination to preserve the worst form of plutocracy before whose throne this nation is subjected to live and move and have its being.

There is no one who questions the appropriateness of a new economic deal. But, for one, I do not plan to smile and swallow the candy-coated pill of a social reform when my whole being cries out for an economic reform, for a just and living annual wage, for production at a profit for the farmer, for the preservation of the small industrialist, for the curtailment of big industry, for the obliteration, though you call me radical for saying so, of the money manufacturers. In one word, I shall support with all my strength the economics of social justice and the conservation of the American standard of living which these social reformers are destroying. But I will not support a new deal which protects plutocrats and comforts communists.

At this juncture may I refer to the book named *"The Economic Consequences of the New Deal"* to point out the economic trends of the new deal which are illustrated, first, by the cigarette industry.

This cigarette business is dominated by four great companies. In 1919 it produced more than 53-billion cigarettes and employed a few more than 24-thousand wage earners. Twelve years later—

196

1931—in the middle of the depression it produced 117-billion cigarettes with 4-thousand less wage earners. In other words, production increased 120 per cent while labor decreased 18 per cent.

Who profited by this tremendous increase in production and efficiency? Foolish question! The workers lost as they have always lost. Their numbers were not only decreased, but those who were left had their earnings cut from $853.00 in 1919 to $727.00 in 1931 and $613.00 in 1933. The industry paid out 30% less wages in 1931 than it did in 1919 though its production more than doubled.

Do you laboring men of America understand these figures? Do you understand that the more you produce, the less you obtain? Do you understand that the more you produce, means greater wealth for big industry and greater poverty for labor?

Do you farmers understand what is implied in these figures? The big four tobacco monopolies exploited the tobacco farmers insofar as tobacco that sold for 32 cents a pound in 1919 was only 8½ cents a pound in 1931.

Who profited? The advertising man, the high priced executives and the stockholders.

Were it not so tragic one would laugh when he learns that the cigarette industry pays twice as much for advertising as it does for labor and that the president of the American Tobacco Company was paid $16,000.00 salary a week while his workers got less than $14.00 a week.

This is a sample of what big industry does to labor, a sample of the exploitation which still marches on under the banner of the new deal which protects big industry and which has not lifted a finger against big industrial profits.

But you will interpose to tell me that the N.R.A. will correct all these abuses. Would that this were so! But here is a story from this same book which indicates the efficiency of the N.R.A. As soon as the N.R.A. got under way, this protected cigarette monopoly sent Mr. Clay Williams, president of the Reynolds Tobacco Company, to Washington to oppose any codification which might involve the least raise in wages. Mr. Williams threatened to fight the N.R.A. if it tried to impose a code contrary to the wishes of the manufacturers. Mr. Williams won his case!

Because he was so clever in upholding his right to exploit the laboring class, Mr. Williams proceeded further. In order to offset a $10-million processing tax levied by the Agricultural Administration Act, he gained permission to raise the wholesale price of cigarettes by $60-million.

197

Big ownership in the cigarette industry added a clear $50-million to its profits in the first year of the new deal. More than that, Mr. Williams was then hired by the Administration to operate the N.I.R.A.!

The authors of *"The Economic Consequences of the New Deal"* are taking the cigarette industry because of its very exaggeration to show how monopolistic capitalism, in its straining for profits, undermines our economic life, and to show that the new deal has been inefficacious in giving the laboring class the least semblance of a new deal. Because it surrenders time and again to men like Mr. Williams whom we do not blame; because the new deal accepts the decision of big industry as against little industry, the decisions of the new deal, up to date, have been invariably against the great middle classes in the majority of economic battles that have been waged. The first two years of the new deal shall be remembered as two years of compromise, two years of social planning, two years of endeavoring to mix bad with good, two years of surrender, two years of matching the puerile, puny brains of idealists against the virile viciousness of business and finance, two years of economic failure. The new dealers themselves, recognizing that they have not produced results, have used the euphemistic term of "experimentation" when everybody knew there was no need to experiment, when everybody knew there was need to drive the money changers from the temple which can only be accomplished by driving the money changers from the temple.

In the meantime, big ownership and private financialism are still with us untouched, unhampered and unafraid. No government can hope to establish a new economic deal unless at every moment and at every move the arrogance and the exploitation of big ownership are deflated, and the tyranny of private financialism is broken. You cannot have a new deal without a new deck. Two more years of this policy which is associated with preserving big business and big finance will be remembered in American history as the sad experiment.

## III

To better appreciate the activities of the new deal which consecrated its vows to break the concentration of wealth in the hands of a few, let us turn back the pages of this same book to the days when Mr. Hoover upheld the principles of modern capitalism and then to the days when the new deal exploitation came into bloom.

From 1923 to 1929 the top 400,000 persons in America who reported incomes of over $10,000 each had increased their revenues by more than 76 per cent; the top 40,000 of these favored few increased their profits by 129 per cent and the top 4,000 plutocrats of this class multiplied their gains by 207 per cent.

But the cream of the top, the 400 real rulers of America, increased their revenues 234 per cent. The bigger the ownership, the bigger the profits was the rule during these six years of rugged individualism.

In sad contrast to this unequal division of profits the little fellow, the laborer at the end of the table, increased his earnings by less than 5 per cent. In other words, during the fictitious prosperity of the Hooverian old deal the national income was being grossly redistributed but always upwards in favor of the concentrators of wealth.

Then came October 23, 1929 with its Wall Street crash. Instead of recognizing that big business and its economic dogmas had wrecked this nation, Mr. Hoover set out to salvage big business by pumping $2-billion of our money into big business through the channels of the R.F.C. For the time being, the over-capitalized railroads were refinanced, the limping banks were loaned a financial crutch which was fashioned from your tax money. As contradictory as it may appear, this money was borrowed at interest from the banks for the banks! The principle was upheld that dividends must keep coming to the stockholders of banks no matter if these dividends were paid with money borrowed from the people of the United States who did not own a penny's worth of stock.

Meanwhile, unemployment increased and the purchasing power of the nation was paralyzed because financial institutions refused to make further capital investment. Mortgages became uncollectible until, eventually, the Michigan moratorium tripped up Wall Street, March 4th., just two years ago.

This appeared to be the death-knell of the privately owned Federal Reserve banking system, the death-knell of plutocracy.

This was the auspicious moment when Mr. Roosevelt came into office to give us a new deal, to thrill us, to electrify us with that unforgettable, that eternally registered promise of driving the money changers from the temple! The new deal, as he called it, was here! At last the joker and the hidden aces were to be removed from the deck of American economic progress. But somehow or other the cards dealt by the new deal contained the same joker, the same hidden cards which were found in the old deal. This time, however, not only the aces of high finance were wild; the kings of big industry were also wild! The cards were dealt out. The first round proved to the disappointment of millions that Mr. Roosevelt's Administration had salvaged private banking and set it back upon its feet. The Administration continued the Hoover policy of lending public cash to private banks. When banks ran short of acceptable collateral, the new deal Administration out-Hoovered Hoover in furnishing them with an additional $850-million through the purchase of their preferred

stock and capital notes. To further entrench and maintain the
private banks with their private right to coin and regulate money
in their Hooverian, old deal position, the unskilled laborer and
the unsuspecting farmer were hoaxed by a deposit insurance law
for the purpose of creating confidence in private banking at the
expense of the taxpayer's money.

While labor and agriculture sat about the table, the second
card was being dealt around. To save the farmer and the small
home owner from foreclosure the new deal refinanced farm mortgages to the tune of $1½-billion and allocated to home owners
$3-billion to refinance their mortgages. But this was a marked
card the value of which neither the farmer nor the laborer knew.
If they could not distinguish its value at least the bankers and the
insurance companies could, because the net result of this $4½-
billion to salvage farms and homes meant that the government
was simply taking over unsound mortgages from unsound banks
and insurance companies who, in turn, obtained from the government either guaranteed mortgage bonds or tax exempt federal
bonds by direct or indirect exchange. The taxpayers were only
enjoying a postponement of the inevitable day. The bad investments of the banks were being protected. Thus there was no
scaling down of debt, there was no significant reduction in interest rates, there was no driving of the money changers from the
temple. It was just a round about way of handing the temple
over to them and of preserving the evils of capitalism and big
ownership upon their gilded thrones.

Then the third card was dealt to the unsuspecting farmer and
trusting laborer. This was the card of the Federal Housing Program which proposed to loan money at 4 per cent to those whose
incomes warranted the loan despite the fact that thousands of
homes were being confiscated, that thousands of others were
on the market at panic prices. The morbid fact is evident that
not one effort put forth by the present Administration to protect
private property has been divorced from its efforts, at least indirectly, to serve private finance as it exsisted under the old deal.

Behold the fourth card which was dealt around! It was the
N.R.A. which contained that famous section 7A guaranteeing to
labor the right of collective bargaining. Maximum hours and
minimum wages were emphasized as far as the laborer was concerned. But the N.R.A. was totally innocent of writing down
maximum profits for industry. The same philosophy which motivated the A.A.A., that destroyed pigs and cotton and wheat and
corn, manifested itself in the N.R.A. with its anti-social obses-
sion for restricting production and its total neglect of limiting
profits. Prosperity must be brought back by traveling that long
forsaken highway of scarcity! Labor must be condemned to work
at a below-level annual wage!

⁺ Finally the fifth card in this poker hand was dealt—the card related to tariff. The tariff is nothing but a sales tax levied on the people of which only a tiny fraction ever reaches the public treasury. The vast bulk of this sales tax is collected by big industry in the form of higher prices. Whatever the laborer gains in wages from these higher prices he loses when he enters the grocery store, the hardware store or the departmental store to purchase the necessities of life.

⁺ *"The legalized thievery of the tariff,"* says Secretary Wallace, *"is probably working more harm to the people of the United States than all other forms of robbery put together."* Even this card was marked in favor of big business!

It is true that Mr. Roosevelt asked Congress' permission to reduce tariffs by as much as 50 per cent which would mean a vast saving in the cost of living to the American consumer. But the joker card upon which this tariff reduction was written contained the provision that tariffs could be lowered only through reciprocal agreements with other governments. Until December 1934 all the new deal managed to do about the tariff was to conclude one reciprocal treaty with Cuba. Big business need not worry if this innocent card is in the hands of the laborer and the farmer and the small business man because the President assured big industry, to quote his words, *"that no wide and important American business will be injuriously disturbed by his tariff policy.*

These are the five cards in the poker hand, and every card in the deck was marked in favor of the old deal of finance. Prices have risen far in excess of wages. Taxation must inevitably rise. Big business is entrenched and so is private finance. Unemployment is still with us. The N.R.A., despite its collective bargaining clause, became a farce. The A.A.A., and its destruction of agricultural produce is a failure, for, at this moment, foodstuffs, including oats and beef and pork and butter are being imported from foreign nations. In view of these facts it is no insult to the intelligence of the Administration to remind them that it has not driven the money changers from the temple.

## IV

Now, let us look at the record of figures compiled by *"The Economic Consequences of the New Deal"* relative to the distribution of wealth under this so-called new deal. The concentration of wealth in the hands of a few was one of the chief characteristics of the old deal. To decentralize wealth was one of the projects of the new deal.

In 1933, the first year of the new deal, income tax payers with less than $10,000.00 per year saw their revenues decrease 5 per cent in comparison with 1932. But income tax payers of more than $50,000.00 increased their takings by 10 per cent; those with

$200,000.00 increased their takings by 16 per cent; while the number of persons with annual incomes of $1-million increased their profits 20 to 46 per cent.

In the last twelve months of the new deal, from October 1933 to October 1934, the real weekly wages of our industrial workers have declined 2 per cent while the dividends of our great corporations have increased 17 per cent in the same period. Is that the decentralization of wealth? Industrial profits in the first nine months of 1934 were 76 per cent greater than during the same period in 1933. Under the new deal the dividends and profits of big ownership have gone far out of the depths of the depression. Business is increasing, so they say, despite the truth that there are 500,000 more unemployed this year than last. My friends, these are the incontrovertible facts which go to prove that big business and big finance were practically the only ones who really benefited from the new deal which, for two long, dreary years, has failed to realize its promises of driving the money changers from the temple and of legislating against the concentration of wealth!

These things I realized, my friends, when on November 11 of last year I ventured to organize the National Union for Social Justice. It is not our purpose to obstruct the main objectives of the new deal. Rather have we devoted our efforts and will dedicate our strength to support the new deal provided it remains true to its original plans. To my mind there can be no new deal if we persist in protecting the right of private individuals to coin and regulate for their own profit the money which belongs to the people of the United States. There can be no new deal as long as big monopolies are encouraged and little industries are starved out of existence.

More than that, there can be no new deal until industrial profits are justly divided with labor and until labor is guaranteed a just and living annual wage that is in keeping with the American standard of decency.

The new deal cannot compromise. Its success depends not upon its social reforms or its political revolutions. Two years of treading the waters long since muddied by the greed of economic abuses have not succeeded in bringing us ashore. These two years, if they have taught us anything, indicate that, with bold strokes, we must set out for the shore of financial independence where, with security and independence, we can enjoy the abundance with which we are blessed—an abundance which is being withheld from us, despite all arguments to the contrary, because the old deal concept of money and wealth still prevails under the auspices of a new deal and thereby forces millions of citizens to withdraw their enthusiastic support.

For the most part these citizens of whom I speak are the laborers, the farmers, the small merchants and the small industrialists. There is not a sane individual amongst them who does not favor supporting the President as long as he supports them. But if he persists in supporting the international bankers and the monopolistic industries either directly or indirectly, he cannot wisely entertain the hope of securing support from the only class that loves him, from the only class that supports him and the only class to whom he can look for re-election and the everlasting glory of his name.

## V

This week marks our entrance upon the second phase of the new deal. Shall these two years to come be characterized by the marked cards which prefer the exploiters to the exploited, the profiteers to the laborers, the consecrated bankers to the sovereign people of the United States?

Time alone can answer that question. Time alone also will vindicate my forecast that unless this Administration has courage to bring about an absolute economic reform, both financial and industrial, it will be repudiated by those who created it.

This is not a wholesome thought, because America, as I know it from millions of conscientious letters, will never revert to the old deal so honestly but unwisely upheld by Herbert Hoover.

Thus I compliment Senator McCarran and his faithful supporters at this present moment because they, at least, seem to have their fingers on the pulse of American life.

As you know, my friends, there will be considered this week a Federal bill which, to quote its exact words, will be enacted into law *"to protect and promote the general welfare by providing relief from hardship attributable to widespread unemployment and conditions resulting therefrom . . . there is hereby appropriated (approximately $5-billion) to be used in the discretion and under the direction of the President in such manner and for such purposes and for such projects Federal or non-Federal of a type such as is or may be authorized by law"* . . . and so forth.

This bill, of course, is designed to promote public works with which everyone has been and still is in sympathy.

Two lamentable features are associated with this bill. The first is that this huge sum of money will be borrowed from the bankers at interest while $9-billion of gold and silver are idle in the treasury vaults.

The full current rate of interest, mind you, will be expended for this loan which, unfortunately, indicates the trend of this second phase of the new deal.

The second regretful feature indicates that, while full current prices will be paid to the manufacturers for any materials supplied on this public works program, a wage less than the prevailing wage, according to the President and his supporters, must be paid to the laborers engaged through this public works program.

Thus the bankers get their full, uncut, undiminished wage for their money. The contractors will get their full prevailing price for their materials. But the forgotten man, the American laborer, who now is idle through no fault of his own, must take a cut to somewhere below $50.00 a month when it is impossible to maintain an average family on less than $1912.00 a year.

Honor the man who manufactures money with his full pound of flesh!

Respect to the last farthing the United States Steel Corporation and its products which come forth from the furnaces embellished by the hand of man!

But the laborer on the public works—disregard him. He is the forgotten man who, with his family, must learn to live upon the crumbs that drop from the rich man's table at less than $50.00 a month!

Is that the philosophy of the new deal?

Is that the method by which prosperity is restored?

Ladies and gentlemen, let me remind you that, according to this bill, none of this public works money may be spent, to quote its exact words, except *as is or may be authorized by law.*

Do you comprehend the meaning of that clause? It has but one meaning. There are twenty-three States in this Union where there are laws demanding that the prevailing rate of wages must be paid to labor on all except direct Federal projects—even on those projects let out by Federal authority to local contractors. That is the law of twenty-three States.

Either in disregard or in ignorance of this law, certain Senators are voting to uphold the slave rate of wages thereby with one ballot injuring both the laborer of America and the welfare of their own States.

Who are these Senators? I shall name them and locate them, for they deserve to be advertised for their part in helping to translate a new deal into a raw deal, if they vote to keep this Federal Works money out of their own States.

Ashurst and Hayden of Arizona
McAdoo of California
Fletcher and Trammell of Florida
Pope of Idaho
Minton of Indiana
Logan and Barkley of Kentucky
Hale of Maine

Tydings and Radcliffe of Maryland
Pittman of Nevada
Moore of New Jersey
Hatch of New Mexico
Copeland and Wagner of New York
Guffey of Pennsylvania
Connally and Sheppard of Texas
King and Elbert D. Thomas of Utah
Duffey of Wisconsin.

These men from the twenty-three States that legislate against paying labor less than the prevailing wage have voted against the McCarran Amendment and plan to vote against it again this week.

Despite the law of their own State Government they favor a slave wage, a wage less than the prevailing wage.

They have proven themselves to be hostile to labor and agriculture and to be friends of the Mammon of iniquity.

Likely the McCarran Amendment will be lost and the slave wages will win. The unemployed have no means of protesting today, but tomorrow—some tomorrow . . . they will remember this policy of the new deal, this unkindest cut of all!

When shall government gain moral courage to pay a decent and living wage and thereby be able to demand the same of industry?

When shall the new dealers realize that the fate of America rests in the hands of the laboring and agricultural class?

Here is represented the majority of American citizens who no longer are ignorant that we are suffering the scourges of this so-called depression for the single purpose of protecting privileged finance and unrestrained monopoly.

Yesterday these citizens were concerned only with the immediate demands of a living wage and of profitable labor. Today the horizon of their vision has widened to comprehend that no just livelihood is obtainable in America until the coinage and regulation of money is restored to Congress and until the profits of big industry are equitably shared, through a process of taxation, with the laborer who, yesterday and today, is worthy of his hire.

To those Senators who still believe in the plainly expressed doctrines of Jesus Christ let me read you the Christian method of dealing with wages and with laborers.

*"The kingdom of heaven is like to an householder who went out early in the morning to hire labourers into his vineyard.*

*"And having agreed with the labourers for a penny a day, he sent them into his vineyard.*

*"And going out about the third hour, he saw others standing in the market place idle.*

*"And he said to them: Go you also into my vineyard and I will give you what shall be just.*

*"And they went their way. And again he went out about the sixth and the ninth hour and did in like manner.*

*"But about the eleventh hour he went out and found others standing. And he saith to them: Why stand you here all the day idle?*

*"They say to him: Because no man hath hired us. He saith to them: Go you also into my vineyard.*

*"And when evening was come, the lord of the vineyard saith to his steward: Call the labourers and pay them their hire, beginning from the last even to the first.*

*"When therefore they were come that came about the eleventh hour, they received every man a penny.*

*"But when the first also came they thought that they should receive more: and they also received every man a penny.*

*"And receiving it they murmured against the master of the house, saying: These last have worked but one hour: and thou hast made them equal to us that have borne the burden of the day and the heats.*

*"But he answering said to one of them: Friend, I do thee no wrong. Didst thou not agree with me for a penny?*

*"Take what is thine and go thy way. I will also give to this last even as to thee."*

The important words in this quotation are first, *"because no man hath hired us."* Through no fault of their own were these laborers standing all the day idle.

The second important group of words is concerned with the payment to every man of a penny, even from the first to the last. You dare not, saving your Christianity, go back to the States and face your Christian population, having voted to give less than a living wage, less than a prevailing wage to those who have stood all this day idle because no man hath hired them. There is a crying want in the midst of plenty due to the supineness of protecting private financial coinage of money and private monopoly of untaxed industry.

Private finance and big industry have had their day of the new deal. This day belongs to the laborer, the farmer and the small industrialist who prefer to die rather than to permit the continuance of the private coinage and regulation of money and want in the midst of plenty.

# THE DECLARATION OF INDEPENDENCE

### (Sunday, March 10, 1935)

## I

OVER a period of more than one hundred and fifty years the spirit of American life has been characterized by a sane desire to establish a homeland wherein liberty might reign supreme. In the dawning of that period our forefathers were oppressed by iniquitous trade laws and silenced by tyrannical political decrees. Against these injustices they appealed to the deaf ears of a stubborn English monarch. In vain were their voices raised; for, to preserve the inequalities of injustice, George III, relying upon the unsound principles that *"Might is right,"* and *"the Divine Right of Kings,"* filled New England with armed troops whom he eventually ordered to shoot and kill those brave patriots who risked their all, preferring honorable death to dishonorable servitude.

At that time England was the unjust aggressor. This truth no one now denies. Most certainly, it was English policies which fomented and brought about a revolution which resulted in giving to the people of this nation the land and the liberty which was theirs by right. Blame not the pioneers for instigating the revolution. Blame those who oppress them!

It is unnecessary to remark that, had George III and his counsellors been reasonable and just, the bloody revolution of 1776 would have been avoided.

In later days the rabid principles of George III reasserted themselves under a cunning disguise. Financial Toryism supplanted political Toryism.

The framers of our Constitution, wishing to avoid the financial abuses which were associated with the privately owned Bank of England, were unalterably opposed to the control of money, to its coinage and regulation by private individuals. In Section VIII, Clause 5, they incorporated the following words: *"Congress has the right to coin money, regulate the value thereof, and of foreign coin, and fix the standard of weights and measures."* They conceived that there could be no liberty in America unless Congress reserved to itself the right to coin and regulate the value of money. For the first few years of our national existence, this right was carefully guarded.

Through various stages of development, however, the control of our money and therefore of our entire economic system was handed over to a small group of stockholders who today own the Federal Reserve banking system. The history which had been enacted in England was duplicated here. In 1694, when threatened by invasion, the British Parliament which had permitted a small group of merchants and goldsmiths to amass the gold of the nation was forced to purchase their support to repel the invaders by granting to these high priced patriots the sovereign right to regulate the money of the realm. In the days of our Civil War Abraham Lincoln, fighting for the freedom of the physical slaves, was constrained to surrender our Constitutional right to the same breed of buccaneers, whose patriotism and loyalty were priced with the same tag. This, of course, was accomplished not according to the spirit of our Constitution but contrary to it.

For more than one hundred years of our national existence we were engaged in pioneering and in producing the necessities and conveniences of life. Pathways were cleared through the forests. Villages and towns were established on the shores of navigable waterways. Ribbons of steel and copper wires were stretched across the continent as sturdy Americans, handicapped with unscientific tools, constantly fought against the forces of a hostile nature. As yet there were no repercussions experienced from the surrender of our sovereign financial rights.

Indeed, the struggle engaged in by our foreparents was an epic nothing short of the heroic.

Within the last thirty years, however, the battle against both the forces of nature and mechanical ignorance has been definitely won. Light conquered darkness! Abundance ruled over want! The age of scarcity surrendered to the age of plenty! Only those of us whose lives have spanned these two ages can appreciate how steam and electricity, how the power-lathe and the power-press, how the tractor and the motor car and a myriad of mechanical devices invented by the genius of our fellow citizens have so completely transformed the world of yesterday into the world of today.

In one sense this same mechanical development was true of most European nations. But it is likewise true that the old system of economy—the economics of scarcity, the economics of the stage coach, the economics of the water mill—are still functioning or trying to function both here and in Europe, when our civilization is demanding the economics of plenty, the economics of the Zephyr locomotive, the economics of the mass production plants. At this stage of our development the chains of financial bondage began to eat deeply into our flesh. At this point in our progress we confronted a barrier of money control which not only impeded further progress but which began to starve us in the very midst of plenty. Despite our miraculous progress in the fields of science and of production, there has not been for the last one hundred and fifty years such widespread poverty and such unbalanced distribution of wealth as there is at the present moment.

Back of it all, under it all, above it all and through it all, both here in America as well as in Europe, is the Central Banking system of a privately owned, privately controlled money system. To those institutions of the Central Bank of England, France, America and to their policies is due more than to every other cause the so-called world depression.

This is neither an intemperate nor an immoderate statement when one considers the basic nature of a Central, privately owned bank. Is it not the Central bank which regulated all the private banks of the nation? Is it not the Central—the Federal Reserve Bank—which issues and regulates the major portion of the currency money which the citizens employ? Is it not the Central Federal Reserve Bank which protects the policy by which you deposit 10 good dollars in a bank and by virtue of which this same bank loans 100 dollars at interest, thereby creating out of nothing the balance of 90 dollars? Is it not the Central Federal Reserve Bank that loans the government $100-million on a million deposited-dollars and thereby through government bond issues gains the profit of interest on $90-million that never existed simply through the process of the printing press and the fountain pen? Is it not the Federal Reserve Bank which expands and contracts credit at will? Is it not this institution which has kept in existence a dishonest dollar containing far more than 100 pennies? These questions must be answered in the affirmative. Their answers cannot be erased from public knowledge merely by vomiting an hour of billingsgate and unproven and unprovable generalities upon the head of him who asks them.

But these points, to which I have here referred and which I have discussed at length in previous addresses, indicate only in part the necessity of restoring America to the Americans by ridding ourselves of the privately owned Central Federal Reserve Bank which, perverting the entire concept of money, exists merely to make real money out of fiction money; to reap where it did not sow!

Here, however, let me stress a more important point which logically follows. Because the Central Banks of the European nations together with our privately owned Federal Reserve Banking system controlled the issuance and regulation of national money; because these same institutions protected the policy of loaning ten times as many dollars as were deposited in the banks, the citizens of these nations and especially the citizens of the United States became burdened with such a heavy yoke of debt that these debts became unpayable. Thus a further expansion of credit was stifled in an economic system which depended totally upon credit. Thus the so-called world-wide depression burst upon us with all its fury!

The world was suffering from a chronic inflation of credit produced by the bankers and their power to loan ten times as much as they possessed. It was a peculiar suffering insofar as its chief victims, namely those who had borrowed manufactured dollars or check book money, were obligated to repay the lenders in real currency dollars, or else, were forced to surrender their homes, their farms, their factories or whatsoever security they had entrusted to the bankers who made the loan.

As a result of this inflation of credit there arose a deflation in property values. As a result of this wicked, greedy inflation in credit there resulted a wholesale confiscation of homes, of farms and of factories because there was not sufficient genuine money in the hands of the borrowers to repay the loans which had been negotiated with the fictitious money manufactured by the bankers. America gradually was being confiscated by the Central bankers.

To develop this point one step further, the Central Federal Reserve bankers who controlled all credit were not satisfied to profit through the manufacture of money. During the last twenty years we find the owners of this institution gradually reaching out their grasping hands to control the industrial activities of the nation.

Mergers and monopolies resulted. The small industries which opposed them were either starved into submission or eliminated from competition. As a result of this great game of greed the laborer, the farmer and the independent merchant were the innocent victims of a system of Tory economics which, counter to the spirit and the letter of our Constitution, has wrought more misery upon the present generation of Americans than did George III impose upon our ancestors. Because they operated for profits only, they cared little or nothing for the jobless laborer whose services were replaced by capitalistic-owned machinery. *"Production for a profit"* was their motto. Where is this better exemplified than in the *"Economic Consequences of the New Deal"* from which I quoted last Sunday—a little book worthwhile reading.

This is the financial Toryism which has developed in our midst. Scoffers at democracy and at the Constitution, these men who support it still believe that *"might is right"* as they reach out to control the government. They adhere to the doctrine of *"the divine right of kings"* as they exploit both the laborer and the farmer and concentrate the wealth of the world in their own possession. He who challenges their kingly right is called a rebel; he who protests against their domination is an inciter of revolution.

My friends and fellow members in the National Union for

Social Justice, are we mongrel Americans or are we thorough-breds? Are we satisfied to pattern our practices after Thomas Jefferson who wrote the Declaration of Independence or have we grown so lily-livered that we dare not voice our resentment?

Jefferson and Washington had courage to demand their God-given social rights. Have we the courage to do likewise in the spirit of the Declaration of Independence which we teach to our children in school but which we fail to employ as a guide in our economic life?

To paraphrase that immortal document: *"It is our duty, out of a decent respect to the opinions of mankind, to declare the causes which impel us to separate from the financial monarchs of this world. When a long train of abuses and usurpations, pursuing invariably the same object, evince a design to reduce us under absolute despotism, it is our right, it is our duty, to throw off such government and to provide new guards for our future security."*

If you have read the Declaration of Independence, you will remember, in general, the twenty-seven indictments of political Toryism which it contained.

In its American spirit, therefore, let us submit our facts to a candid world, against the Rothschilds of Europe, the Morgans and the Baruchs of America, against the financial Tories who dominate us.

Thus, in deadly parallel to the points expressed by the Father of American Democracy, I submit the following twenty-seven indictments against the Federal Reserve banks, against the pluto-crats whose policies have reduced us, in this land of plenty, to a state of poverty:

1. They have refused to permit Congress to coin money and regulate the value thereof.

2. They have kept banking in private hands, alloting both money and credit at will to their friends.

3. They have promoted the growth of giant corporations to the extent that 200 of the 300,000 corporate entities in America possess $61-billion out of the $165-billion total corporate assets.

4. They have loaned abroad in private loans over $8-billion of our peoples money, leaving worthless securities in lieu thereof.

5. They drove America into the World War, to secure the credit of the British Empire, at the consequent cost of thousands of lives and $40-billion cost to the taxpayers of the United States.

6. They have secured the loans of over $11-billion of public monies to foreign nations, now wholly in default.

7.  They have so promoted foreign trade by inducing the sale of American goods abroad in exchange for foreign goods, that we have imported at an estimated loss of $22-billion, since the beginning of this century.

8.  They have prompted, as far back as the Civil War, the system of National Banks which permitted the banker to obtain interest on his investment as well as paper currency for his capital.

9.  They have floated foreign and worthless issues of German bonds and South American bonds in this nation, robbing the people of our surplus, to meet their inordinate demands for interest and commission.

10.  They have promoted wild-cat issues of stocks and bonds of domestic corporations.

11.  They have dominated the Treasury of the United States and dictated its policies.

12.  They have placed their representatives before the people for selection in the highest places of preferment.

13.  They have covered the country with false and lying propaganda, prostituted the press and invaded the schools, with their campaign for so-called sound money.

14.  They have sent their lobbyists to Washington, against the interests of the people and for the protection of their selfish interests.

15.  They have induced the government of the United States to refuse to issue adequate currency, but rather to issue interest bearing bonds, in exchange for book credits issued by the banks, over-subscribing each issue till now the national debt is reaching its all time high of $34-billion financed largely by banks which never had a full billion of actual currency in their vaults.

16.  They have accepted as deposits the savings of the people and issued in credit ten times the amount of currency in the counterfeit, fiction money of credit.

17.  They have sent their salesmen into municipalities and all forms of local government with the offer of loans for public works in order to secure a supply of tax-exempt securities for their wealthier customers.

18.  They have opposed every effort to reform taxation and placed the burden on all classes of people and on all forms of wealth.

19.  They have financed rebellions in friendly nations in order to take over the very governments themselves.

20.  They have financed wars for the profit on war and in-

duced armament races for the profits on armaments and munitions.

21. They have expanded credit periodically and taken the profit on rising markets only to sell securities before a pre-ordained period of deflation. They have called loans, caused a wide contraction of credit, destroyed values and purchased or confiscated property at bankrupt prices.

22. They have destroyed the opportunity of America becoming the financial and foreign exchange market of the world and have induced even the Treasury to buy and sell in London.

23. They have filled the vaults of little banks with worthless securities and caused endless bank failures in the nation.

24. They have opposed the economic welfare of the farmer, played the game of the city against the rural community, the manufacturer against the industrial laborer, and the foreigner against the American citizen.

25. They have pitted large industry against small industry, denying credit to the 97 per cent of our manufacturers who employ less than 250 men each and concentrating credit with large industry, thus adversely affecting 48.1 per cent of all the wage earners of the nation.

26. They have, through their political manipulator, Baruch, induced this government to establish the N.R.A. as a device of letting industries write their own codes, which means that the power and resources of big industry have dominated the codes.

27. In the executive department of our present Administration they have seated their "Council of 52"—representatives of the largest corporations in America, for the purpose of actually framing the laws through the department of Commerce; and in the legislative department they have appeared in the guise of associations—the American Bankers, the Chamber of Commerce, the Manufacturers Association—opposing every salutary law contemplated for the public economic welfare.

In short they have manipulated the wealth of the nation and the very State itself, which, rather than ruling in kingly majesty, has become their tool in concentrating wealth and power and domination in the hands of the few.

More than any other factor the misconceived policies of these men have been the chief cause of the worst depression which this or any other nation ever experienced although in the preamble of the law which created Federal Reserve banks it was stated that these privately owned financial institutions would end future depressions.

These indictments I enumerate against the Federal Reserve

Banking system which the owners thereof operate to the disadvantage of a stricken people.

In the spirit of Thomas Jefferson, in league with those patriots who had any part in the signing of the Declaration of Independence, I stand behind these assertions in the name of liberty, in the name of humanity. Jefferson's twenty-seven points of grievance against the person of King George III cried out in that bygone day for redress no louder than do those grievances cry to the Father of justice for remedy and relief!

As our forefathers proved that George III was the real subversive element in the civilization of that day, so do I point out with twenty-seven specific truths that the imperialism of Wall Street is the true subversive movement in America today. In that early day when we battled for our political independence, we found our beloved Washington ragged and starved on the hillside of Valley Forge while the English Howe and his imperialistic treasury lived in arrogance and luxury in the city of Philadelphia.

Today twenty-million of my countrymen are ragged and desolate on the farm sites and valleys of the richest land in this world while the agents of Baruch and Morgan and Warburg, protected by their imperialistic system, by their control of the press, by their control of money, feast in arrogance in the halls of the Waldorf-Astoria Hotel.

I have been accused of being an inciter of revolution. So were Washington and Jefferson!

I have been accused of stirring up the masses and of consorting with sinners—political and otherwise. So was Jesus Christ!

Infinitely unworthy even to whisper the name of the Master or to parallel my services to those of the first patriots, I do confess that I have attempted, in season and out of season, to convince the elected representatives of our people and their executives to abolish the privately owned Federal Banking system and to erect in its stead a nationally owned Central Bank, if for no other purpose than to prevent a continuance of the present despotism, which is far more acute than was taxation without representation.

If there ever flare the fires of red revolt in this harrassed nation of ours let the international bankers—the Baruchs and the Rothschilds, the Kuhn-Loebs and the Morgans—remember 1776. In that day it was the tyranny of a King George which kindled the flames. History will but repeat itself if the protestations of 80-millions of peace-loving citizens are unheeded!

## II

If it has been my privilege to organize the National Union for Social Justice, it is also my consolation that at least I have built

214

a lightning rod down whose length there has crackled into the innocuous ground the pent-up wrath of an overtaxed, an exploited, an injured citizenry. It is and always will be a union designed to uphold the Constitution of our country and, if necessary, to defend it. Its members are neither communists who are bent on nationalizing the wealth of the nation nor plutocrats whose aim is to concentrate that wealth in the hands of a few. Its principles are pledged to increase private ownership and to restore to Congress those common goods which, by nature and by common design, are intended to remain sacred for the common usage.

The National Union for Social Justice may be referred to as the National Revolutionary Party by the plutocrats because it demands a living, decent, annual wage for the laborer and a fair profit for the farmer. The real reason for the assaults being made against it is because it is attempting to restore to Congress the right to coin and regulate the value of money.

But I ask you, what have the plutocrats, the Federal Reservists, the Baruchs accomplished or even suggested that was practical for the laborer or for the farmer except to put two or three million idle men back to work at less than a living wage?

What has their maximum hour and minimum wage achieved? What has their philosophy of destructionism gained? What solid, sound or sane program have they offered?

Unfortunately, not a single one!

You, my fellow members in the National Union, have offered a workable, a sane, an unmolested program. Not once have your enemies, the plutocrats, attacked it successfully. They have been content to hurl their blasphemies at me as if I counted for anything. I am not important. But my doctrine is important. I am but a voice crying in the wilderness and always will remain as such. But my doctrines, borrowed from the Scriptures, gleaned from the fields of philosophy, garnered from the books of justice —my doctrines are supremely important. Nor are they hidden doctrines. They have been published throughout the nation. They have been broadcast to a people hungry for truth. They have been accepted by millions of Protestants, of Catholics, of Jews and irreligionists.

"*My doctrines*," say I? Oh no! They are the truths of social justice which I have made vocal; truths which have smouldered in every honest heart; truths which I fanned into glowing embers; truths which no winds of intemperate passion can ever extinguish!

Therefore, my friends, be not perturbed by any venomous charges hurled against you for what you believe. You are not inflationists—a cry raised by those who have perpetrated the greatest credit or debt inflation which this world has ever witnessed. You do not support any creation of printing press money. It is this very thing to which you are opposed.

Inflation properly so-called is related to the printing of worthless money. It is associated with manufacturing paper money that has no value behind it. An inflationist is best represented by the Federal Reserve banker who writes, or permits to be written more than $10.00 worth of check book money for every genuine dollar deposited with him.

An inflationist is again represented by the German Republic which printed billions of marks when the nation was already bankrupt and when its treasury was despoiled of its last ounce of gold.

An inflationist, if we can judge by the Federal Reserve Act of 1913, is also represented by a person who advocates that, for every dollar's worth of gold or silver possessed by the nation, we print more than 2½ paper dollars of currency money.

Realizing that our nation possesses more than $11-billion of gold and silver; realizing that the Federal Reserve Act permits 2½ paper dollars to be issued against every metallic dollar, did you ever hear me advocate that we should print paper money to the extent of $25-billion? Never! But you have heard me ask and receive no answer from the government or from the bankers why it is that we have almost two metal dollars sterilized, idle and as unproductive as a blue eagle's decayed egg—for every paper dollar existing in the nation?

Because the National Union has put this embarrassing and unanswerable question to the Baruchs we, the members, and I, the mouthpiece of the National Union for Social Justice, are branded as inflationists!

The next time you hear this term applied to us by speaker or by newspaper, please remember that you are being played upon by a thief, as it were, who is yelling *"Stop, thief!"*

We do not want to create money out of nothing. But we do want a reasonable explanation why the Government imprisons the gold and the silver belonging to its citizens instead of freeing it, instead of putting it to work.

It is likewise embarrassing to inquire why billions of dollars —of manufactured credit, checkbook dollars—are borrowed from the Federal Reserve Bankers at interest, if you please, when the Government could employ this idle gold and silver as a base against which it could issue its own credit. Must we believe that the influence of the Baruchs is so omnipotent that our Government is more concerned in sustaining the profits of the money manufacturers than it is in relieving the burden of debt—of untold accumulated interest debt—from the backs of the burdened taxpayers and from the obligations of the unborn generations?

At this juncture I wish to encourage you in your campaign to restore America to the Americans. Thus, may I inform you that Congressman Martin Sweeney, Democrat of Ohio has introduced our monetary bill before the House of Representatives. To him do we extend our heartiest thanks and support.

In the United States Senate, the Honorable Gerald Nye, Republican Senator from North Dakota, was our leader. We have proven by the choice of these two standard bearers that the National Union for Social Justice is independent of party politics, is wedded to principles and not to men, is devoted to the success of social justice rather than to the depravity of party politics.

Because our bill to restore America to the Americans has been introduced into Congress the barons of Wall Street are excited.

Our goal is constitutional—to restore to Congress *"the right to coin and regulate the value of money."*

It is my hope that our method of attaining this goal shall be peaceful and just as constitutional.

Throughout the ages classes became privileged only because they controlled the wealth of a nation, only because they made either physical or political or economic slaves of their fellow citizens. It was true with the Romans under their Caesar Augustus and his millions of slaves who were shackled to the oars of the galleys. It was true with the baronial lords of the middle ages who lived their lives of leisure while the tenants upon their princely estates lived the lives of serfs. It is still true in America today, through the grace of an Alexander Hamilton and through those who practically assassinated the character of Lincoln by forcing him, as the price of their patriotism, to establish the privately owned Bank of the United States.

It is just as logical to expect a Caesar to unshackle the chains of the galley slaves, it is just as logical to expect a feudal baron to distribute his far-flung acres to his serfs, it is just as logical to expect a George III to bestow political liberty to the exploited colonists as it is for us to expect the Rothschilds, the Morgans, the Baruchs to give up without a struggle the financial domination which they possess—the financial domination which, like a wall, obstructs our progress; the financial domination which creates want in the midst of plenty. It is a new kind of slavery, this financial slavery. But as long as it exists you can prate of your physical liberty, you can talk of your political liberty, you can even speak of your religious liberty, all in vain. They are all inconsequential unless there is, as set forth in the Declaration of Independence, the right to life, to liberty and to the pursuit of happiness which today is denied by the absence of our sovereign right of circulating the goods of our fields and our factories because the money is controlled by the few.

Therefore, it is our business as members of the National Union to support good government, to look forward to peace, and to stand by the Constitution. Let the money changers be the Judas Iscariots who betray the Constitution of our nation! Let them explain why we must omit from its teachings today the right of Congress to coin and regulate money! But as for us we still believe in America, and shall do our utmost, despite every onslaught, to restore America to the Americans by first restoring to Congress the right to coin and regulate money without which no other principle of social justice is probable or possible. Towards this goal we will bend our efforts.

# A REPLY TO GENERAL
# HUGH JOHNSON

*(Monday, March 11, 1935)*

## I

**I** AM truly indebted to the National Broadcasting System by whom this time is contributed and to General Hugh Johnson for having provided the occasion and the opportunity for me to address you.

I am mindful that I am a Catholic priest whose voice is being carried into the homes of millions of persons who do not share my faith. I am thoroughly mindful that despite differences of religion, of race, of color and of profession, I am also an American citizen privileged as such to speak to American citizens.

The economic disaster which overwhelmed our nation proved beyond question that, independent of all racial or religious differences, there was common need for Catholic, Protestant, Jew and irreligionist to solve a common problem. Together did we not enjoy a common citizenship? Together did we not rejoice in the common appellation of American? Together have we not worried through the dark years of this depression? Thus, when through the inevitable sequence of events, a crisis had been reached in the development of our social well being; when it became necessary to bridge the chasm that separates this day of our economic affliction from the tomorrow of our hoped-for benediction, some one, irrespective of his Catholicity, or of his Protestantism, or of his Jewish faith was required to raise his voice, if for no other reason, than to condemn those who, refusing to leave this land of sorrow, obstructed our passage to the land of prosperity.

While it was and always will be impossible for me to divest myself of my Catholic priesthood, nevertheless, in accepting the dignities which my religion conferred upon me, I sacrificed in no respect the rights identified with my citizenship. It is still my prerogative to vote. It is still my privilege to be interested in good government. It is still my duty as a common citizen to engage in the common efforts for the preservation of our commonwealth as chaos clamors at our doors.

I regret sincerely that a man who once held such high office in our nation, either ignorantly or maliciously, has called into question this fundamental principle of citizenship. It has been intimated in words more forceful than mere suggestions that a priest's place is at his alter; that a priest, on becoming such, should sacrifice his privileges, his prerogatives and his rights as a democratic citizen. Thus, with the logic of a braggart, I have been challenged to divest myself of my priestly vocation, if I wish to participate in national affairs. Does our concept of Americanism instruct the teacher that his place is always in the classroom? Does it teach the lawyer that his proper place is circumscribed by the walls of his office? Does it tell the barber that his activities are limited to the tools of his trade? Does it cling to the out-worn theory of the divine right of kings by which is implied that the affairs of good government and the direction of national progress must be surrendered into the hands of professional politicians?

Unfortunately this erroneous doctrine has been openly intimated by the spokesman of a group which has gained control of the democratic liberties of a free people. It is just as logical to conclude that a general must be perpetually occupied in leading troops, if a clergyman must be constantly engaged in his sacerdotal duties.

Our concept of government so far transcends the bigotry of race, of creed, of color and of profession that, through our forefathers, we refrained from writing into the Constitution of the United States any impediment to disbar any citizen from engaging in the activities of good citizenship. I am compelled to rehearse this plain truth for your consideration because a demagogic utterance, by its appeal to thoughtlessness, to religious and to professional bigotry, has questioned it. The money changers, whom the Priest of Priests drove from the temple of Jerusalem both by word and by physical force, have marshaled their forces behind the leadership of a chocolate soldier for the purpose of driving the priest out of public affairs!

While always a priest I address you neither as the spokesman of the Catholic Church nor as the representative of its Catholic following. I speak to you as American to American.

While always a priest I carry to you the fundamental doctrines of social justice which are intended both for religionist and irreligionist, for black and white, for laborer and farmer for everyone who shares with me the citizenship in which I rejoice.

Therefore, away with that prostituted bigotry which, at one time, has been the poisoned rapier of arrant cowards and, at another, the butcher's cleaving axe wielded to destroy a national unity!

The object of the National Union for Social Justice is to secure economic liberty for our people. So well is this truth known that the concentrators of wealth are resorting to musty methods, long since in disrepute, to preserve America for the plutocrats and to retain its quarreling, divided citizens for their own exploitation.

Our program, which is interested in restoring America to the Americans, can be accomplished peacefully only through a national solidarity. Peacefully, I say, because I believe in the Prince of Peace and dare not disregard His warning that they who use the sword shall perish by it.

In the meantime, therefore, let the Tories of high finance learn from their prototype, George III. Let the unjust aggressors, who for generations have mismanaged the economic affairs of our nation, assume the entire responsibility of their own Tory stubbornness. The laborer has not sabotaged our factories! The farmer has not created a man-made scarcity of food! The 80-million cry babies, to whom General Johnson referred, have not concentrated our wealth! These people, played upon by paid-for propaganda, did not hurl us into the seething maelstrom of a bloody war! These cry babies—80-millions of them, so confessed —were not responsible for the concentration of wealth in the hands of a few and for the destruction of small industry! They did not force 22-million hungry men and women to stand in a bread-line nor, with the lash of poverty, did they drive 11-million laborers into idleness and insecurity!

I am characterized as a revolutionary for raising my voice against these palpable injustices while the blind Bourbons cannot see the writing on the wall nor read the pages of history written in crimson by pens which were dipped into bleeding hearts at Concord, Lexington and Valley Forge!

In 1776 Washington and Jefferson and their compatriots had hurled at them the vile epithet of "revolutionary." Their lands had been over-taxed. Their laborers and farmers had been exploited. Their liberties had been denied. Their right to free speech and to petition had been scoffed at! They, too, were called "revolutionary."

Today, when the rights to life, to liberty and to the pursuit of happiness have been obstructed by an economic system of high finance far more vicious in its implications and results than were the unjust political aggressions of a George III, they who protest against them are classified and indexed with the patriots of 1776.

This, indeed, is a high compliment inadvertently paid by the new deal's greatest casualty, General Hugh Johnson, who never faced an enemy nor successfully faced an issue.

Today he and the Wall Streeters whom he represents become distorters of history and perverters of logic as they, the unjust aggressors, garb themselves in the raiment of patriotism and cast upon those who have suffered from their misdeeds the scarlet cloak of the rebel!

## II

For a moment I plan to pause to answer the charges and insinuations which General Johnson so intemperately made against my person. First he said: *"This political padre . . . may or may not now be an American citizen, but certainly once was not."*

My dear General, I am as much, if not more, of an American citizen as you are or ever will be. Your parents are but one generation removed from Ireland. My paternal grandfather's bones are buried in Lackawanna, New York. My great-grandfather dulled many a pick with the pioneers who dug the Eric Canal. If you mean that I have sprung from the laboring class and chance to be born of American parents on Canadian soil I have no apologies to make. By an Act of Congress of February 10, 1855, Sec. 1993 U.S.R.S. I was always an American citizen!

Secondly, you categorically accuse me of breaking the religious vow of poverty. The truth is, as my religious superiors will testify, I never made a vow of poverty and therefore could never break one. More than that I never belonged to any religious order although I was associated with a group of priests whose lives were dedicated to the teaching of Canadian and American students.

Thirdly, you have cleverly insinuated that I was a modern Talleyrand, who, as a Catholic cleric, was excommunicated by his Church because, among other reasons, he protected the plundering Bourbons. This you did in one breath while in the next you praised the good Catholic laity. For what purpose? For none other than to turn not the Protestants nor the Jews against me but rather to confuse the people of my own faith. It is sufficient for me to say that, up to the present date, I have not been classified with a Talleyrand by those whose business it is to judge whether or not I am in good standing in the Catholic Church.

Fourthly, *"compared to me Judas Iscariot is a piker"*—the same Judas who betrayed his Lord and Master. It is not my province to classify myself with the eleven faithful Apostles. I am content to leave to the justice of history and to the judgment of God this decision.

What insanity possessed you to say such things? What desperation forced you to utter such exaggerations?

I remember how in 1933 Mr. Roosevelt pleaded with the people to cease their hoarding. I remember how he promised to raise the price of commodities. It was in those days that the committee in charge of the financial affairs of the Radio League of the Little Flower heeded the President's word and believed the President's promise. This committee, having more faith in Franklin D. Roosevelt than you and your kind ever placed in him, expended some of the surplus money under their care in silver contracts. As a result of this action more than $12,000 was gained for the Radio League of the Little Flower. Not one ounce of silver have I ever purchased for myself. Not one penny of gain from it have I ever made for myself. And I am the Judas Iscariot!

But you and your kind, wedded to the belief that the Baruchs are the only ones who should make gain by transacting business in commodities, have spewed your venom not upon me but upon an organization of people whose membership runs into the millions, because their legally constituted officers gained for them enough money to pay for the broadcasting activities which are designed for the people and paid for by the people.

It is perfectly ethical for your task-master, Bernard Baruch, to profit by his gold and silver transactions. But it is totally unethical for the people who have been exploited by him and his group of speculators and international bankers to gather the crumbs of profit which fall from the table of the commodity market.

To malign me you have more than insinuated that personally it was I who profited and, therefore, that I am the modern Judas Iscariot who has betrayed Jesus Christ! I rejoice that never once have I sold Jesus Christ nor did I betray the brothers of Jesus Christ! Can you say as much?

General Johnson, your enemies and, if I must say it, some of your fair-weather friends, have heaped upon my desk the fulsome record of your personal life. General, I disdain to refer to it. Need I remind you, however, that of old it was said that Christ stirreth up the multitudes; that He was a wine bibber, a consorter with sinners? Or need you remind me how the Master, crowned with the thorns which were woven by the fingers of the money changers, nailed to the cross by the spikes which were forged in the furnace of hatred, said: *"Father forgive them for they know not what they do."* Dare I claim title to Christianity, General, and forget that prayer?

My dear General Johnson, I am not important nor are you. But the doctrines which I preach are important. While you were content to vomit your venom upon my person and against my character the American public is fully cognizant that not once did you dare attack the truths which I teach. I need not condemn you before the court of public opinion. You have condemned yourself. More than that, you have appeared before a jury of 80-million people—your own figures, General—who, through your lack of Christian charity and justice, are today prejudiced against you. These "cry babies" whose tears have welled to their eyes because you and your kind have lashed them at the pillar of poverty; these brothers and sisters of Christ whom you and your masters have crowned with the thorns of worry and insecurity; these sterling American citizens whom you first fastened to the cross of hunger and nakedness and then pierced their hearts with the spear

223

of exploitation—these inarticulate people for whom I speak will never forget you and your Wall Streeters!

These people, so you have intimated, are rats being led by a Pied Piper. Must that be the metaphor which you employ to describe the wreckage which your kind has created?

✝ My friends, I appeal to your charity, to your good judgment, to your sense of social justice to bear no ill will against General Johnson. Your intelligence informs you that he is but a faithful, obedient servant willing to express in his own grotesque manner the thoughts which are harbored in the mind of his master. Today he appears before us as a figure to be pitied and not condemned. He has been cast out by an Administration because he and his plans were failures. Thus, as he appears before you on future occasions, remember that he is to be regarded as a cracked gramaphone record squawking the messages of his master's voice.

My dear General, if I am constrained from indicting your person, it is simply because you are the first great casualty of the new deal experimentation. Whether you know it or not, you are but a political corpse whose ghost has returned to haunt us. Although I believe that your unquiet spirit will not rest in peace, nevertheless, I still believe in that ethical axiom—*"De mortuis nil nisi bonum"*—*"Of the dead let us speak kindly."* When real soldiers come forth to fight, having facts for targets and truths for ammunition, I shall oppose them with the most forceful weapons which my wits command, but never shall I adopt dishonest tactics or dishonest warfare or be accused of fighting a ghost. I shall draw my reasons from that school of militancy presided over by Jesus Christ, Who, 1900 years ago, refrained not from attacking in scathing terms the scribes and Pharisees. *"Woe to you scribes and Pharisees, hypocrites, because you devour the houses of widows, praying long prayers. For this you shall receive the greater judgment. For you bind heavy and insupportable burdens and lay them on men's shoulders; but with a finger of your own you will not move them."*

Yes, General Johnson, Christ, for having made that statement, is accused of stirring class against class by the Voltaires, the Rousseaus, the Louis Sixteenths, the atheists and the pussyfooters of all times. But there are times when certain classes must be forcefully reminded that there is such a thing as Christian charity which bids us love our neighbors as ourselves, and which warns us that whatsoever we do even to the least, we do to Christ. That is what the Pharisees refused to learn. That is what their descendents in Wall Street refuse to accept as they continue to devour the houses of widows and tax our citizenry into slavery and idleness.

Remembering the method of attack employed by Christ's Precursor, John the Baptist, I will dare confront the Herods by name and by fact even though my head be served on a golden platter; even though my body be sawed in twain as was that of the prophet Isaias for having scorned into disrepute a prince by the name of Manasses!

Today there is another Manasses, your lord and master, General Johnson. I refer to Bernard Manasses Baruch whose full name has seldom been mentioned but which name from this day forth shall not be forgotten in America. This was the name which his parents gave him, the name Manasses. This is the name, General Johnson, of your prince of high finance. Him with the Rothschilds in Europe, the Lazzeres in France, the Warburgs, the Kuhn-Loebs, the Morgans and the rest of that wrecking crew of internationalists whose god is gold and whose emblem is the red shield of exploitation—these men I shall oppose until my dying days even though the Bernard Manasses Baruchs of Wall Street are successful in doing to me what the prince, after whom he was named, accomplished in doing to Isaias. I am well apprised of the fact that your own vociferous volubility, which you characterized last Monday night as *"howling,"* is but the opening gun in a well organized attack against me. I fear it not because I am protected by the moral support of the *"cry babies"* and the *"rats"* whom you have forced into the ranks of the National Union for Social Justice. Therefore, I shall doubly bend my efforts to the task of handing back America to the Americans and of rescuing our beloved country from the hands of the Baruchs, your masters.

### III

There are two remaining charges which you made against me. I rejoice in this opportunity to answer them. The first respects money. You said that my plan is *"to make money out of nothing, which would therefore make it worth nothing."* At least you admit that I have a plan. I need not inform this audience that since 1930 and long before then I had a plan to establish social justice. Long before you or the financial puppet-masters, who are expert in manipulating the strings of Punch and Judy oratory, became prominent in the desperate struggle for economic independence, I was associated with pioneers who were protesting against the profitless labor of our farmers and against the slavery of modern mass productionism.

Where were you in 1930 and 1931 while we were advocating a new deal on Sundays and feeding thousands in the bread line on Mondays, made necessary by the cold-blooded individualism of an ancient economic system to which you belong?

Where were you in 1932 when our same group was advocating the election of Franklin D. Roosevelt and the birth of a new deal long before Franklin Roosevelt was even nominated for the presidency?

Where were you in 1933 and 1934 when our beloved leader, consecrated to drive the money changers out of the temple, was hampered and impeded by your master, Bernard Manasses Baruch, the acting president of the United States, the uncrowned prince of Wall Street?

I say this in no disparagement because everyone appreciates that you are nothing more than his man Friday. With Bernard Manasses Baruch's plan in your pocket to regiment industry, to destroy competition, to institute a wage system designated to share poverty, to create monopolies and eliminate small industries —you strutted upon the stage of this depression like a comic opera cream puff general. You organized a comic opera parade on the streets of New York.

Why, General, before your name and your under-slung vocabulary became household words in this nation these pioneer associates of mine had been fighting in the front trenches against the enemies of the new deal, bearing its heaviest burdens and carrying its heaviest crosses!

And now you accuse me of planning to make money out of nothing. But let us become more specific on that point. The man who put this thought into your mouth is nothing but a thief yelling *"Stop, thief!"* Bear with me, General, as I refresh the memories of this audience on the nature of money and how it is manufactured out of nothing by your masters.

1. As you confess, money is merely the medium of trade. It is not wealth. It is only the transportation system, as it were, by which wealth is carried from one person to another.

2. For more than one hundred years the people of this nation have permitted a small group of men to possess the privilege of making money, and thereby, of controlling the flow of wealth. Many of us began to believe that money was the real wealth instead of the truck, as it were, whose only reason for existence is to carry the precious freight of food, of clothing, of shelter, of human beings and their labor from one point to another— from the producer to the consumer—. There are many kinds of transportation, such as the railway, the truck, the steamboat. There are three kinds of capitalistic money all monopolized for use by the banker—metal, paper currency and credit. In round figures there are $9-billion of idle metal in the Treasury, $5½-billion of paper currency throughout the nation and at least $250-billion of credit or of debt money such as mortgages, loans, bonds, etc. Credit money or check money is really the major portion of all our money by 90 per cent. Credit money is check book money.

3. How is this check book money created in this nation? First, a group of wealthy men petition the Government for a

bank charter, or, in other words, for the right to counterfeit legally.

4. These men deposit, for example, $100-thousand with the Treasury. In return, the Treasury gives them $100-thousand worth of interest-bearing bonds which are kept at Washington as security. But the interest accumulating on the bonds belongs to these new bankers.

5. These men return to their home town after they have the Government print for them, at scarcely no cost, $100-thousand worth of paper dollars which they deposit in their new bank.

6. John Smith comes to these bankers for a loan of $10-thousand which he obtains at 6 per cent on depositing as security the deed for his $20-thousand farm.

7. Then the banker gives John a check book—no actual cash, mind you—and immediately writes on his own books that $10-thousand has been deposited, whereas in truth it was simply loaned.

8. Fifty, eighty, one hundred John Smiths go through the same process until the bank which started with only $100-thousand of printed money has loaned $1-million at 6 per cent. That was their rule, to lend ten times what they actually had. Therefore, the first year in business grossed the bank $60-thousand interest profit on an investment of $100-thousand which all this time was bearing interest for them through the bonds which they deposited originally at Washington at 4 per cent.

9. Of course, Jim Jones and one thousand other neighbors of Jim Jones placed their savings in the town bank. They thought that this money was safe and that the bank would surrender it on demand. But Jim did not read the fine print in his bank book. Had he done so, he would have discovered that he had actually loaned his money to the bankers; that he had become a creditor and, therefore, had to take his chance of getting his money back with all the other creditors and patrons of the bank.

10. Meanwhile, from the bankers' bank, the Federal Reserve Bank, word went out that too much money had been loaned by their fellow bankers. It was time to call in the loans. It was time to cut down on credit. Thus Henry Doe, the manufacturer, John Smith, the farmer and Peter Adams, the merchant, all of whom borrowed from the bank were ordered to pay back in currency money, mind you, what they obtained in check book money. Simultaneously this happened all over the nation. Ten, twenty, thirty billion dollars of loans were called. There were only five billions of dollars of currency money in existence. It was an impossible situation. Therefore, a depression arose. The deeds and mortgages were claimed by the bankers and homes and

farms and industries were confiscated by him because there was no currency money.

11. Did the banker close up shop? He did not. At least the big bankers did not. They liquidated the homes and farms and industries which they confiscated when the borrowers had no currency money to save them. They sold them for what they could obtain on a depressed market. Then they turned around with this new fresh currency money and bought government bonds at 4 per cent or less.

12. Meanwhile, bread lines were established. Unemployment was rife. Poverty stalked through the nation. Of necessity the government must obtain money to feed the poor and must undertake public work to salvage the unemployed. Therefore, it borrowed $8-billion from the bankers who, playing their game even in the face of national distress, loaned the government a fat check book and, perhaps, for good measure, a bottle of ink and a fountain pen. Still there were only $5-billion of actual currency in the nation. But, through a banker's magic and a gambler's instinct, they loaned the $8-billion because they knew that in eighteen years hence, $6-billion in interest would be returned by the government for the privilege of using a banker's check book —$14-billion in all!

There, General, is the true story of how money is made out of nothing. Can you or any Wall Streeter controvert this?

To this process of manufacturing money I have been opposed simply because our Constitution says that it is the right of Congress to coin and regulate the value of money. In the year 1694 this right still belonged to the British people and to their Parliament but, when threatened by invasion, the merchants and goldsmiths of London forced Parliament to surrender this right to them. This was the price of their patriotism. This was the birthday of the privately owned Bank of England.

During the days of our Civil War, when Abraham Lincoln was engaged in realizing a dream that was born in the crib of Bethlehem, he needed gold to purchase arms and ammunition. In that day the international bankers were willing to loan gold to Lincoln on the one condition that he would abrogate and cancel Article I, Section VIII, Clause V of our Constitution which says Congress has the right to coin and regulate the value of money. This right they themselves coveted; this right they themselves demanded.

From that day forward until 1913 when the Federal Reserve Banking system was created—a system owned by a group of your masters and not by the American people, as many in this audience formerly believed—from that day forward the economic destinies of our country have been controlled by these private, Central bankers who extended and contracted credit at will.

Because I have, in season and out of season, demanded that we Americans go back to the Constitution and restore to Congress its right and duty to coin and regulate the value of money you have assailed me and in doing so have stultified yourself.

When did I ever propose to make money out of nothing? I have pointed to $9-billion of idle gold and silver, sterilized in the vaults of our Treasury. I have questioned time after time the wisdom on the part of our government running to the Federal Reserve Bank for dollars created out of nothing, borrowing this manufactured money for relief purposes, for public works activities, with the understanding that the bankers would be repaid either with good currency, at interest, or else the security of the United States could be confiscated by them.

I have advocated that the government employ this idle gold and silver instead of building up unpayable debts to be shouldered by the unborn children of future generations. You and your group have been the inflationists, the makers of money out of nothing. But mindful of the Federal Reserve Act which was passed in 1913 and which permits 2½ currency dollars to be printed against each gold dollar; mindful that we have only 5¼ billion paper dollars in the country and over $9-billion of gold and silver in the Treasury, I have asked and I still ask why we do not employ it for the welfare of the American people instead of utilizing the bankers' manufactured money for the welfare of the Warburgs, the Rothschilds, the Kuhn-Loebs, the Morgans and your own master, Bernard Manasses Baruch?

Only yesterday afternoon I asked that same question. And this morning, to the gratification of every patriotic American, Franklin D. Roosevelt has made the initial step in our direction. Today he has given the answer to you and your false charge by ordering the use of approximately $650-million of that idle gold and silver, thereby giving his benediction to the principles for which I have fought for more than three years.

## IV

The few minutes which remain at my command I shall devote to your last set of charges which I need not rehearse. My record is clear in that neither you nor Bernard Manasses Baruch can justify any statement to the effect that the National Union for Social Justice or that I, its President, are allied with Republican or Democrat, with Catholic or Protestant or with any other individual or group of individuals. The principles which I have enunciated and the principles upheld by other organizations are ample proof to substantiate this statement. My dear General, you have gone on record as categorically stating that, ever since the exposition of the silver list, I have been opposed to Franklin D. Roosevelt, our elected President. An entire nation knows that this statement is palpably untrue. On that point my record is clear.

Who originated the slogan of Roosevelt or Ruin?

Who repeated it again this year? When only last January the President's magnificent message was read to Congress, did not your master's associates condemn it, while openly and nationally I advocated its support?

The real enemies who are boring from within have been you and your group of Wall Streeters, of international bankers.

Who have been the President's advisers over a period of two years? Not the farmer or the laborer, not the National Union for Social Justice, not his close and disinterested friends! Surely they were not responsible for 11-million men who are still unemployed, for 22-million persons who are still in the bread lines, for our national debt which has risen to the unscalable heights of $34-billion. If our people are growing disheartened, it is not because they have lost faith in Franklin D. Roosevelt, but because they are rising in their wrath against you and your group who have surrounded him.

It was Bernard Manasses Baruch and the international bankers who whispered into his perturbed ears the philosophy of destruction, the sophistry of social reforms and policies, all of which have prevented a magnificent leader like Roosevelt from rescuing a nation still bound to the rock of depression by the chains of economic slavery? Did they not, in season and out of season, obstruct our President from driving the money changers from the temple? Did not your master, the acting President of the United States, actually sit in at the gold plate banquet of the Supreme Court before the gold clause decision?

My friends in this audience, I still proclaim to you that it is either "Roosevelt or Ruin." I support him today and will support him tomorrow because we are neither going back to the individualism of the past nor are we going forward to the communism of the future. But I am not that type of false friend who, mangling the very meaning of the word friendship, praise policies like N. R. A. when criticism is required or betray my millions of supporters throughout this nation by preaching to them the prostituted slogan of " 'Peace, Peace,' when there is no peace."

The fantastic fussilade of false charges which the genial general of generalities, the kind chocolate soldier, and the sweet Prince of Bombast so engagingly publicized, certainly were not potent enough to arouse my wrath. More important things must be accomplished. I dare not be diverted from my course by a red herring, even though it chances to be a dead one.

America's destiny is in the process of fulfilment. The ancient world set aside the bondage of physical freedom. Throughout the middle centuries civilization struggled to disentangle itself from an agrarian serfdom which prevented men from owning their own homes or farms. In later days, in the spirit of the Magna Charta, there was lifted aloft the first standard for political freedom. Physical, agrarian, political—these freedoms has the world obtained. But, as the finger of Providence weaves on the wall of time the fabric of this life's story, there is still another golden thread which must be spun from north to south, from east to west—the golden thread of economic liberty and financial freedom. Palestine has given us our religion — our faith and hope and charity. Greece has bestowed upon us her culture. From the Tiber's banks at Rome came law and order. It was left to England and Spain, and especially to the Nordic nations, to teach the world the story of commerce and carry across the seven seas the glory which they inherited.

What part must America play? There is only one. We, the great creditor nation of this world, who today control its gold are in a position to strike the first and telling blow for economic freedom, for financial independence! This shall be our contribution. As long as there is a God in heaven and power within my soul I will stand out first and foremost to lead in driving the money changers from the temple. This is the destiny of Columbia. This will be her contribution to civilization. To this task I invite you to dedicate your lives.

# "PROGRAM—NOT A PANACEA"

## (Sunday, March 24th, 1935

I T is evident to any thinking citizen that the economic breakdown which we have experienced cannot be cured by a single remedy. Our national ailments are too numerous and diverse. Finance, industry, labor, agriculture and politics, like five different organs of the economic body, are afflicted all at one time. In one sense, our national sickness is similar to a patient whose heart, lungs, spine, stomach and brains have suffered from the ravages of specifically different diseases. When planning for the patient's recovery, it is necessary, first, to place him in the environment of the hospital of good morals. Once situated there, it is then scientific to ascertain the causes which produced the diseases. This progressive step is followed by the skillful application of medicine and surgery.

There is no candy-coated pill which will cure a broken spine and heal a diseased heart. There is no panacea or nostrum which will restore America to prosperity.

With this homely metaphor in mind, may I partially develop for you the thought that the National Union for Social Justice, while abhorring all panaceas, is dedicated to the theory that afflicted America cannot be restored to healthful prosperity unless it submits to a program that is designed to cure its various major ailments.

That is why our prescriptions, as it were, could not be compounded in one bottle. That is why sixteen different treatments, each designed for a specific ailment, were incorporated in our program for social justice. This afternoon I shall touch upon these in order, in this final discourse, to give a resumé of the ailments and of the remedies which we have incorporated in our program for recovery.

### I

Relative to the disease of unprofitable unemployment and a just, living annual wage for all citizens willing and able to work, it is well to recapitulate the following points.

It is certain beyond dispute that while production has increased, employment decreased. It is likewise certain that the laborer has been laboring at a loss. According to the American Federation of Labor's survey, a family of five required, in 1934, $1,912.00 to live and meet the necessary humble expenses. The actual average wage which approximately 14-million laborers received was $1,120.36½. Thus, our laboring class, who were fortunate enough to secure employment, were living and working at a loss of $712.00 per year. Disregarding for the moment the 11-million unemployed, the National Union realizes that the unhealthy condition of low wages which has been prevalent for many years must be rectified. It views with concern the ever increasing profits gained by the industrialist and the stockholders in mass production corporations. Therefore, unafraid to face realities and deeming it entirely radical to nurse the exorbitant concentration of wealth resulting from an age that is dedicated to mass productionism, we set down the principle that the profits accruing to industry must be more equitably divided with the laborer. The laborer is justified in demanding a just and living annual wage if, through no fault of his own, he is forced to spend a portion of his time in idleness.

The acceptance of this principle is advantageous to both the laborer and to the industrialist. Without purchasing power in the hands of the laborer, profits will cease flowing into the purses of the industrialist.

## II

It is evident to every observing person that agriculture is suffering as much, if not more, than labor. Therefore, the National Union realizing how imperative it is to cure this economic ill, prescribed the principle that the American farmer must receive for his efforts the cost of production plus a fair profit. If one diagnoses the agricultural disease he will discover some alarming facts. In 1920 the value of farm property in America was $78½-billion. In the ten prosperous years immediately following, this value depreciated to $58-billion—a loss of $20-billion!

According to the official figures published by the United States Department of Agriculture we are astounded to learn of a further $20-billion decrease in value from 1930 to 1934!

Forty billion dollars, or more than 50 per cent, has been wiped away from the value of American farms in a period of fourteen years!

This serious economic ailment becomes more alarming when we learn from official figures that the cash income to farmers has been decreasing with a rapidity that is startling. In 1929 the farmers' financial receipts amounted to $10½-billion. Last year, despite the agricultural doles administered by the AAA, the American farmer received only $6-billion. His revenue had decreased by 40 per cent!

Here we have one third of our population suffering from an economic malady that will be fatal to our national life unless it is cured immediately. Does any fair minded critic discover the taint of radicalism in our principle which prescribes not only the cost of production but also a fair profit for the farmer?

## III

When I speak of the American farmer and laborer I am speaking of those persons who are responsible for carrying the major portion of our nation's tax burden. Forced in common by social injustice to eke out a profitless existence, how can these persons hope to meet the exorbitant demands of taxation?

Does not this aggravated situation claim our common attention? Its analysis shows that we have one federal government and forty-eight state governments each supreme in its proper sphere. Under the forty-eight states there are 3,070 counties, 16,000 cities, towns and villages, 128,000 school districts, 19,000 townships and more than 14,000 special assessment districts. In all there are 182,658 governments or agencies or districts each with its own power to levy and assess taxes.

The National Union, believing in the simplification of government, prescribes that, at least in part, the burden of taxation should be lifted from the slender revenues of those laborers and farmers who pay the major portion of this bill. With this principle in mind, we suggest that thousands of our present taxing governments and agencies be co-ordinated or abolished. For the alleviation of the poor and the security of the wealthy we advocate that taxation should be organized upon the theory of the ownership of wealth and according to one's capacity to pay. To encourage private ownership, we advocate that the first $5,000 of real property wealth possessed by an individual should be exempted from taxation. The iniquitous sales tax whose burden rests upon the great mass of people living below the American standard of decency should be abolished. The excise taxes on tobacco and on gasoline, both of which bear more heavily upon the shoulders of the poor than upon those of the rich, should be eliminated.

If the perfection of citizenship is related to property ownership, why not encourage this by deed as well as by word? "Every man a citizen in deed as well as in name" should be our common ambition.

Thus it is in keeping with the philosophy of social justice to substitute for the multitude of taxes now being levied a simplified system of equitable taxation. Basing the rule for assessment upon one's wealth, the National Union prescribes that those who possess less than $5,000 of real wealth should be exempt from any Federal, State or Land tax. From this point forward, all owners would be obliged to pay their proportionate land tax.

Over and above this land tax, those possessing between five and ten thousand dollars' worth of any wealth should be assessed one per cent for State and Federal purpose; two per cent for those in the $25,000 classification; three per cent for those in the $50,000 classification—and upwards, by graduation, until ten per cent would be levied on those whose capacity to pay is so limitless that this assessment in no way would injure their personal fortune.

## IV

While dwelling upon this subject of taxation let me clarify the attitude of the National Union on those bonds which are classified as non-productive and which, under our present system, are generally free from taxation. Most bonds have been issued for productive purposes such as school bonds, highway bonds, railroad bonds. Others were issued to supply money for digging shell holes, for filling hospitals with cripples, for destroying cities and fertilizing the fields of France with the corpses of young men. Is it patriotic to profiteer upon bloodshed? Is it just to profit upon human misery? The National Union prescribes that all these non-productive bonds should be recalled. It does not advocate that currency be traded for these bonds, but it does suggest that the coupons on these interest bearing bonds be reduced to a minimum, and subjected to taxation. Many billions of dollars of our wealth is represented by these bonds which, under modern capitalism, permit their holders to escape taxation. This burden, then, is, at present, borne by the poor—who were not able to indulge in the purchase of such choice and unjust profit-making securities. All bonds should be taxed.

## V

Pursuing our principles in the program for social justice, permit me to refer to the attitude of the National Union towards public and private property. In diagnosing the economic ills of America we are convinced that there is a growing tendency to diminish the ownership of private property. In one sense, there is too little of private ownership. This is caused, first, by an economic system which persistently tends to concentrate wealth in the hands of a few, and, second, by an obnoxious system of taxation which discourages private ownership.

On the other hand, there are some things which, by their nature, should be owned nationally or publicly. Among these things there are listed the Central Bank which will have the sole right of issuing, coining and regulating the value of money be it currency or credit. In no sense does the National Union propose to nationalize any other bank. The local banking system must be kept intact. Its functions of safeguarding depositors' money and of extending local loans upon a reasonable basis must not be destroyed. It is regrettable that more than $773-million, or 23 per cent of the capital stock of these banks, is now owned by the government. It would be a benediction, however, if the government nationalized the Federal Reserve Bank, whose capital stock is valued at approximately $140-million.

Then there are the natural resources scattered throughout the nation. The ownership and development of Niagara Falls, of the St. Lawrence Waterway, which is capable of generating one million two hundred thousand horsepower, of Boulder Dam, of the

Tennessee Valley project, of the Grand Coulee on the Colorado—these and other natural resources should be owned and developed by the nation. In no sense should they be farmed out for private exploitation. The National Union further subscribes in its principles to a permanent public works program of reforestation, of land reclamation, of slum clearance, of national highway building and of other public activities whereat the idle factory workers may be employed during slack industrial seasons.

Relative to the many public utilities, the National Union regards the great majority of their holding companies as economic maladies. In many cases these holding companies were born in iniquity. By their nature they deceived the investing public. By their desire for greedy gain, oftentimes they marked up their values three, four and five times the tangible value of their physical properties. On this false basis they sold their securities to an unsuspecting public.

However, the National Union is not convinced that the ownership and the operation of public utilities should be nationalized. We prescribe that these should be kept in private hands subject to governmental supervision. At all times we must avoid the communistic tendency to sovietize industry or public service enterprises. Two extremes confront us: The one is advocating the national ownership of those things which should be retained in private hands; the other is advocating and supporting the private ownership of those things which should be owned in public.

Thus, while we cling to this twofold principle of ownership—one public, the other, private—let it also be noted that even private ownership must be subject to public regulation for the public good.

Relying upon that principle, the theory is sustained that, for the public welfare, the government may enact salutary laws to regulate not only personal liberties but also property and industrial liberties. Private ownership must be protected against corporate ownership. Small business must be safeguarded reasonably against monopolistic business. Were we to permit private ownership and small business gradually to be assimilated by corporate and monopolistic creations, then we are only preparing the way either for state capitalism or for communism.

## VI

In the rapid resumé of the economic ills of America and the citation of remedial principles which the National Union suggests as guides for treatment, I am well aware that the observant critic will suggest the question relative to unemployment, to the living annual wage, to a profitless farming and to the program for public works: "What will we use for money?" Although he accepts the other principles and subscribes to their adoptions insofar as they are practical, he seriously doubts if the spine, which is labor, and the stomach, which is agriculture, can be cured.

It is readily admitted that these cannot be cured unless, first of all, the heart of the patient is cured so that it can supply the entire body with an abundant flow of healthy blood.

By the heart, I refer to banking. By the blood, I refer to money —both currency and credit.

Before I forsake the metaphor permit me to observe that the patient's heart is sorely misplaced and, as a result, the blood flow is totally inefficient. This organic ailment must be rectified immediately before we can discuss realistically a permanent public works program and profitable farming for the unemployed and the under-paid citizens of our nation.

In the United States there are more than 15,000 privately owned local banks. These banks are controlled either directly or indirectly, in matters of extending loans to industry, to commerce or to individuals by the gigantic bank known as the Federal Reserve Banking System which is not owned in any shape, form or manner by the Government. It is purely a private corporation owned by a group of private bankers.

When we consider that, at least, 90 per cent of our money is credit money or check book money, it follows that, if the Federal Reserve Bank controls the credit policies of the local banks, it controls 90 per cent of the nation's money. This was totally true until the Reconstruction Finance Corporation was established and is true, in a great degree, at the present moment.

The Constitution of our country explicitly states that Congress has the right to coin and regulate the value of money. Here, then, when confronted with the private ownership and control of money, is an organic misplacement of the heart upon which depends all of our economic activities.

In the cure of our financial ailments, the National Union prescribes the establishment of a government owned Central Bank, subject to Congress, to replace the Federal Reserve Banking System. This principle is incorporated in the Nye-Sweeney Central Banking Bill.

This is an absolutely essential prescription which must be compounded and administered immediately before we can entertain valid hope for the patient's survival.

On March 10th I listed twenty-seven specific indictments against this Federal Reserve Banking System and its credit policies.

Throughout the tragic history of its twenty-two years' existence it has fathered two major depressions. It has proven to be devoid of judgment in the extension of loans. Through that period of time it was chiefly responsible for loaning $8-billion of our people's money to private foreigners, and for accepting worthless securities in lieu thereof. In 1915 and 1916 its policies were so concerned with saving the credit of the British Empire, that we were driven into war at the consequent cost of thousands of lives and $40-billion of taxpayers' money. In 1919 and 1920 it succeeded in persuading our government to cancel $14-billion of European war debts, the burden of which fell upon the backs of American citizens. In 1922 and the several years following it secured the loans of more than $11-billion to foreign nations— loans which are now in default. In 1925, and in the years preceding the Wall Street crash of 1929, it promoted the sale of foreign bonds, and of worthless or near-worthless securities to our un‧ suspecting public.

+During these same years of malicious credit inflation it sanctioned the sending of salesmen into municipalities and counties with the offer of loans for unneeded public works in order to secure a supply of tax-exempt securities for wealthy clients.

During these twenty-two years the policies of this institution have dominated our Treasury Department, have fostered and protected the existence of a dishonest dollar, have expanded and contracted credit at will and have filled the vaults of local banks with worthless securities. Its Boards of Directors appeared to be obsessed with the single mania of manipulating the privately controlled credit of the nation for private profit.

Not only was the heart of our entire economic system misplaced when Congress, twenty-two years ago, surrendered to the Federal Reserve Bank System the right to coin and regulate money, but the life blood of the nation—our credit—was stifled and contaminated with the filth of greed.

Our life blood, I repeat! Instead of carrying throughout the economic body the vivifying elements of health, history has proven that the Federal Reserve Banking System was the conveyor of destruction. Instead of rescuing finance from the hands of politicians, it betrayed it into the bondage of financial overlords!

There is no secret about money. Nor is there any secret about this fatal complication of diseases referred to as a depression. The history of the case has unveiled the causes! If the financial debauchery, resultant from the Federal Reserve credit inflation, is any criterion upon which to gage the future, history has proven eloquently but sadly that it is impossible to cure ourselves or our multiple maladies by placing confidence in the quack panacea of Federal Reserve dictatorship.

My friends, our beloved nation is neither bankrupt nor verging upon bankruptcy, as the Federal Reservists intimate. According to the National Industrial Conference Board, there are approximately $200-billion of actual wealth and immediate potential wealth within our confines.

Credit, I repeat, represents at least 90 per cent of the money which we use in our daily domestic, commercial and industrial lives. Under our present system where does this credit money originate? Briefly, the banks create credit. On the dollar you deposit, bankers were accustomed to lend 10 credit dollars. Against the valuable stocks, bonds and securities in their vaults they issued more credit. The total amount of credit, therefore, could never be more than 10 times the actual money or wealth owned by the bankers. Today there is scarcely more than $30-billion of credit available under our present banking system because the theory of modern banking which operates on issuing credit against its privately owned property, does not permit a further extension of credit. I repeat that the present actual wealth of the nation is practically $200-billion although in 1920 it was estimated to be $488-billion. Thus, of this stupendous amount, at least $170-billion of credit is unattachable and therefore unusable by the Federal Reserve private banking system. Let me stress that point: The usable credit of this nation is, at present, limited and measured by the actual wealth owned and controlled by the bankers. It is not limited by the vast amount of wealth which is over and above what the bankers own. With this new viewpoint we discover that here is a new, uncharted ocean of available credit which, by its constituted authority, Congress may utilize, if it restores to itself its original right of coining and regulating the value of money for the benefit of the nation at large instead of permitting the ship of State to rust and rot upon the dry bottom of a private financial mud pond which has been drained dry.

This project, if I may continue to change the metaphor for a moment, this project of launching America upon the depths of a credit ocean which is sustained by the consolidated wealth of the nation is but part of the program which is embraced by the Nye-Sweeney Bill and which is sponsored by the National Union.

Idle factories and a population hungry for the goods which could be produced; unused wheat and pork and a hungry population suffering from undernourishment. Yes! Idle credit—and we fear to reach out and use it!

Last Sunday, my friends, I developed for you the fact that the United States Government already owns 23 per cent of the capital stock of 13,896 banks, including 5,400 odd National banks, 958 State banks in the Federal Reserve System, 7,459 State banks not in the Federal Reserve System, and a few Morris Plan and Industrial banks. By the investment of 773-million-344 thousand dollars of R.F.C. money belonging to the people of the United States, we already have secured a 23 per cent interest in the three-billion 319-million dollar total capital stock of 13,896 private banks. The figures I have quoted to you are taken from a combined statement of the condition of all banks in the Federal Deposit Insurance Corporation, and the figures were as of June 30, 1934.

We are in the banking business today, but we are playing the game according to the bankers' rules. Instead of utilizing the power of eminent domain to extend the credit of the nation, we are content to piddle with the policies of utilizing the meagre credit created by the bankers! However, I want to carry that thought one step further. I want to show you how far the United States Government is in the business of bankers' banking today. When the financial system of the United States failed in 1929 and brought upon us one of those periodic depressions which has been our lot for over a century, the greatest bank in the world was formed. From a table compiled by the California Bank of Los Angeles, I find that the Midland Bank of London is termed a 2 billion 100 million dollar bank. The Barclays of London rates $1 billion 900 million, the Lloyds of London $1 billion 879 million, the Westminster of London $1 billion 500 million, the National Provincial of London $1 billion 486 million, the Chase National of New York, is $1 billion 338 million, the National City $1 billion 117 million, the Guaranty Trust of New York $1 billion 19 million. These are the only banks in the world, according to this list, that have deposits of over 1 billion dollars.

+After 1929 the United States of America went into the banking business. The largest bank in the world has become the R.F.C., the Reconstruction Finance Corporation. Private credit collapsed; so the Government of the United States started a bank to make loans and subscriptions to those institutions which the private banks of America could not handle. The banks themselves came to the R.F.C. for loans of 591-million dollars, the railroads for $343-million, mortgage loan company for $160-million, the Federal Land Bank for $116-million, the insurance companies for $30-million, the building and loan associations for $28-million, the Joint Stock Land Banks for $7-million 600-thousand, the Regional Agricultural Credit Corporation for $4-million 300-thousand—so that the total in loans and subscriptions outstanding on a single day, June 30, 1934, was 1 billion 287-million dollars. But all this time the Government was in the old fashioned banking business content to use as a base of credit the privately owned loans which it borrowed from the banks. Although this appears to be contradictory and an insult to your intelligence, nevertheless it is the truth.

Beyond all these loans, the R.F.C. subscribed to preferred stock and capital notes in weak banks to the extent of 805-million dollars. The total of these loans and subscriptions amounts to 2-billion 803-million dollars. In addition to these items, the R.F.C. has allocated funds under the Emergency Relief Act of 1932 and 1933 to the extent of 797-million dollars. And still in addition to these, it has extended to the Federal Home Loan Banks $81-million, to the Home Owners Loan Corporation $200-million, to the Land Bank Commissioner $147-million, to the Federal Farm Mortgage Corporation $55-million, to the Federal Housing Administration $10-million, and to the Secretary of Agriculture, for crop loans, $115-million. It has supplied, in addition $44-million in capital to the Regional Agricultural Credit Corporation, and, in addition to that, $40-million to the Farm Credit Administration. The grand total of its outstanding loans, subscriptions, and allocations on September 30, 1934, was 3-billion 874-million 458-thousand dollars!

In actual loans to banking institutions, to railroads, and to corporations the R.F.C. has had, since its creation, over $7-billion 900-million. On a single day it has had over 3 billion dollars outstanding. The loans and discounts of the 13 thousand odd banks which I have referred to on June 30, 1934, were 15-billion 180-million dollars. Therefore, the R.F.C. extended the governmental credit facilities, aside from any relief allocation, to the extent of 3-billion 180-million dollars. In other words, the R.F.C. has been doing 17 per cent of the total loan and discount business of this nation, but has been predicating its entire loaning business on the credit owned and controlled by the bankers. Believe it as true, the R.F.C. borrowed the money it loaned to the banks from the banks—at interest.

Of the remaining 83 per cent of loans and discounts by the commercial banks of the nation, the Government of the United States is represented by its ownership of 23 per cent of their capital stock.

I feel justified in concluding that on June 30, 1934, the Federal Government provided directly 17 per cent of all the loans and discounts in the United States, and, in addition thereto, the Federal Government, by its ownership of the capital stock in private banks, furnished the facilities for 19 per cent of all the loans and discounts. Therefore an amazing fact faces the critics of the Nye-Sweeney Bill. That bill provides for a Central Bank of the United States. That bill provides that the people of the United States, who are now in the banking business to the extent of 36 per cent of all the credit available in commercial loans and discounts in the United States, will have a bank of their own, a Central Bank, and not leave the Federal Reserve in private hands while the government is in the banking business. It further provides that the new government Central Bank will tap the ocean of credit that at present is idle while the Ship of State is stranded.

The Bank of the U.S.A. has another objective, namely, the raising of a price level of the farm commodities of this country. Behold the status of the American farmer! The value of all farm property in the United States is estimated by the Department of Agriculture to be but $37 billion 27 million, which, I repeat, is a drop of 40 billion dollars in 14 years.

## VII

To this thought I shall return at a future date. Thus far I have touched upon twelve of the sixteen points contained in our program for social justice—a program that is not a panacea. There still remains to be mentioned in this resumé the right of liberty of conscience and liberty of education; the right of the laboring man to organize in unions and the duty of the Federal Government to protect these unions; the necessity of preferring the sanctity of human rights to property rights. These social medicines must be administered to our national body before the benediction of complete health will have been restored.

## VIII

As an agitated world gropes through the appalling darkness of the clouds of war, it is befitting that I terminate my remarks on that topic.

Of the four men who had most to do in framing the Peace Treaty of Versailles, David Lloyd George is the only living survivor. Woodrow Wilson is dead. Orlando of Italy and Clemenceau of France have passed away. In these trying hours of intemperate charges and counter-charges it is well to remember the sober words which Lloyd George recently pronounced. An old man, heavy with years and laden with wisdom, warns us that all the Allies already have broken the Peace Treaty. Why, then, is there such passionate denunciation of Germany's transgression? That is his observation.

I hold no brief for France or for Germany. Nevertheless, I advance no defense for the pugnacious attitude assumed by the French Chamber of Deputies.

Consider that Germany is unarmed compared to France.

Consider that the Treaty of Versailles was coined from the philosophy of pagan hatred which aimed at the destruction of a vanquished foe rather than at the establishment of peace.

Consider that western civilization, already tottering to its fall, cannot withstand successfully another military disaster.

Consider these things—and then pray to God that in His mercy, He will stem the imminence of war!

As for America, our duty, our necessity is to remain aloof. Fortunately we refrained from entangling ourselves in the World Court. Fortunately there is no necessity for us to commit ourselves to any judgment issued by the World Court. Nevertheless, our policy is to warn France and Italy and England, who already have repudiated their just debts, and who already have repudiated the terms of the Treaty of Versailles, that we will not sustain them with money; that we will not supply them with munitions; that we will not comfort them with moral support as they plan to marshal their millions of men to celebrate the suicide of civilization.

If ever in the history of this world the blessing of peace was required that day has arrived.

For that we pray. To that principle do we, the members of the National Union for Social Justice, dedicate our strength.

This, too, is a part of our program which, we are proud to say, is no panacea!

From time to time, although I have been one of the ardent supporters of the new deal, I have criticized the National Recovery Act because it is not a recovery act.

From time to time I have criticized the Agricultural Adjustment Administration because it was responsible for the destruction of foodstuffs and raw materials as it leaned towards the philosophy of "less-and-lessism" while the population of our nation was clamoring for "more-and-moreism."

Without cessation I have inveighed against a vicious philosophy of money not because they who operate it were vicious men. On the contrary they are deservedly classified as outstanding gentlemen in our midst. But the system which they upheld was vicious.

By restoring to Congress the right to coin and regulate the value of money, the right to extend and contract credit, the right to use every acre, every home, every factory, every railroad, every motor car, every property in the United States as a base against which that same Congress can issue loans to those who deserve them and to those who wish to use them for productive purposes—by doing this the age of prosperity will dawn upon us. There is no need to look with longing eyes towards the flesh pot of Egyptian communism. There is no need to assail the sanctity of private property ownership. There is no need to regiment industry, to nationalize local banking institutions and to socialize the lives of a democratic people.

Banking, money and credit—these three are identical with

the heart, the arteries and the life blood of our national economic existence. These three are suffering from the disaster consequent upon disease. These three must be cured. Therefore, this is only one remedy which I have suggested relative to banking, money and credit. For industry there is another remedy. For agriculture there is a third remedy. For the burdens of taxation there is a fourth remedy.

This program which, during the past five months, I have explained to you is the program for social justice. We, the members of the National Union for Social Justice, shall stand together steadfastly until these principles have either been disproved as impractical or until they will have been adopted.